Through the Needle's Eye

Other books by David Kirkwood

Christ's Incredible Cross

Forgive Me for Waiting so Long to Tell You This

God's Tests

Modern Myths About Satan and Spiritual Warfare

Your Best Year Yet

The Great Gospel Deception

The Disciple-Making Minister

Through *the* Needle's Eye

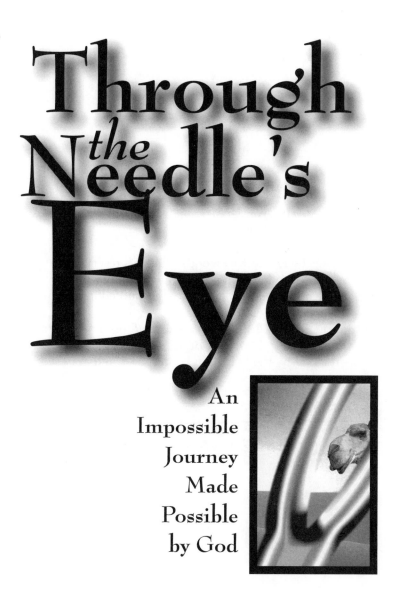

An
Impossible
Journey
Made
Possible
by God

DAVID S. KIRKWOOD

ETHNOS PRESS
Pittsburgh, Pennsylvania

Through the Needle's Eye
An Impossible Journey Made Possible With God
First printing: February, 2006

All Scripture quotations in this book, except those noted otherwise are from the New American Standard Bible, © 1960, 1962, 1963, 1971, 1972, 1973, 1975, and 1977 by the Lockman Foundation, and are used with permission.

Cover Design: Charity Kirkwood
Printed in the United States of America
Internation Standard Book Number: 978-0-9629625-9-2

To my fellow camels

Acknowledgements

When I first began writing about two decades ago, I was disadvantaged in at least one respect. From first through twelfth grade, I had been subject to an experiment by my local school district that adopted a "modern" way to teach English. I consequently never learned how to diagram a sentence. Neither was I taught about adverbs or prepositions. When my class graduated from high school, the school district abandoned its experimental English program, having our class as proof of its failure. (I am thankful, however, for the typing class that was offered in tenth grade.)

The Lord must have known before I was born of the devil's plot to keep me from writing, and so He provided me with a mother who was an English major in college. Her name is LaVerne. When I first began submitting my writing to her scrutiny, there could be as many as twenty corrections on a page. Nowadays I have it down to one or two. But without her, I would be in trouble. Who knows what misteaks might've made it into the books I've wrote?

My wife, Becky, has also been a valuable proof reader and genuine source of encouragement. When you write a book that you know is destined to be an international worst-seller, you need all the encouragement you can get.

My greatest thanks to the Lord, through whom all things are possible, even the squeezing of camels through needles. May He use this book to squeeze a few more through.

Contents

Introduction

Anyone who reads through the Gospels cannot avoid repeatedly encountering Jesus' startling and often troubling words about money, possessions and stewardship. He commanded His followers to sell their possessions and give to charity.[1] He forbade them to lay up earthly treasures.[2] He told stories about rich people who went to hell.[3] He warned that eternal damnation awaited those who don't help the very poor among His family.[4]

What are we to make of these "hard sayings," as they are commonly called?

Regrettably, some within the realm of Christendom, certain that their eternal salvation is secure by means of a faith that requires no obedience to Christ, simply ignore them. They mistakenly trust in a grace that is foreign to Scripture, one that gives them license to sin. In their minds, Jesus' commandments serve no higher purpose than to show them their sinfulness, thus motivating them to receive Him as Savior as they continue to reject Him as Lord. Repentance and obedience are optional.

I've exposed these fatally-flawed assumptions in another book titled *The Great Gospel Deception* (Ethnos Press, 1999). Jesus and His apostles continually warned that faith without works cannot save and that heaven does not await the unholy. Jesus declared that it is not those who call Him Lord who will be saved, but those who do the will of His Father (see Matt. 7:21). Only *they* are His true brothers (see Matt. 12:48-50). Paul taught that those who practice sin, including the greedy and covetous, will not inherit God's kingdom, even if they profess to believe in Jesus (see 1 Cor. 6:9-10;

[1] Luke 12:33

[2] Matt. 6:19

[3] Luke 12:16-20; 16:19-31

[4] Matt. 25:31-46

Eph. 5:3-5). John declared that only those who keep Jesus' commandments actually know Him (see 1 John 2:3-4). The author of the book of Hebrews tells us that without holiness, no one will see the Lord (see Heb. 12:14). Jude warned against the heresy of turning God's grace into a license to sin (see Jude 1:4). All of this being so, it is certainly not wise to ignore Jesus' hard sayings about money, possessions and stewardship.

Those who don't ignore Jesus' difficult statements about stewardship often soften or explain them in such a way that troubled consciences are soothed. How relieving it is to discover "what Jesus must have really meant," so that we can convince ourselves that we have been, after all, obeying Him right along.

Both of those "solutions" are only temporary solutions at best. Eventually we all must stand before the One who gave those commandments that we currently ignore or modify. And just the fact that we resist what the Lord Jesus plainly said indicates that we have a problem right now that needs fixed.

Let's face it, rich people like us don't like to think that God might appraise us as being selfish, materialistic, greedy, deceived or disqualified for heaven. We'll do just about anything to avoid those kinds of thoughts, including believing lies. The only other alternative—taking what Jesus said honestly—is just too difficult, perhaps impossible.

God, of course, knows better than anyone how hard it is for rich people to enter His kingdom. After all, it was *Jesus* who said it was easier for a camel to go through the eye of a needle than for a rich person to be saved (see Matt. 19:24-25). Even if you've believed the legend of an alleged "Needle Gate" in Jerusalem where camels had to unload before entering, the idea conveyed is still the same—everything must be shed or you don't get in. We should be thankful that Jesus offered some hope to His despairing disciples who, after hearing His camel and needle analogy, asked, "Then who can be saved?" He responded, "With men it is impossible, but not with God; for all things are possible with God" (Mark 10:26-27).

So there is hope for us, with God's help.

It is obvious, however, that Jesus did not mean that God would make the impossible possible by changing His mind and lowering His requirements for rich people to enter His kingdom. Rather, He would make the impossible possible by helping rich people to meet His requirements.

It is also obvious, however, that God doesn't help rich people without their cooperation. Jesus didn't stop the rich, young ruler from sadly walking away. God isn't in the business of making holy robots.

That being said, God helps us by first helping us to face up to what Jesus plainly said. He exposes the lies we've believed in light of His Word. *He makes us feel guilty.* Then He helps us change our desires and repent. He turns greedy people into generous people. He helps us to do what it is not possible to do without Him. It is nothing short of a miracle, and it happens to very few people. *But you can be one of them.* You must be prepared, however, to let God help you *His* way and to cooperate with *His* help.

I can assure you that you will be challenged by what you are about to read, but that is part of the process. You must understand that *there is no other way.* May I add that I can certainly sympathize with you. As I've personally faced up to what Jesus taught, I've often felt like a camel going through the eye of a needle. For many years as a pastor, I lived and taught in contradiction of much of what I've written in this book. But God helped me, first by showing me how I had been ignoring numerous scriptures as well as twisting the clear meaning of many others.

He also showed me my selfishness. I had been a poor steward of His money with which I had been entrusted, and I was not ready to stand before Him to give an account. It wasn't an easy pill to swallow, but I'm so glad God opened my eyes. *Better now than later.*

Since then, and after conversing with many people on this subject, I've become convinced that none of us can honestly receive what Jesus said about money, possessions and stewardship unless God Himself does a work in our hearts. If our hearts are not open to God's work, however, no amount of Scripture or logic will change us. Jesus Himself could not open the eyes of the Pharisees, whom the Bible states were "lovers of money" (Luke 16:14), and who scoffed when He spoke about stewardship. He told them, "You are those who justify yourselves in the sight of men, but God knows your hearts" (Luke 16:15). We, too, may justify ourselves in the sight of people, but God knows our hearts. He knows if we are self-deceived or not.

"But I'm certain that I'm not deceived!" you may claim. Do you realize, however, that every deceived person would claim that very thing? If deceived people knew they were deceived, they wouldn't be deceived. That is why it is imperative that we adopt a sincere, humble attitude that says, "I may be deceived, and if I am, I pray that God would help me to see it." Otherwise, there is little hope that we will accept what Jesus taught.

The Bible promises that God resists the proud (see 1 Pet. 5:5), and as long as we are not open to self-examination and correction, our pride is exposed and God resists us. Scripture also teaches, however, that God gives grace to the humble (see 1 Pet. 5:5). As we sincerely humble ourselves and ask God to show us the truth—to open our eyes to any lies we've believed and to reveal if we're displeasing to Him in any way—He will pour His grace upon us. God hides truth from those who consider themselves "wise and intelligent," but He opens the eyes of "babes" (Luke 10:21).

A Word about Guilt

So the very first step through the needle's eye is the decision to be willing to face up to what Jesus plainly taught. We must be willing to examine ourselves in the light of His words and accept guilt if we find ourselves falling short. That being so, it is imperative that we understand that guilt is not the bad thing it is often made out to be. Guilt, in fact, is the great catalyst of spiritual progress. The truth is that we *don't* change unless we are *motivated* to change. *Repentance is always preceded by guilt. That is God's way, and the only way that He can even begin to get camels through needles.*

Guilt is the simple recognition that we are not pleasing God whom we ought to please. The only people whom God doesn't want to *feel* guilty are those who *aren't* guilty. And the only people who are not guilty in God's eyes are those who are not sinning, or those who have sinned, repented, and been forgiven by Him. If one repeats his sin after he has received God's forgiveness, he is once again guilty, and should feel guilty. It's just that simple.

Scripture says, "My son, do not reject the discipline of the Lord, or loathe His reproof" (Prov. 3:11). What is guilt but God's reproof? We should therefore not reject guilt, but welcome it, embrace it, and allow it to work God's goal in us, which is our repentance and obedience.

On the other hand, Scripture declares that fools spurn God's reproof (see Prov. 1:22-30). Foolish indeed are those who are adverse to guilt or any teaching that makes people feel guilty. *If one is adverse toward guilt, he is adverse toward God.* Amazingly, many such people claim to be Christians.

What so many professing Christians reject as "condemning" really ought to be embraced as "convicting." The primary difference between condemnation and conviction is the existence or absence of hope. Condemnation is void of hope. Conviction is bursting with it. The whole purpose of guilt is to motivate us to repent; thus the very concept of guilt implies that forgiveness is available. Praise God! But those who don't yield to guilt's conviction do not experience God's forgiveness.

Another difference between condemnation and conviction is the motive behind each. Condemnation originates from a motive of justice, whereas conviction is born from a motivation of love and mercy. This book is convicting and not condemning in the least, and anyone who claims otherwise is hiding behind a smokescreen because he feels convicted and doesn't want to change. (Ear-tickling preaching is actually the most condemning preaching of all, because those who buy into the false grace that is proffered through it are sealing their eternal condemnation.) I write from a motivation of love, as one who once was completely brainwashed ("brain dirtied" would describe it better) by beliefs that contradicted Christ's commandments. I've also wrestled with the conviction that every reader will face. It hasn't been easy for me and it won't be easy for you. But to keep silent now would be criminal, because God ultimately does condemn those who resist His conviction. Then there is no longer any hope.

When guilt is based on the unconfessed, unforgiven transgression of

God's will, guilt is a *very good* thing. It is a means of God's communication. It is an indication of His love. Please, as you read, don't resist His love for you. Don't resist what can motivate you to change. We can deal with guilt either by confession and repentance or by justification. Confession and repentance reveal a humble heart that chooses to believe the truth; attempting to justify one's actions reveals a proud heart that willfully believes a lie. If we believe in and love Jesus, we will not be adverse to what He plainly said. He declared, "If you love Me, you will keep My commandments" (John 14:15). It's just that simple.

So let us begin with a sincere prayer on our knees, or better, on our faces. Pray for God's help to get through the needle's eye. Then let us begin to consider honestly what Jesus taught about money, possessions and stewardship. You are about to begin a journey that leads to true joy.

David Kirkwood

ONE

The Untimely
Passing of a Wealthy Fool
Luke 12:13-34

So you've decided to continue reading. Good. That is a hopeful indication that your heart is open to be challenged. Now your journey toward true joy begins, and it begins at the only place it can, by honestly considering what Jesus said.

We'll start with His words found in Luke 12:13-34, which include His parable of the rich fool, and we'll be challenged to examine our own lives in light of what He taught. We'll probably feel guilt, but as I stated in the introduction, *there is no other way.* Get ready. We'll also be tempted to find a way to resolve our guilt by some means other than confession and repentance. Thus we must be wary of inconsistent, illogical "explanations" we've previously heard that soften what Jesus said or help us understand "what He really must have meant." Let's read slowly and honestly:

> And someone in the crowd said to Him [Jesus], "Teacher, tell my brother to divide the family inheritance with me." But He said to him, "Man, who appointed Me a judge or arbiter over you?" And He said to them, "Beware, and be on your guard against every form of greed; for not even when one has an abundance does his life consist of his possessions." And He told them a parable, saying, "The land of a certain rich man was very productive. And he began reasoning to himself, saying, 'What shall I do, since I have no place to store my crops?' And he said, 'This is what I will do: I will tear down my barns and build larger ones, and there I will store all my grain and my goods. And I will say to my soul, "Soul, you have many goods laid up for many years to come; take your ease, eat, drink and be merry."' But God said to him, 'You fool! This very

night your soul is required of you; and now who will own what you have prepared?' So is the man who lays up treasure for himself, and is not rich toward God."

And He said to His disciples, "For this reason I say to you, do not be anxious for your life, as to what you shall eat; nor for your body, as to what you shall put on. For life is more than food, and the body than clothing. Consider the ravens, for they neither sow nor reap; and they have no storeroom nor barn; and yet God feeds them; how much more valuable you are than the birds! And which of you by being anxious can add a single cubit to his life's span? If then you cannot do even a very little thing, why are you anxious about other matters? Consider the lilies, how they grow; they neither toil nor spin; but I tell you, even Solomon in all his glory did not clothe himself like one of these. But if God so arrays the grass in the field, which is alive today and tomorrow is thrown into the furnace, how much more will He clothe you, O men of little faith! And do not seek what you shall eat, and what you shall drink, and do not keep worrying. For all these things the nations of the world eagerly seek; but your Father knows that you need these things. But seek for His kingdom, and these things shall be added to you. Do not be afraid, little flock, for your Father has chosen gladly to give you the kingdom. Sell your possessions and give to charity; make yourselves purses which do not wear out, an unfailing treasure in heaven, where no thief comes near, nor moth destroys. For where your treasure is, there will your heart be also" (Luke 12:13-34).

Imagine for a moment, Jesus preaching to thousands of people (see 12:1), a multitude that consisted of His followers and the curious. Within the crowd stood a man who felt he'd been treated unfairly by his brother in regard to the family inheritance. We don't know if he had been defrauded of his entire share or if he simply felt that his half wasn't as large as his brother's. Neither do we know his brother's side of the story, who may have had some good justification for his apparently selfish actions. Regardless, the outspoken man had hopes that Jesus would settle their dispute. Perhaps he thought that if this very popular rabbi publicly rendered judgment in his favor, it would motivate his brother to acquiesce. So he said to Jesus, "Teacher, tell my brother to divide the family inheritance with me" (Luke 12:13).

Jesus, however, refused to get involved in the man's dispute, asking him, "Man, who appointed Me a judge or arbiter over you?" (Luke 12:14).

Jesus didn't believe it was His place to render a decision in the matter. And He certainly didn't have the time to listen to both sides of the story, oversee an appraisal of every item in the estate, and then determine who got what. He had much more important things to do.

Jesus did, however, seize the opportunity to warn of a much more serious matter that had surfaced. A danger flag was waving that He wanted everyone to see. Greed was rearing its head. This man was much too preoccupied with getting his inheritance, evidenced by his publicly speaking evil of his own brother and his inappropriate, ill-timed and even foolish request of Jesus.[1] Just imagine seeing someone walk up to a preacher at the end of his sermon and publicly say to him, "Preacher, tell my brother to divide the family inheritance with me!" I'm sure you would conclude that such a person was overly occupied with his inheritance.

Jesus then said to the crowd, *"Beware, and be on your guard against every form of greed; for not even when one has an abundance does his life consist of his possessions"* (Luke 12:15).[2]

Let's consider several very significant points of that divinely-uttered statement.

Four Significant Points

First, note in verse 15 the unmistakable connection Jesus drew between greed and a person thinking that his life consists of his possessions. The two are intrinsically linked. When a person becomes convinced that life is about material possessions, whether he has many or few, greed becomes an inevitable and normally irresistible temptation. If one's joy is found in the ownership of possessions, he will soon become discontent with what he has, and will then devote himself to the pursuit of gaining more. Money then becomes His master, directing his life. It will lead him along selfish paths, away from what his life's pursuit should be. This leads us to the next point.

If one's life does not consist of his possessions, then there must be something else in life of greater importance. What is it? Jesus makes that very clear in the remainder of this passage. The pursuit of one's life should be knowing, loving, enjoying and pleasing His Creator, or as Jesus puts it, being "rich toward God" (12:21). Our life's focus should not be for what is material, but for what is spiritual. We should "seek for His kingdom" (12:31), just as Jesus said.

---

[1] A friend has suggested that Jesus may have been thinking about the man's brother as being the one who was guilty of greed. I will admit that is a possibility, but because of Jesus' refusal to arbitrate the dispute, I doubt that He would have jumped to a conclusion about the man's brother after hearing only one side of the story. Also, there is no proof within the text that Jesus' warning against greed was spoken in reference to the man's brother, while there is certainly some evidence to suggest that the man who made the request was in danger of yielding to greed. Regardless, Jesus' subsequent warning about greed had application to the man, his brother, the crowd that day, and everyone since then. Greed is often the reason that people fight over inheritances and money.

[2] The *King James Version* translates the last part of Jesus' statement in 12:15 slightly different: "For a man's life consisteth not in the abundance of the things which he possesseth."

The greedy man in this story was standing among a crowd that was listening to a live sermon by God in the flesh, but all he could think of was gaining more material wealth via his inheritance! What a pity! Many pastors know the pain of having one of their parishioners ask some trite question of them immediately after a sermon in which they had poured out their hearts. Such pastors may be smiling on the outside, but inwardly they are groaning, realizing that their impassioned message obviously had no effect upon *that* parishioner. That example, however, pales in comparison to someone asking the Son of God, perhaps even interrupting Him during His sermon, to settle a dispute about an inheritance. This man was spiritually dull to say the least.

A third point that can be derived from Jesus' warning is that greed stalks rich and poor alike. Note that He said, "Not even when one has an abundance does his life consist of his possessions" (Luke 12:15). If I said, "Not even when one owns many cows does he find true happiness," my declaration has application to those who own no cows as well as those who own many cows. In fact, it would seem more likely that my words were addressed to those with few cows. Those who have little are often just as deceived as those who have much, thinking that life consists of possessions. Jesus would shortly elaborate on greed's deception of rich and poor as He continued His discourse.

A fourth and final point that surfaces is that greed is something that we must beware and stand guard against, just as Jesus said. Greed never announces its arrival, but rather slithers silently into one's heart like a snake. It always looks for opportunities, such as when inheritances are received. Unguarded hearts are easily infiltrated, and *the person who believes that life consists of possessions might as well have a welcome mat laid out for greed.* Moreover, once greed has taken up residence in a heart, it specializes in making itself invisible to the heart's owner, hiding behind an innumerable number of smokescreens. Only God's Word and Spirit are able to expose its presence.

When the Greedy Define Greed

If we are to obey Jesus' commandment to beware of greed, we must first be able to identify it. And that presents a problem. Too often we define greed like Mafia mobsters define evil people, never suspecting that they themselves exemplify the true definition. We similarly define greed with a strong cultural bias and without reference to God's standards. For example, Webster defines greed as "excessive desire for getting or having, especially wealth; desire for more than one needs or deserves."

By this definition, I wonder, *How can I determine if I'm greedy?* Can anyone tell me what constitutes a desire for wealth that is excessive? How many people would consider *their* desire for wealth to be excessive? We may judge others as having an excessive desire for wealth, but we would never judge our own desire for wealth as being excessive.

And if greed is the "desire for more than one needs or deserves," how much does one need? And how does one determine what he deserves? You can see how just about anyone who reads this somewhat vague, modern definition of greed might easily appraise himself as not being guilty. Webster has indeed accurately defined greed by the modern usage of the word, because no one considers himself or herself to be greedy.

Not only is our modern definition of greed very vague, it is also often inconsistent. We sometimes fool ourselves by supposing that greed is a sin that can be committed only by the ultra-rich, or by those who gain their money immorally or illegally. Yet we tell our children not to be greedy in relationship to cookies in a cookie jar. We know that it is selfish for one child to eat the three remaining cookies when that child's brother and sister are equally desirous of one. And such selfishness we call greed— "Don't be greedy, Johnny! Just eat one cookie!" Obviously, we don't really believe that greed is a sin that can only be committed by the ultra-rich or by those who gain their wealth immorally or illegally. We know otherwise. We intuitively understand that what makes greed wrong is the way it affects others, those who don't get the cookies that we gorge. It has something to do with inequality.

There is another way by which we fool ourselves through a customary definition of greed. It is commonly believed that greed is only an attitude of the heart and that it has nothing to do with our actions. We imagine that we can accumulate and keep as much as we want, just as long as we don't allow greed into our hearts. We might just as well claim that hatred is only an attitude of the heart that has nothing to do with actions. Could it be rightly said that there is nothing wrong with murdering another person just as long as the murderer doesn't allow hatred into his heart? Greed is indeed an attitude of one's heart, but one that manifests itself by actions. We would never tell our children, "Go ahead and eat all the cookies while your siblings go without any—but just make sure you do it without an attitude of greed!"

Greed Biblically Defined

How does God define greed? That is what matters. When the Bible speaks of greed, should we assume that Webster's definition is valid? What makes greed wrong in God's eyes?

As we progress in our study of Scripture, God's definition of greed will become increasingly clearer to us. Most fundamentally, however, greed is a violation of the two greatest commandments ever given to humanity— to love God with all one's heart, soul and mind and to love one's neighbor as one's self (see Matt. 22:36-39).

Greedy people do not love their neighbors as themselves—they love themselves and ignore their neighbors. They take for themselves what belongs to their neighbors or they keep for themselves what they should share with their neighbors. It is just that simple. How could one not be guilty of greed if he lives in abundant self-indulgence while he knows that his brother is starving? Please pause and think about this, as there is no escaping its truthfulness.

Neither do greedy people love God as He should be loved because material things have usurped His rightful place. Money is directing their lives, not God. They are finding their happiness in their possessions, not in knowing, loving, enjoying and pleasing Him. Nothing competes with God for the hearts of people like money and possessions, which is no doubt why Jesus warned that one can't serve God and money (see Matt. 6:24). If money is one's master, God is not.

Of course, people don't actually serve money; they serve themselves by what they do with their money. Paul warned that people in the last days would be, first of all, "lovers of *self*, lovers of *money*" (2 Tim. 3:2, emphasis added). It is interesting that Paul placed these two loves right beside each other. The love of money is really the love of self. Greed indicates that self is on the throne of one's heart and that God is not. Jesus is not Lord of greedy people, which is precisely why Scripture tells us that greed is equivalent to idolatry (see Eph. 5:5; Col. 3:5). In God's eyes, greedy and covetous people are just like those who bow before false gods. In this case, however, they are bowing before photographs of themselves. These kinds of people are not God's people, even if they claim to be. The Bible warns that greedy/covetous people will not inherit the kingdom of God (see 1 Cor. 6:9-10; Eph. 5:3-6). There is no such thing as a greedy Christian. Greedy people are not Christians. Greedy people don't go to heaven. That is why it is so crucial to examine ourselves in this matter, to put it mildly.

All this being so, Jesus, whose love is so great, is concerned about anyone yielding to greed's temptation, which is why He so earnestly warned the crowd that day. The outspoken man, in particular, was in dire danger of gaining an inheritance at the expense of forfeiting any hope of eternal life. What a tragic error.

The Similarities Between Greed and Covetousness

While we're beginning to search for a biblical definition of greed, let's also take a minute to consider the sin of covetousness, also mentioned in the New Testament. How does it differ, if at all, from greed?

In the original Greek language of the New Testament, there is little obvious difference in meaning between the two words most often translated *greed* and *covetousness*. In fact, the Greek word that is most often translated *greed* (pleonexia) is derived from the root word that is most often translated *covetous* (pleonektes). Additionally, even pleonexia is sometimes translated *covetousness* or *coveting* (for example, see Mark 7:22 and 2 Cor. 9:5 in the NASB). The *King James Version* translates pleonexia as *covetousness* in Jesus' warning about greed that we're currently considering: "Take heed, and beware of covetousness (pleonexia)" (Luke 12:15). All of this indicates that even Bible translators have difficulty finding any discernible difference in meaning between the words that are most often translated *greed* and *covetousness* in the New Testament.

In the English language, greed and covetousness share very similar meanings. Both terms are meaningless apart from people's relationships with others. Both express a desire to possess what rightfully does or should belong to another. Although I may not jealously desire what another person currently possesses (commonly thought of as covetousness), I may be wrongfully keeping in my possession what God wants me to share with another (which is one manifestation of greed). For example, if God entrusts me with money to feed a starving person and I keep that money for myself, I'm greedy. I'm keeping for myself what should belong to someone else. Again, pause and think about this, for there is no escaping its truthfulness.

Back to Our Story...

Jesus continued His warning against greed that day by relating a story of a rich man who yielded to greed and died soon after. May I refresh your memory by quoting it again:

> The land of a certain rich man was very productive. And he began reasoning to himself, saying, "What shall I do, since I have no place to store my crops?" And he said, "This is what I will do: I will tear down my barns and build larger ones, and there I will store all my grain and my goods. And I will say to my soul, 'Soul, you have many goods laid up for many years to come; take your ease, eat, drink and be merry.'" But God said to him, "You fool! This very night your soul is required of you; and now who will own what you have prepared?" So is the man who lays up treasure for himself, and is not rich toward God (Luke 12:16-21).

The rich man in this parable is an example of a man who thought his life consisted of his possessions. That is, the primary pursuit in his life was the acquiring and selfish enjoyment of material things. Eating, drinking, and pleasure were what he worked and lived for. And with a little help from the weather his hard work paid off. He found himself with more crops and goods than he had barns in which to store them. Then, as is the case every time one finds himself with more than he needs, greed tempted him. His prosperity made it possible for him to retire long before he became elderly or unable to work. Now his ultimate dream could be real-ized—he could selfishly enjoy the remaining years of his life without hav-ing to labor. Every day would be a party. He would have been the envy of almost everyone who knew him.

God, however, considered the man to be a fool, and there are at least four reasons for such an appraisal.

First, the rich man thought only of himself when he considered what to do with his prosperity. He made his decision as if he were the only person in the world. It never occurred to him to think of those who had little or no food. He didn't love his neighbor as himself. He only loved himself. He acted selfishly.

Second, the rich man thought of his life only in terms of its earthly du-ration, and not its eternal duration. As Jesus said, he laid up treasure for himself on earth, not considering the eternal ramifications of his decision. The remainder of his earthly life might be enviable, but how about his life throughout eternity? He possessed earthly treasures, but what about heavenly treasures?

Third, he never considered God in his circumstances. It never occurred to him that God, the one responsible for the good weather that brought abundant crops, had blessed him in order to make him a blessing to others. He never saw his opportunity to glorify God by obeying Him and loving his neighbor as himself. Although he was rich in earthly material things, he was not "rich toward God" (Luke 12:21) as Jesus said. His lifestyle was a testimony to his unbelief, as he ignored the two greatest command-ments. He could have labored for many more years under God's blessing, working to show his love to God and others by sharing his abundance.

And fourth, he assumed he had "many years to come" (Luke 12:19), something that no greedy person should assume, as God certainly has no vested interest in keeping greedy people alive. The rich man in Jesus' parable died on the very night he made his selfish decision. The final deci-sion of his life was a selfish, damning decision. His death that night may well have been God's judgment upon him because of his selfish decision. Jesus certainly didn't leave us much room to think that the rich fool went to heaven that night.[3] In a moment of time, he lost everything he lived for. One second, he owned an abundance, and the next second he owned nothing. God asked him, "And now who will own what you have pre-pared?" (Luke 12:20). It wouldn't be him.

Clearly, Jesus described for us a greedy man, as that was the topic that the parable was meant to illustrate. Note that Jesus didn't describe a rich man whose actions would have been approved by God if he had only

---

[3] I suspect that some will object, saying that Jesus never said that the man went to hell. But are we to believe that this man, who served as Jesus' illustration of greed in action, was saved and went to heaven, only forfeit-ing certain rewards there, in light of the fact that the New Testament teaches that no greedy/covetous person will inherit God's kingdom? (see 1 Cor. 6:10; Eph. 5:3-6).

adjusted his *attitude* about what he possessed, still keeping it all and retiring. *Greed is an attitude that is always manifested by actions.* If one repents of greed, he must not only change his attitude, he must also change his actions. *If he doesn't change his actions, he has not changed his attitude.*

Note also that this rich man was guilty before God, not because he desired what wasn't his, but because he decided to keep what God had given him and wanted him to share with others. He was selfish in the use of his money and possessions. He, as Jesus plainly said of him, laid "up treasure for himself" (Luke 12:21). He was greedy. All who lay up treasure for themselves are greedy. Such people are "not rich toward God" (Luke 12:21), just as Jesus said. God thinks they are fools.

The Application

Now let us begin to pinpoint some application for our own lives from this parable of the rich fool. Let us pray that Jesus' words will have the impact upon us that He intended they would have.

How would you respond to someone who, after reading Jesus' story, said, "I'm so glad that I'm not a farmer, because if I were and I had an abundant harvest, I'd have to consider what Jesus taught"?

Surely you would point out to him that what Jesus said in this parable has application to other people besides farmers. Such a comment would be as foolish as claiming that the Parable of the Good Samaritan only applies to people journeying on the road to Jericho.

What if someone said, "I'm so glad that I've accumulated my wealth gradually rather than by a sudden windfall like that farmer in Jesus' parable. Otherwise, what Jesus said would have application to me."

Would you not realize that person was also fooling himself? What Jesus said has application to everyone who has more than he needs, anyone who might "lay up treasure for himself," whether he's accumulated it slowly or suddenly. I might also add that there is nothing in Jesus' parable that states the rich man accumulated his wealth suddenly. His wealth was more likely acquired gradually, through seasons of fruitful harvests. I suspect that it would be difficult to retire on just one year's crop.

Suppose someone said, "I'm glad I'm not faced with the option of an early retirement, or else I'd have to give some thought to what Jesus taught"?

Although what Jesus said has application to those faced with the option of an early retirement, it clearly has application to those not faced with such an option. Jesus Himself revealed to whom the parable applies—anyone who has opportunity, like the man in the parable, to "lay up treasure for himself" (Luke 12:21), something that Jesus forbade all of His followers to do (see Matt. 6:19-24; Luke 12:33). It makes no difference if we are farmers or flight attendants, if we've accumulated our wealth quickly or gradually, or if we are young or old. The rich fool in Jesus' parable is representative of anyone who has more than he needs and yields to the sin of greed.

How We Might Be Just Like the Rich Fool

When I first began to read this parable honestly and contextually, I realized that I was in many ways similar to the rich fool. I initially assumed that my practice of tithing set me apart from him, and perhaps to some degree it did. But it occurred to me that the rich fool could have been a good Jew who faithfully tithed all of his life. And certainly it is possible to tithe and still lay up treasures for oneself if one has enough abundance. Surely it is possible to tithe and still be selfish with the remaining abundance. One may tithe and remain guilty of greed. The Pharisees *scrupulously* tithed, but according to Scripture, they were also lovers of money (see Luke 11:42; 16:14), and they were also hell-bound (see Matt. 23:13-15).

Are we to think, for example, that God would have fully approved of the rich man if he had tithed on his increase and then decided to take his ease and selfishly retire at that point in his life with his remaining abundance? That doesn't seem very likely, does it? Just because a rich man tithes his income, is he fulfilling the commandments to love God with all his heart and love his neighbor as himself? Although I had tithed my income for many years, I used the remainder of my abundance to enrich my own life, just like the rich fool did. As my income increased, I just kept spending more on myself, "building bigger barns," as it were, never content.

But there are other ways that this parable applies to so many of us. Certainly we are just as foolish as the man in the parable if we think our lives consist of our possessions—when the primary pursuit in our lives is the acquiring and selfish enjoyment of material things. But isn't that the picture of so many of us who profess to be Christians? Our lives completely revolve around acquiring, selfishly spending, and selfishly enjoying wealth. That's what we live for. We aren't seeking first the kingdom of God, as Jesus commanded us (see Matt. 6:33). We are trying to find happiness in material wealth, not in knowing, loving, enjoying and obeying God. We are rich, but not "rich toward God" (Luke 12:21), and the evidence is overwhelming.

Why isn't the average professing Christian in wealthy countries like ours involved at all in the basic things that Jesus said mark authentic believers, such as visiting the sick or providing food and clothing for poor believers (see Matt. 25:31-46)? Why do we give so little money to help fulfill the Great Commission, the large majority of us not even attaining to the Old Covenant standard of tithing? Why do we respond to charitable appeals with the line, "I'll need to pray about that," but we don't need to pray about spending discretionary income on ourselves? In short, why do so many of us who profess to be Christians show so little commitment to Christ in relation to how we spend our time and money? Why are so many of us so lukewarm?

The answer to all these questions is that we are primarily pursuing the American dream, and we are focused on enjoying the material fruits of our labor.

From our earliest years we are programmed to believe that happiness is found in "things." We're encouraged by everyone to perfect those virtues that will reap material rewards. Hard work, honesty and thrift can all really "pay off" in the future. If we work hard in school, then we can get a "good job," which means a job with a high salary.

We choose our careers based on their financial potential, and then work long hours for years and years to pay the leases on our late model cars and the mortgage on a house that speaks of our success. And who has time for something as trivial as raising children? So we drop off our babies at the day care center in servitude to the Almighty Dollar. How can we deny that money controls our lives? The obvious goal in life for so many of us is to earn more money, acquire more possessions and enjoy more pleasures, and then retire comfortably. The sooner, the better.

More Similarities

But the evidence that we think our lives consist of our possessions does not end there. We collect *stuff*. More furniture, more clothing, more tools, more figurines, more golf clubs, more china. While billions wait to hear the gospel and thirty thousand children die each day, we keep right on collecting more. Ultimately, our possessions possess us, consuming all of our God-given time and energy. There is no time to do God's will because we're slaves to our money and possessions. We've got one thousand things that must be used, enjoyed, polished, repaired, dusted, insured, stored and maintained. Don't forget to purchase the service contract that will get it back up and running if it breaks down! How can we honestly say that we are not convinced that our lives consist of the abundance of our possessions? Jesus couldn't have made it more plain. He said that the one who "lays up treasure for himself" is not "rich toward God" (Luke 12:21). It is just that simple.

Not only must we have what advertisers say we must have, but we must have it all *now*. So we borrow to the limit, wasting a huge percentage of our wealth on interest payments, again, while millions starve and billions wait to hear that Jesus died for them. Many of our monthly payments are a continual testimony to our greed.

Then there are our many activities that all cost money—sports, hobbies, entertainment and so on, too often pursued with devotion that could only be defined as religious. Over our lifetimes we waste hundreds of thousands of dollars on things that are nothing more than pure self-indulgence. How can we claim that we are ready to stand before Jesus while being such poor stewards of the time and money He has entrusted to us? If the essence of following Jesus is self-denial (see Matt. 16:24), then where are the people who are following Jesus? Are not our lives more characterized by self-indulgence than self-denial?

Moreover, we spend the majority of our money on things that no one *could* spend their money on a hundred years ago and on which the majority of people in the world will never spend their money. Our lives could be summarized by two words: *acquire* and *indulge*. Worse yet, we are never satisfied. We need a bigger house, a newer car, a more exotic vacation. And we don't even recognize our greed, just as insane people can't detect their insanity. Our culture of materialism has callused our consciences. The only real difference between the rich fool and many of us is that God is still giving us time to repent of our greed. The rich fool has faced His judgment—we are waiting our turn.

If your conscience is being pricked, remember, guilt is good when it is based on God's Word. Don't resist it. Embrace it. God is speaking to you.

Still More Similarities

We are equally as foolish as the rich fool if we don't consider the eternal ramifications of our earthly decisions regarding money and possessions. If no greedy or covetous person is going to inherit the kingdom of God (see 1 Cor. 6:9-10; Eph. 5:5), should we not seriously consider if we are guilty in this matter? Eternity depends, at least in part, on what we do with our money. Jesus expressly forbade us to lay up treasures on earth, but commanded us to lay them up in heaven by sharing what God entrusts to us. All of us will have to stand before Him one day to give an account of our stewardship. Will He accept our excuses?

We are just as foolish as the rich fool if we don't consider that God is the source of our every material possession—if not by direct blessing, at least by His permissive will. Thus He has the absolute right to direct our use of what He entrusts to us. I might think, "I worked my way through college, and I've worked hard ever since. I've *earned* my wealth, so I *deserve* to enjoy spending it on myself." But have I considered how my life would have turned out had I been born to a cocaine addict in a New York City housing project, or to a prostitute in Calcutta? Have I considered that God allowed me to be born in the wealthy country in which I live, and that He is the one who made me as intelligent as I am, and who made it possible for me to work hard or attend college? Thus, I am just as accountable to God for my wealth as the rich fool was in Jesus' parable. If God has blessed me, it is because He intends that I share His blessing with others. What would

Jesus have thought of His disciples if, upon receiving the multiplied fish and bread from His hands, they had piled up for themselves what He intended for them to share? What must He think if we indulge ourselves with that which He intends for us to use for His glory? Are we faithful stewards?

Finally, we are just as foolish as the rich fool if we assume that we have many years left in our lives, especially when we are living so selfishly. We should live every day as if it were our last one. We could be standing in front of Jesus' throne one minute from now. In fact, Jesus concluded His thoughts about greed that day by warning His disciples to be ready for His return (see Luke 12:35-48).

Unless we have a rich relationship with God, we're not ready. If all we've done with our lives is acquire more for ourselves, we're fools, because everything we've lived for will be gone in a moment. The only thing that is eternal is our relationship with God.

A Warning to Those with Little

Jesus had still more to say on the subject of greed. He didn't want us to think that greed is a sin that is committed only by those who have abundance. I again quote His elaboration to His disciples:

> For this reason I say to you, do not be anxious for your life, as to what you shall eat; nor for your body, as to what you shall put on. For life is more than food, and the body than clothing. Consider the ravens, for they neither sow nor reap; and they have no storeroom nor barn; and yet God feeds them; how much more valuable you are than the birds! And which of you by being anxious can add a single cubit to his life's span? If then you cannot do even a very little thing, why are you anxious about other matters? Consider the lilies, how they grow; they neither toil nor spin; but I tell you, even Solomon in all his glory did not clothe himself like one of these. But if God so arrays the grass in the field, which is alive today and tomorrow is thrown into the furnace, how much more will He clothe you, O men of little faith! And do not seek what you shall eat, and what you shall drink, and do not keep worrying. For all these things the nations of the world eagerly seek; but your Father knows that you need these things. But seek for His kingdom, and these things shall be added to you. Do not be afraid, little flock, for your Father has chosen gladly to give you the kingdom. Sell your possessions and give to charity; make yourselves purses which do not wear out, an unfailing treasure in heaven, where no thief

comes near, nor moth destroys. For where your treasure
is, there will your heart be also (Luke 12:22-34).

Notice that Jesus began by saying, "For this reason I say to you..." Those
words tie everything He has just said to what He was about to say. The
subject was still greed and the folly of those who think that life consists of
their possessions. Notice also the similarity of Jesus' words here about *life
being more than food* and His previous words about *life not consisting of the
abundance of one's possessions.* The subject hasn't changed.

Now, however, Jesus applies what He has just said to those who, by
normal North American standards, have very little. It is possible for them
to be just as deceived as the rich if they are primarily focused on earthly
possessions, even if those possessions are basic necessities such as food
and clothing. Just because a person has few possessions, he is not automatically more devoted to God or less of a servant of mammon. Anyone,
rich or poor, who thinks that life consists of possessions, is making a grave
mistake.

Jesus does not want His disciples to be preoccupied with even the necessities of life, because God will take care of those things. Certainly, if
God doesn't want us to be preoccupied with life's basic necessities, how
much more does He not want us to be preoccupied with non-essentials?

Needs and Wants

I used to question where to draw the line between my needs and my
wants. In the just-quoted passage about food and covering, however, Jesus made it very clear. He said, "Your Father knows that *you need these
things*" (Luke 12:30; emphasis added). Those things are all we actually
need. Everything besides food and covering is a want.[4] That is why Paul
wrote,

> For we have brought nothing into the world, so we can-
> not take anything out of it either. And if we have food and
> covering, with these we shall be content. But those who
> want to get rich fall into temptation and a snare and many
> foolish and harmful desires which plunge men into ruin
> and destruction (1 Tim. 6:7-9).

Can we honestly claim that we would be content if all we had was food
and covering (that is, clothing and shelter) when we are obviously not
content with the abundance we now possess, but are continually striving
to acquire and selfishly enjoy more and more?

Can we say we are convinced, like Paul, that the desire to be rich (which
Paul seems to define as desiring more than food and covering) is poten-

---

[4] The concept that our real needs consist of only food and covering is found in other scriptures. See, for example, Gen. 28:20; Prov. 25:2; Luke 3:11; 12:22-30.

tially damning because of the many temptations to be selfish and greedy that confront those with such a desire?[5]

All of Christ's followers are supposed be seeking for His kingdom, just as He said (see Luke 12:31). His kingdom is the only thing that is eternal, which is precisely why Jesus instructed all of His disciples (as we just read) not to lay up treasures on the earth. All of our earthly possessions are destined to perish; in fact, most are perishing before our eyes right now. Thus it makes perfect sense to sell our possessions and lay up eternal treasure in heaven as Christ commanded.

As martyred missionary Jim Elliot said, "He is no fool who gives up what he cannot keep to gain what he cannot lose." But how many Christians do you know who have obeyed Christ's clear command (that we just read) to sell their possessions and give to charity, as did all the first Christians? (see Acts 2:45; 4:34-35). Most of us seem to be gathering more possessions.

Jesus couldn't have made His point more clear. He does not want our hearts to be fastened to this world. Rather, He wants our hearts to be in heaven (see Luke 12:34). When our lives revolve around temporal gain and selfish pursuits, can we honestly say that our hearts are not on the earth? Can we honestly say our hearts are in heaven, and that what we do with our money and possessions reflects that heavenly affection? *Or are we rich fools?*

I warned you that this wasn't going to be easy! If you've been convicted, embrace it. Confession and repentance will be the result. When I was first convicted, I was so full of pride that it was very difficult for me to admit my sin. But I just couldn't ignore what Jesus taught, and as I would humble myself just a little, confessing my sin, God poured out more of His grace and opened more of His Word to me. Remember that He resists the proud but gives grace to the humble.

If you find yourself resenting what I've written so far, it's time to get back on your knees. Pray fervently for God's help and grace, admitting your desperate need for both. Then go back and reread this chapter. Believe me, you aren't ready for the next chapter until you can face up to this one. You may still have some questions or objections, but I assure you that we'll cover them in following chapters.

Search me, O God, and know my heart;
Try me and know my anxious thoughts;
And see if there be any hurtful way in me,
And lead me in the everlasting way (Ps. 139:23-24).

---

[5] The *King James Version* does not soften Paul's warning here as much as the NASB seems to: "But they that will be rich fall into temptation and a snare, and into many foolish and hurtful lusts, which drown men in *destruction and perdition*" (emphasis added).

TWO

Jesus Loves a Rich, Young Ruler
Mark 10:17-30

I hope you are still praying fervently for God's help. If you are intending to read this chapter, that is a good indication that He's answering your prayers. Now pray that God will help you read with an open heart, honestly, just like a child. The reason that Scripture is often "difficult to understand" (as we say) is because we don't want to accept its simple message.

The study of the rich, young ruler will require two chapters, because we must consider the very means and nature of salvation, and there are so many unbiblical ideas on that subject that are entrenched in our minds. Pray that God will give you clarity of understanding. He will!

Let us read the story of the rich, young ruler as it was told by Mark:

> And as He [Jesus] was setting out on a journey, a man ran up to Him and knelt before Him, and began asking Him, "Good Teacher, what shall I do to inherit eternal life?" And Jesus said to him, "Why do you call Me good? No one is good except God alone. You know the commandments, 'Do not murder, Do not commit adultery, Do not steal, Do not bear false witness, Do not defraud, Honor your father and mother.'" And he said to Him, "Teacher, I have kept all these things from my youth up." And looking at him, Jesus felt a love for him, and said to him, "One thing you lack: go and sell all you possess, and give to the poor, and you shall have treasure in heaven; and come, follow Me." But at these words his face fell, and he went away grieved, for he was one who owned much property.
>
> And Jesus, looking around, said to His disciples, "How hard it will be for those who are wealthy to enter the kingdom of God!" And the disciples were amazed at His

words. But Jesus answered again and said to them, "Children, how hard it is to enter the kingdom of God! It is easier for a camel to go through the eye of a needle than for a rich man to enter the kingdom of God." And they were even more astonished and said to Him, "Then who can be saved?" Looking upon them, Jesus said, "With men it is impossible, but not with God; for all things are possible with God." Peter began to say to Him, "Behold, we have left everything and followed You." Jesus said, "Truly I say to you, there is no one who has left house or brothers or sisters or mother or father or children or farms, for My sake and for the gospel's sake, but that he shall receive a hundred times as much now in the present age, houses and brothers and sisters and mothers and children and farms, along with persecutions; and in the age to come, eternal life" (Mark 10:17-30).

This well-known story of the rich, young ruler, recorded in three of the four Gospels, disturbs us for several reasons. First, it seems as if Jesus required the rich ruler to give up his wealth in order to inherit eternal life. That certainly doesn't fit well with our theology. It sounds to us like salvation by works, not by grace through faith.

Second, Jesus broadened the application of what He said to one man that day to include all wealthy people, saying that it is "easier for a camel to go through the eye of a needle than for *a rich man* to enter the kingdom of God" (Mark 10:25, emphasis added). If we're wealthy, then what Jesus said apparently applies to us, just as much as it did to the rich, young ruler. If you work forty hours each week and are paid the minimum wage in the United States, you are enjoying an annual income that is higher than 87% of the world's population.[1] It would seem that what Jesus said has application to most of us.

So what are we to make of this whole incident? It's likely that you've heard somebody's explanation that has made the whole thing easier to swallow.[2] But let's try to consider the story without preconceived ideas. Let's try to read it honestly, without changing what Jesus actually said. If we can, we'll see that Matthew, Mark and Luke recorded some vital spiritual truths that should not be discounted or ignored by anyone, truths that harmonize perfectly with the rest of the New Testament. For many readers, just like the rich ruler, eternity will depend on their understanding and application of what Christ said in these passages. This story is not recorded three times in God's one book without good reason.

[1] You can find out exactly where your particular annual income puts you in comparison to the rest of the world by visiting www.globalrichlist.com and typing your annual income.

[2] What a shame it is when preachers, striving to win the favor of their audiences, expend so much effort trying to explain what Jesus must have really meant. Their goal seems to be to undo the normal guilt people feel when they read the plain words of Christ. Such ministers work against the Holy Spirit.

A Look at the Man

The first thing we notice about this wealthy man is his apparent sincerity and spiritual hunger. Mark tells us that he ran to Jesus and then publicly knelt before Him to pose his question (see Mark 10:17). How many people do you know who run to and publicly kneel before preachers to ask spiritual questions? Such a thing is exceedingly rare (to say the least), and I would suspect it is even more rare when it is done by people of wealth and position.

We additionally note that he respected Jesus greatly, again indicated by his kneeling before Him, and by his addressing Jesus as a "good teacher" (Mark 10:17). He apparently did not know or believe, however, that Jesus was divine, which makes his kneeling before Him an even more telling revelation of his sincerity, spiritual hunger, and respect.

He then asked the most intelligent question that anyone could ask: "What shall I do to inherit eternal life?" (Mark 10:17). It shows that he was thinking about the most significant and important issue that exists. Wouldn't it be wonderful if everyone in the world were as wise as this young man, who realized the importance of learning what a person must do to inherit eternal life?[3] He certainly asked the right question.

God Responds

Jesus began to answer the young ruler's question with a question of His own, followed by a related declaration: "Why do you call Me good? No one is good but God alone" (Mark 10:18).

Jesus, of course, was not attempting to deny or discount His own goodness. He knew that He was worthy to be called good and that He was God. So perhaps Jesus was gently prodding the man to think about His identity. Did he sincerely believe that Jesus was worthy to be called good? If so, Jesus also deserved to be called God, because only God is truly good. Is it not possible that Jesus wanted this man to realize that He was much more than just a good teacher? Certainly.

At the same time, Jesus was subtly telling the rich, young ruler something about himself—that he was a sinner. *No one is good*, said Jesus, except God. So if anyone is going to gain eternal life, it will require God's grace.

Thus, Jesus was already beginning to answer the man's question by prodding him to consider two questions that everyone must ponder before receiving eternal life. Jesus, in essence, asks everyone, "Do you know who I am?" and, "Do you know who you are?"

Jesus next said to the young ruler, "If you wish to enter into life, keep the commandments" (Matt. 19:17). That is pretty straightforward, wouldn't you say? Not complex at all.

---

[3] Although the phrase, *eternal life*, is not found in the Old Testament, the word *forever* is found in more than 250 Old Testament verses. Anyone who takes such verses seriously must conclude that eternal life is the promised inheritance of God's righteous people. This the rich, young ruler knew.

Although it is so straightforward and simple, this is where our confusion begins, because what Jesus said contradicts our theology about salvation. If someone asked us what he should do to inherit eternal life, we would be much more likely to tell him to believe in Jesus. We certainly wouldn't tell him to keep the commandments, because we know that salvation is received by faith, not earned by works. So why did Jesus tell this sincere seeker of eternal life to keep the commandments in order to "enter into life"? There are only a few possible answers to that question. Let us consider them one by one.

It has been suggested that because Jesus never lied, He could only have been endorsing the idea that eternal life can indeed be earned by perfectly keeping God's commandments. Certainly such a method of salvation would seem theoretically possible. If a person never sinned, living a perfectly sinless life, would God cast him into hell at his death? Certainly not, as that would be completely unjust. Thus, that person would have inherited eternal life by keeping God's commandments. If a person never sinned, Jesus would not have had to die for his sins, because that person would have no sins for which to die, and he wouldn't need to be forgiven. He wouldn't need to be saved by grace.

The problem is that no such sinless person has ever existed (other than Jesus). Thus it would seem odd for Jesus, who surely knew that the man had already broken at least some of God's commandments, and who just told him that no one is good, to tell him that he could be saved as long as he never broke any of God's commandments. What might have been theoretically possible was in all practicality utterly impossible for the young ruler (and for all the rest of us as well). Surely Jesus would not have attempted to deceive the rich ruler into thinking he could be saved by a means that was impossible for him to attain. So we can eliminate this particular explanation.

Another Explanation

Others suggest that by telling the rich ruler to keep the commandments, Jesus was only attempting to help the man realize his sinfulness so he would then comprehend the impossibility of being saved by his works. Once that was accomplished, he could then just have "accepted Jesus as his Savior" (a modern formula for salvation). He could have been saved by grace through faith, and not by works.

This theory is based on some biblical truth, and for that reason, many accept it. Against this interpretation, however, is the plain fact that Jesus said, "If you wish to enter into life, keep the commandments" (Matt. 19:17). It was a direct answer to the man's sincere question of how to obtain eternal life. And it was an answer that directly contradicts the idea that keeping the commandments has nothing to do with inheriting eternal life. Jesus certainly wouldn't have lied to the man. The way to enter life is to keep the commandments. That is what the Son of God said.

Have we misunderstood Jesus? No, He reinforced the same message seconds later. When the rich ruler asked which specific commandments he needed to keep in order to inherit eternal life, Jesus listed seven from the Old Testament. And Jesus didn't stop there. When the man claimed to have kept, from his youth, the commandments Jesus listed, Jesus told him he still lacked one thing, and then instructed him to sell his possessions and give the proceeds to charity, a commandment to love the poor as he loved himself.

Note: Jesus let the man walk away thinking that he had to keep at least seven commandments and liquidate his possessions if he wanted to inherit eternal life. If Jesus only wanted the man to realize his sinful state so he would understand that works couldn't save him, (thus opening his heart so he could be saved by the modern method), then Jesus blundered in a major way. Although perhaps He succeeded in getting the rich man to realize his sinfulness, He let the man walk away thinking that he couldn't inherit eternal life unless he kept God's commandments and liquidated his wealth to benefit the poor. *Jesus did the exact opposite of what this particular theory says was His actual intention.*

Not only did Jesus blunder regarding the rich man, misleading him into believing the very lie He supposedly set out to remove from his mind, but Jesus also misled His disciples to believe the same lie. Note that as the rich young ruler walked away sadly, Jesus did not back down at all on what He had said. Rather, He only reinforced one more time what He had already said, declaring to His disciples, "How hard it will be for those who are wealthy to enter the kingdom of God!....It is easier for a camel to go through the eye of a needle than for a rich man to enter the kingdom of God" (Mark 10:23, 25).

Jesus thus "misled" His disciples into thinking that all rich people, and not just the one rich fellow who was walking away, had to sell their possessions and give to charity in order to inherit eternal life. That was obviously how the disciples interpreted what He said, because they were "very astonished" (Matt. 19:25) with His statement about the camel and needle, and exclaimed, "Then who can be *saved*?" (Mark 10:26, emphasis added). They clearly believed Jesus was talking about requirements for salvation, and that one of those requirements involved selling possessions and giving to charity, something wealthy people find difficult to do.

Moreover, when Jesus responded by telling them that only with God was it possible for wealthy people to be saved, they reminded Him that they had left everything to follow Him. Peter asked, "What then will there be for us?" (Matt. 19:27). They wondered if they had met the stringent requirements for inheriting eternal life. Would they be saved? They hadn't sold everything, but they had left everything behind, demonstrating that their love for Him superseded their love of possessions. Money was not their master. Jesus then reassured them of great future rewards and eternal life (see Mark 10:30).

Note that Jesus did not say in response to their astonishment, "Now don't get so worked up! I was just trying to help that rich man see his sinfulness so he would realize his need for a savior and then receive salvation by grace through faith. He didn't really need to sell all his possessions to be saved and neither does any other rich person."

No, Jesus could not have done a better job in making His point clear. He never backed down for a moment. We can be certain that if Jesus, who loved the man and also loved His disciples, thought that any of them had misunderstood what He was saying, He would have clarified what He actually meant. But He didn't.

Thus we can lay to rest the theory that Jesus was only trying to help the man realize his sinfulness so he would then understand the impossibility of being saved by his works, thus leading him to simply "accept Jesus as his Savior," without actually needing to liquidate his wealth. That theory doesn't harmonize at all with what Jesus actually said. In fact, it completely contradicts what Jesus said.

A Third Explanation

A third interpretation of Jesus' words to the rich ruler is that Jesus was revealing a way of salvation that was temporary, one that had application only to those under the old covenant. Were not those people saved by works, but now we are saved by faith? And was not Jesus ministering under the old covenant?

This is a bad theory, due to the fact that Scripture teaches that no person has ever been saved by works, before, during, or after the old covenant. Salvation has always been received by faith. For example, Paul taught that Abraham (*before* the old covenant) and David (*during* the old covenant) were both saved by faith and not by works (see Romans 4:1-13). Additionally, twice in the New Testament, Paul quoted old-covenant prophet Habakkuk's Holy-Spirit inspired words, "But the righteous man shall live by faith" (Rom. 1:17; Gal. 3:11), as well as from the writings of Isaiah and Joel (see Is. 28:16; Joel 2:32; Rom. 10:11, 13) to prove that old covenant people were justified by faith. Jesus, too, once told a woman whom He had forgiven that her faith saved her (see Luke 7:50). This He did while the Jews were living under old covenant. Thus, salvation has always been received by faith. Jesus could not have been endorsing a temporary means of salvation to the rich ruler.

The Answer to Our Question

The only possible conclusion that harmonizes with the rest of what Scripture teaches about salvation is that Jesus was indeed affirming that salvation is received by grace through faith, even though it may not seem so to us. Our problem is that we don't understand what faith is, nor do we see the grace that Jesus was offering.

Scripture teaches that eternal life is given to those who believe in Jesus (see John 3:15-16). But Scripture also states that Jesus "became to all those who *obey* Him the source of eternal salvation" (Heb. 5:9, emphasis added). This is not a contradiction, however, for the simple reason that it is only those who obey Jesus who truly believe in Him. Scripture affirms this again and again. For example, we read in John 3:36: "He who *believes* in the Son has eternal life; but he who does not *obey* the Son shall not see life, but the wrath of God abides on him" (emphasis added). The words *believe* and *obey* are used synonymously in a single verse.

In order to be saved, the rich, young ruler had to become a true believer—and thus a follower of Jesus—and that is the same requirement Jesus made of anyone who wanted eternal life. To be saved, the rich ruler had to repent, just like anyone else, and he specifically needed to turn from money as his master in order to make Jesus his Master, because it is impossible to serve God and mammon (see Matt. 6:24). He had to repent of greed, just like any other greedy person who wants to be saved, because greedy people will not inherit the kingdom of God (see 1 Cor. 6:9-10; Eph. 5:5). Had he believed that Jesus was God's Son, he would have repented of His greed and started following Jesus. But he didn't believe, and thus he did not obey.

How important it is that we understand that Jesus was offering the rich ruler eternal life on the same conditions that He offers eternal life to everyone else. We must believe in Jesus, and thus we must repent and start keeping His commandments. If we are guilty of greed, we must repent of it. That is salvation by grace through faith. Those who truly believe will show their faith by their obedience to His commandments.

"But where is the grace in that?" some question. God's grace (at least in part) is found in the forgiveness granted to those who believe. Their past sins are erased. That is grace, and it can be nothing other than grace. But God has never offered a grace that says, "I forgive you of your past sins, and from now on you can continue sinning without fearing My wrath." That is a grace that is utterly foreign to Scripture. Jesus didn't say, for example, to the woman caught in adultery, "I don't condemn you for what you've done, and you can keep on committing adultery as much as you want without fear of My condemnation." No, Jesus said to her, "Neither do I condemn you; go your way. From now on sin no more" (John 8:11). That is exactly what Jesus in essence said to the rich ruler, and that is the true grace of salvation.[4]

---

[4] Note that Jesus was doing nothing for the woman caught in adultery that He is not doing for every other living person. He is currently not condemning us, and is currently giving us the opportunity to repent. His current grace, however, is no guarantee of His eternal grace. If this woman did not repent, she is now in hell with all unrepentant adulterers (see 1 Cor. 6:9-10).

A Similar Example

The rich ruler is not the only person whom Jesus told to keep the commandments if he wanted to inherit eternal life. We read of Jesus once being asked by an expert in Jewish law, "Teacher, what shall I do to inherit eternal life?" (Luke 10:25). Jesus responded, "What is written in the Law? How does it read to you?" (Luke 10:26). Clearly, Jesus believed the answer could be easily found in the Old Testament. God had not been keeping the most important issue of life, the way to eternal life, a secret!

The lawyer then gave his best answer: "You shall love the Lord your God with all your heart, and with all your soul, and with all your strength, and with all your mind; and your neighbor as yourself" (Luke 10:27). Jesus then replied, "You have answered correctly; do this, and you will live" (Luke 10:28). How much more plain could it be? Jesus said that the man answered correctly. Also note that Jesus used the words, "You will live" to mean, "You shall inherit eternal life." The phrase, "You will live" is borrowed from the Old Testament, and many translations of Luke 10:28 highlight it as a direct Old Testament quotation.

Again we see that Jesus told someone who wanted to know what to do to inherit eternal life that he should keep God's commandments, in this case, the two greatest commandments that summarize all the others. For reasons already stated, we cannot rightfully conclude that Jesus was telling a sinful man that he could be saved as long as he lived a perfectly sinless life. Nor can we, for reasons already stated, rightfully conclude that Jesus was only trying to make the man realize his sinfulness so He could then tell him that salvation was by faith. And neither can we rightfully conclude that Jesus was revealing a temporary means of salvation. The only possibility is that Jesus was affirming salvation by grace through faith. Unlike so many modern professing Christians, however, Jesus knew that faith without works is dead, useless, and cannot save (see Jas. 2:14-26). He would offer no false assurance of salvation to anyone who would not repent and obey, demonstrating a living faith.

There is no other way to interpret what Jesus said to the Jewish lawyer without making Jesus say something He didn't actually say (which is done by Bible interpreters all the time). Jesus never backed down from what He said, even when the lawyer tried to justify himself by asking Jesus to define the word *neighbor* as it was used in the second greatest commandment. After Jesus told the story of the Good Samaritan, in which He defined what God meant by the word *neighbor*, His final words to the lawyer were, "Go and do the same" (Luke 10:37). That is, "Obey the second greatest commandment as the Good Samaritan in the story did." And the lawyer walked away believing that he must do what Jesus said in order to inherit eternal life. There can be no mistake about this. What would the lawyer have said if you had asked him ten minutes later, "What did Jesus tell you to do in order to inherit eternal life?" He would have responded, "I must keep the two greatest commandments, and obeying the second greatest commandment requires that I practice love, not only toward Jews, but also toward Samaritans." That is salvation by grace through faith, and it harmonizes perfectly with the rest of Scripture.

An Old Testament Example of Salvation by Faith

As I've already stated, salvation has always been received by grace through faith. This Paul proves in his letter to the Romans (see Rom. 1:17; 4:1-13; 10:11, 13). Salvation has always been received by faith, not just under the new covenant, but before and during the old covenant.

We, however, often miss this truth as we read the Old Testament, simply because we don't understand the inseparable correlation between faith and works. We think that faith and works are diametrically opposed to one another. The truth is, however, that works are an intrinsic component of true faith. Faith is not a substitute for good works. Rather, faith is a catalyst for good works.

Consider the following Old Testament passage from Ezekiel. Can you find the offer of salvation and eternal life by grace through faith in the promises it contains? Read carefully! These are the actual words of God:

> "Behold, all souls are Mine; the soul of the father as well as the soul of the son is Mine. The soul who sins will die. But if a man is righteous, and practices justice and righteousness, and does not eat at the mountain shrines or lift up his eyes to the idols of the house of Israel, or defile his neighbor's wife, or approach a woman during her menstrual period—if a man does not oppress anyone, but restores to the debtor his pledge, does not commit robbery, but gives his bread to the hungry, and covers the naked with clothing, if he does not lend money on interest or take increase, if he keeps his hand from iniquity, and executes true justice between man and man, if he walks in My statutes and My ordinances so as to deal faithfully—he is righteous and will surely live," declares the Lord God.

> "Then he may have a violent son who sheds blood, and who does any of these things to a brother (though he himself did not do any of these things), that is, he even eats at the mountain shrines, and defiles his neighbor's wife, oppresses the poor and needy, commits robbery, does not restore a pledge, but lifts up his eyes to the idols, and commits abomination, he lends money on interest and takes increase; will he live? He will not live! He has committed

all these abominations, he will surely be put to death; his blood will be on his own head.

"Now behold, he has a son who has observed all his father's sins which he committed, and observing does not do likewise. He does not eat at the mountain shrines or lift up his eyes to the idols of the house of Israel, or defile his neighbor's wife, or oppress anyone, or retain a pledge, or commit robbery, but he gives his bread to the hungry, and covers the naked with clothing, he keeps his hand from the poor, does not take interest or increase, but executes My ordinances, and walks in My statutes; he will not die for his father's iniquity, he will surely live. As for his father, because he practiced extortion, robbed his brother, and did what was not good among his people, behold, he will die for his iniquity.

"Yet you say, 'Why should the son not bear the punishment for the father's iniquity?' When the son has practiced justice and righteousness, and has observed all My statutes and done them, he shall surely live. The person who sins will die. The son will not bear the punishment for the father's iniquity, nor will the father bear the punishment for the son's iniquity; the righteousness of the righteous will be upon himself, and the wickedness of the wicked will be upon himself.

"But if the wicked man turns from all his sins which he has committed and observes all My statutes and practices justice and righteousness, he shall surely live; he shall not die. All his transgressions which he has committed will not be remembered against him; because of his righteousness which he has practiced, he will live. Do I have any pleasure in the death of the wicked," declares the Lord God, "rather than that he should turn from his ways and live?

"But when a righteous man turns away from his righteousness, commits iniquity, and does according to all the abominations that a wicked man does, will he live? All his righteous deeds which he has done will not be remembered for his treachery which he has committed and his sin which he has committed; for them he will die. Yet you say, 'The way of the Lord is not right.' Hear now, O house of Israel! Is My way not right? Is it not your ways that are not right? When a righteous man turns away from his righteousness, commits iniquity, and dies because of it, for his iniquity which he has committed he will die. Again, when a wicked man turns away from his wickedness which he has committed and practices justice and righteousness, he will save his life. Because he considered and turned away from all his transgressions which he had committed, he shall surely live; he shall not die. But the house of Israel says, 'The way of the Lord is not right.' Are My ways not right, O house of Israel? Is it not your ways that are not right?

"Therefore I will judge you, O house of Israel, each according to his conduct," declares the Lord God. "Repent and turn away from all your transgressions, so that iniquity may not become a stumbling block to you. Cast away from you all your transgressions which you have committed, and make yourselves a new heart and a new spirit! For why will you die, O house of Israel? For I have no pleasure in the death of anyone who dies," declares the Lord God. "Therefore, repent and live" (Ezek. 18:4-32, emphasis added).

It Couldn't be More Clear

First, note that God speaks of two categories of people in this passage—righteous and wicked. The righteous are characterized by obedience and the wicked are characterized by sin. The righteous are promised by God that they will live and the wicked are promised that they will die.

If *physical* death and life were all that God had in mind in this passage, then it is quite obvious that the wicked man didn't die physically immediately, as there existed the possibility that he might turn from his sins and live, as we just read. In fact, in the final admonition in this passage, God pleads with sinful Israel to turn from all their sins so that they might live and not die. Thus we see God's grace in His giving sinners an opportunity to repent, and His forgiveness granted to them when they do repent.

But did God have only *physical* life and death in mind in this passage? Or did He perhaps have *spiritual* and *eternal* life and death in mind? As I have noted earlier, Jesus used the same phrase we've just repeatedly read in Ezekiel 18, "You shall live" to mean, "You shall inherit eternal life" when He spoke to an inquiring lawyer.

Did God's promise to the righteous that they would *live* have any application to what happened to them after they died? It is certainly reasonable to think so. Imagine a person who falls into the category, mentioned in Ezekiel 18, of one who is disobedient to God but who turns from his sins. He who was formerly wicked begins to obey God's commandments. According to God's promise through Ezekiel, that person is forgiven of his past sins, becomes righteous, and God is holding nothing against him. He, according to God's promise, will live and not die. Yet we can be certain that he will eventually die physically. Thus, may not God's promise to him that he will live and not die have something to do with eternal life? Additionally, are we to think that the possibility exists that such a righteous person might be cast into hell when he dies, even though he died in an obedient state, was forgiven by God of all his past wickedness and was declared righteous by God Himself? Is it even remotely possible that God might say to such a person at his judgment, "You repented while you were on the earth, turning from your sins. I forgave you and declared you righteous. I promised you that you would live and not die. But My promise was only good until you died (which, incidentally, means I didn't keep My promise to you). Now that you are dead, I'm going to cast you into hell forever. The reason is because you didn't have faith, because salvation is by faith"? Isn't such a thought utterly absurd?

If it is possible for such a repentant person *not* to have saving faith, may I ask, *What would he have done differently if he would have had saving faith?*

All this being so, we can safely and logically conclude that this repentant person mentioned by Ezekiel was one who *believed*.[5] His faith resulted in his repentance and continued obedience. He was saved through faith by *grace*, as he was *forgiven*, and forgiveness can only occur because of grace. That is a picture of how salvation works and how it has always worked. "Let the wicked forsake his way, and the unrighteous man his thoughts; and let him return to the Lord, and He will have compassion on him; and to our God, for He will abundantly pardon" (Is. 55:7). When such a person dies, he inherits eternal life. So "if you wish to enter into life," as Jesus said, "keep the commandments" (Matt. 19:17). It is just that simple.

This may be different than the way salvation is often proclaimed today, but it does not differ from the salvation Jesus proclaimed. He continually called on people to repent, and He told them, "Not everyone who says to Me, 'Lord, Lord,' will enter the kingdom of heaven; but *he who does the will of My Father* who is in heaven" (Matt. 7:21, emphasis added). How could He have said it more bluntly than that? The one who is saved is the one who keeps God's commandments. Jesus proclaimed a salvation that was promised only to those who repented and obeyed, because only those kinds of people believed in Him.

Understanding Saving Faith

I cannot stress this fact too much: What Jesus told the rich young ruler

---

[5] Obviously, under the old covenant, although people were saved by faith, it was not faith in the Lord Jesus Christ, but faith in God. Since Jesus is God, salvation by faith during old and new covenants is really not any different.

to do to be saved was no different than what He told anyone else to do to be saved, that is, repent and follow Him, keeping His commandments. That is true "salvation by grace through faith."

Unfortunately, the faith that is often expected of Christian "converts" today is nothing more than a mental acknowledgement of some historical or theological facts. People think they are saved because they know that salvation is received by faith and not by works. True saving faith, however, is not faith in a *doctrine*, but faith in a *person*—the Lord Jesus, the divine Son of God. And if one believes that Jesus is God's divine Son, he will begin to follow and obey Him. Had the rich ruler believed that Jesus was the Son of God, he would have done what Jesus told him to do. The root of his disobedience was his unbelief, as is always the case. Likewise, the root of sincere obedience is faith.

It can indeed be rightfully said that faith is the sole condition of salvation. But true faith submits. True faith is always working, revealing itself by obedience. If you remove works from faith, faith dies. Consider what the apostle James had to say to professing Christians who claimed to have faith yet had no works:

> What use is it, my brethren, if a man says he has faith, but he has no works? Can that faith save him? (Jas. 2:14).

The obvious answer to James' rhetorical questions is *No*. Faith without works is not saving faith. James continues:

> If a brother or sister is without clothing and in need of daily food, and one of you says to them, "Go in peace, be warmed and be filled," and yet you do not give them what is necessary for their body, what use is that? Even so faith, if it has no works, is dead, being by itself (Jas. 2:15-17).

It is interesting that the example James used to illustrate faith without works is that of a professing believer who verbalizes concern for the pressing needs of a fellow believer, but who does nothing to help. His words are empty. He is no Good Samaritan. This is true also of the one who claims to have faith but who has no works. His profession of faith is meaningless. As James said, when works are removed from faith, faith is dead.

> But someone may well say, "You have faith, and I have works; show me your faith without the works, and I will show you my faith by my works." You believe that God is one. You do well; the demons also believe, and shudder. But are you willing to recognize, you foolish fellow, that faith without works is useless? (Jas. 2:18-20).

The Jews of James' day were proud to verbalize their faith in one of their cardinal doctrines, that God is one (see Deut. 6:4). James chided them for their dead faith in the one God, saying that demons believed the same doctrine, but *their* faith was evident by their *actions*—they shuddered! Only foolish people, wrote James, think that faith without works is anything but useless. Unfortunately, many professing Christians are very foolish in this regard. Many of them are preachers and theologians.

James then cited two Old Testament examples of living faith:

> Was not Abraham our father justified by works, when he offered up Isaac his son on the altar? You see that faith was working with his works, and as a result of the works, faith was perfected; and the Scripture was fulfilled which says, "And Abraham believed God, and it was reckoned to him as righteousness," and he was called the friend of God. You see that a man is justified by works, and not by faith alone. And in the same way was not Rahab the harlot also justified by works, when she received the messengers and sent them out by another way? For just as the body without the spirit is dead, so also faith without works is dead (Jas. 2:21-26).

Neither Abraham nor Rahab possessed dead faith, void of works. Their faith was evident by their works. James was very bold in stating that faith by itself will justify no one. Saving faith always has works with it. When works are removed from faith, it is similar to what happens when the spirit is removed from the body. How could James have made his point more clear?

A living faith immediately begins obeying, and the biblical term for that initial obedience is repentance, the turning away from sin. If there is no repentance, there is no faith. Repentance is the natural initial fruit of a living faith. That is what Jesus was demanding of the rich ruler—a faith that showed itself alive by repentance and obedience. Jesus wanted a true follower, not a phony Christian.

Does This Not Contradict Salvation by Grace?

Some unfortunately think that obedience and repentance are contrary to the concept of God's grace. If we tell people that they must repent in order to be saved, or that they must obey God, then we are supposedly not preaching a salvation that is based on God's grace. Grace is always absolutely unconditional, they say, or it is not grace. Thus, if there are conditions for salvation, salvation is supposedly not of grace.

But these people misunderstand God's grace, and grace in general.

If something is offered with conditions attached, must it be said that it was not offered in grace? Certainly not. Let's say you are notified that you've inherited one million dollars. There is, however, a condition attached. You must drive to an attorney's office to pick up the check. Because you keep the condition, does that mean the million-dollar inheritance was not given to you because of the grace of your benefactor? Must you say that you earned or *deserved* the money? The answers to these questions are obvious.

Here's another example that correlates a little more closely with God's grace in salvation: Imagine you are a serial murderer, averaging about one murder per week for a year. Imagine that you are apprehended in the act of killing someone and are brought to trial. Imagine that the judge shows you grace, not sentencing you to death, but letting you go free without punishment. He requires, however, that you stop murdering people. So there is a condition placed on the grace he is showing you. You must repent of being a murderer. As long as you don't murder anyone else, you will continue to enjoy freedom and will not be punished for your crimes. Does that mean your life was not saved by the grace of the judge? Will you say that you earned or deserved your freedom?

Thus you can easily see that just because something is offered conditionally, it does not automatically indicate that grace is not the basis for the gift. This is especially evident when there is great disparity between the gift given and the condition attached. Had the rich ruler sold all as Jesus commanded, he could never have rightfully said, "I purchased my salvation." No, he could only rightly say, "I spent my entire life as a religious hypocrite, ignoring His second greatest commandment. However, because of His amazing grace, God gave me an opportunity to receive eternal life, a gift of unparalleled worth. I only had to believe in His Son, which I did, and because I believed, I began obeying Him from that time on, repenting of my greed and finding true joy in the process. Praise God for His wonderful grace by which I'm saved!"

When we consider what our salvation cost Jesus and the punishment we deserved for our sins, is there any way we could rightfully boast?

The Myth of God's Unconditional Grace

God's grace is clearly conditional. That is so obvious it is a wonder that anyone would argue otherwise. If God's grace were *un*conditional, then everyone would be saved automatically, because there would be no conditions for salvation. But to use just one biblical example, when the Philippian jailer asked Paul, who certainly understood that salvation was by God's grace, what he needed to do to be saved, Paul didn't reply, "You don't need to do anything, because salvation is purely of God's grace! There are no conditions! You, and everyone else, are already saved!"

No, Paul said, "Believe in the Lord Jesus, and you shall be saved" (Acts

16:31). Faith was the condition of his salvation by grace. And notice it was faith in the *Lord* Jesus, indicating that he had to believe in a Jesus who is Lord.

The Philippian jailer did believe, and his faith went right to work, as he repented, immediately washing Paul and Silas' wounds, then served them a good meal and received baptism in obedience to Christ's command (see Acts. 16:33-34).

What if that jailer had said to Paul, "I'm so glad to have learned that salvation is all by God's unconditional grace. Wow, is it ever great to be saved! Now get back in your cells you prison scum and starve! I'm going home to eat!"? He would have been trusting in a grace that doesn't exist, an unconditional grace that God has never offered. And that is the very thing that many professing Christians are doing. To them, obedience is optional, because they think God's grace is unconditional. Or they have mistakenly thought that believing in Jesus is nothing more than knowing about Jesus. They are indistinguishable from non-Christians because they actually are non-Christians, even though they think otherwise.

God's grace is clearly conditional. At the present time, for example, God is giving every living person an opportunity to repent. They are in a "grace period." At the end of their lives, however, the grace period ends. Thus, God's grace extended to them is conditional. They must receive salvation by faith before they die, or they will go to hell, forfeiting any future possibility of being saved. Does that condition of a limited period of time nullify God's grace? Are sinners *earning* their right to continue in sin while they live? Or is their opportunity to continue sinning or repent due only to God's grace? The answers are obvious.

God's grace is clearly conditional. He "gives grace to the humble," Scripture declares (Jas. 4:6; 1 Pet. 5:5). Humility is a *condition* of receiving God's grace. Salvation begins when a person humbles himself, admits his sinfulness, and cries out for God's mercy. Then, and only then, does God's grace regenerate the sinner (see Jas. 4:6-10).

The Intention of God's Grace

God has not extended His grace to us to give us a license to continue sinning. On the contrary—His plan is that His grace will result in our turning from our sins. "The kindness of God leads [us] to repentance" (Rom. 2:4). Isn't that the same reason you extend grace to other people? You are hoping that your grace will motivate them to change, and that they will repent out of gratitude. And are you not hoping they won't misunderstand your grace as being an indication of your approval of their behavior?

For example, suppose you catch your young daughter disobeying you. She deserves to be punished, but you decide not to punish her, showing her "undeserved favor," or grace. You have shown her grace hoping that she will repent and not repeat her disobedience. You certainly don't want her to think that you approve of her actions, do you?

Your continued grace, however, is based on her repentance. If she repeats her sin, your conditional grace will end. This time she'll get what she deserves.

Likewise, God has not extended His grace so we can continue sinning. Paul, an authority on God's grace, wrote,

> For *the grace of God* has appeared, bringing salvation to all men, *instructing us to deny ungodliness and worldly desires and to live sensibly, righteously and godly* in the present age (Tit. 2:11-12, emphasis added).

Likewise, the apostle Jude warned of a perversion of God's true grace, one that relinquished people's responsibility to be holy:

> For certain persons have crept in unnoticed, those who were long beforehand marked out for this condemnation, ungodly persons who *turn the grace of our God into licentiousness* and deny our only Master and Lord, Jesus Christ (Jude 1:4, emphasis added).

These false Christians were obviously not publicly proclaiming, "We deny the Master and Lord, Jesus Christ," otherwise they would not have "crept in unnoticed." No, by their perversion of God's grace, turning it into a license to sin, they were effectively denying Christ's lordship by their daily lives.

The Necessity of Repentance for Salvation

We will return to the story of the rich, young ruler. But please allow me to continue for a while considering the *biblical* gospel, *biblical* grace and *biblical* salvation. Repentance and obedience are part and parcel of all of these and none of them nullifies God's grace. If requiring repentance and obedience for salvation somehow stands in opposition to or nullifies the concept of God's grace, then Jesus nullified salvation by grace, because He spoke of the necessity of repentance and obedience for salvation. First, let's consider Jesus' proclamations of repentance.

Jesus declared that He came to call sinners to repentance (see Luke 5:32). From the outset of His ministry He preached, "Repent, for the kingdom of heaven is at hand" (Matt. 4:17). Unless His hearers repented, they wouldn't be ready for the kingdom, over which a King will rule. Repentance was an integral part of His message.

Jesus reproached cities that did not repent at His preaching, telling them that hell was their destiny (see Matt. 11:20-24). He declared that His generation would be condemned at their judgment because they did not repent (see Matt. 12:41). He warned people that if they wouldn't re-pent, they would perish (see Luke 13:3, 5). He revealed that there is joy in heaven over one sinner who repents (see Luke 15:7). He commissioned His disciples after His resurrection to preach "repentance for [that is, *as a condition of*] forgiveness of sins" (Luke 24:47). If preaching repentance as a requirement for salvation nullifies God's grace, then Jesus nullified God's grace by His preaching.

What it Means to Repent

Repentance is too often edited from the gospel today, and when it is mentioned, it is often redefined as being only a change in a person's mind about who Jesus is, a change that doesn't necessarily result in any change of his actions. But are we really to think that a person could have a change of mind about who Jesus is, now believing that He is the Son of God, the One before whom he must stand to give an account of his life, and it not result in a change in that person's actions? What an absurd thought! We might just as well say that a person could believe that his children were trapped in a burning house and it not affect his actions.

Paul certainly wouldn't have accepted such a senseless definition of repentance. He declared everywhere that people should "repent and turn to God, *performing deeds appropriate to repentance*" (Acts 26:20, emphasis added).

Neither would John the Baptist have stood for such obvious heresy. He told his convicted audience, "Bring forth fruit in keeping with repen-tance" (Matt. 3:8), and warned that if they didn't, they would be cast into hell (see Matt. 3:10).

Incidentally, when members of John's audience once asked what they should do specifically, he responded by telling them to stop breaking the second greatest commandment and repent of greed: "Let the man who has two tunics share with him who has none, and let him who has food do likewise" (Luke 3:11).

In fact, practically every specific deed of repentance that John men-tioned had something to do with money and greed. To the tax-gatherers he said, "Collect no more than what you have been ordered to" (Luke. 3:12). To some soldiers he said, "Do not take money from anyone by force…and be content with your wages" (Luke. 3:14). Greed was such a pervasive sin that it touched the lives of everyone, just as it does today. It is so common that even those in the church don't recognize it. Preaching the gospel, as Luke calls it (see Luke 3:18), John made it clear that unless his listeners repented of their greed, they would end up in hell. *John would have had no theological problem with what Jesus expected of the rich, young ruler.*

If the two greatest commandments are to love God with all one's heart, mind, soul and strength and to love one's neighbor as oneself (as Christ taught; see Mark 12:28-31), then it could be rightly said that the two greatest sins are not loving God with all one's heart, mind, soul and strength, and not loving one's neighbor as oneself. If repentance is turning from sin, then the most important sins that one should turn away from are those two. Greed is a sin that violates both of the two greatest commandments. People who are not willing to repent of greed cannot have a relationship with God, because their god is money.

The need to repent of greed has been removed from the gospel in our materialistic culture. When anyone even remotely suggests that such repentance may be necessary for salvation, he is immediately branded a legalist. "You are proclaiming a salvation by works!" is the impassioned accusation. But if what I'm saying is legalism, then Jesus and John the Baptist were legalists.

The Necessity of Obedience for Salvation

Jesus also spoke of the necessity of obedience and holiness for salvation. He declared,

> For I say to you, that unless your righteousness surpasses that of the scribes and Pharisees, you shall not enter the kingdom of heaven (Matt. 5:20).[6]

> And if your right eye makes you stumble, tear it out, and throw it from you; for it is better for you that one of the parts of your body perish, than for your whole body to be thrown into hell. And if your right hand makes you stumble, cut it off, and throw it from you; for it is better for you that one of the parts of your body perish, than for your whole body to go into hell (Matt. 5:29-30).

> Not everyone who says to Me, "Lord, Lord," will enter the kingdom of heaven; but he who does the will of My Father who is in heaven. Many will say to Me on that day, "Lord, Lord, did we not prophesy in Your name, and in Your name cast out demons, and in Your name perform many miracles?" And then I will declare to them, "I never knew you; depart from Me, you who practice lawlessness" (Matt. 7:21-23).

> For whoever does the will of My Father who is in heaven, he is My brother and sister and mother (Matt. 12:50).

> The Son of Man will send forth His angels, and they will gather out of His kingdom all stumbling blocks, and

[6] When this statement is read contextually, we cannot rightfully conclude that Jesus was alluding to the imputed legal righteousness that believers receive as a gift. Rather, Jesus was talking about practical holiness. For further explanation, see my book, *The Great Gospel Deception*, pp. 136-139.

51

those who commit lawlessness, and will cast them into
the furnace of fire; in that place there shall be weeping and
gnashing of teeth (Matt. 13:41-42).

Do not marvel at this; for an hour is coming, in which all
who are in the tombs shall hear His voice, and shall come
forth; those who did the good deeds to a resurrection of
life, those who committed the evil deeds to a resurrection
of judgment (John 5:28-29).

All of the above statements speak of the necessity of obedience for salvation. Did not "the author of [our] salvation" (Heb. 2:10) know that people are saved by grace through faith? Certainly He did. Thus, we can only
conclude that what He said does not nullify the true saving grace that God
is extending to humanity.

Taking Up the Cross

Consider also the following words of Christ:

And He summoned the multitude with His disciples, and
said to them, "If anyone wishes to come after Me, let him
deny himself, and take up his cross, and follow Me. For
whoever wishes to save his life shall lose it; but whoever
loses his life for My sake and the gospel's shall save it. For
what does it profit a man to gain the whole world, and
forfeit his soul? For what shall a man give in exchange for
his soul? For whoever is ashamed of Me and My words in
this adulterous and sinful generation, the Son of Man will
also be ashamed of him when He comes in the glory of
His Father with the holy angels" (Mark 8:34-38).

When we read these words honestly, we realize that they are not an invitation to a deeper walk addressed to Christians, but a revelation of what
is required of nonbelievers if they are to be saved.

First, note that Jesus' words here were addressed to nonbelievers and
believers. Jesus "summoned the *multitude* with His *disciples*" (Mark 8:34,
emphasis added).

Second, Jesus declared at the outset that what He was about to say applied to anyone who wished to "come after" or "follow" Him (Mark 8:34).
That person must deny himself and take up his cross. So there are conditions. There is a cost.

The very next sentence is related to the first one, as it begins with the
word *for*. Jesus then contrasted the one who denies himself and takes up
his cross with the one who doesn't. The former "loses his life" for Jesus
and the gospel's sake and consequently saves his life; the later "wishes

to save his life" and consequently loses it. Obviously, Jesus was talking about the outcomes of commitment and non-commitment. The terms He used couldn't have been stronger: denying oneself, taking up one's cross, losing one's life. Unreserved devotion is what Jesus had in mind.

Jesus continued to contrast the committed and non-committed in the next two sentences. The one who does not deny himself, take up his cross, follow Christ, and lose his life for Christ and the gospel's sake might "gain the whole world." *Gaining the world* speaks of the ultimate accomplishment of the one who is not committed to Christ. He might gain power, pleasure, wealth and so on, those things the world offers to those who have not made Jesus Lord. But the consequence is that one "forfeits his soul," the ultimate foolish exchange. Does one who "forfeits his soul" sound like the description of a saved person? The answer is obvious.

Clearly, Jesus was talking about salvation, and what one must do to receive it. Are we to think that there will be people in heaven who did *not* desire to "come after" and "follow" Christ, who did not "deny themselves and take up their cross," who did not "lose their lives for Jesus and the gospel's sake" but who "desired to save their lives," and who "gained the world" and thus "forfeited their souls"?

Jesus ended with a warning to those who chose not to deny themselves, take up their crosses, follow Him and lose their lives. Because they are ashamed of Him and what He said, when He returns He will be ashamed of them. They will forfeit their souls at His judgment. Matthew's version adds, "For the Son of Man is going to come in the glory of His Father with His angels; and will then recompense every man according to his deeds" (Matt. 16:27).[7]

In the next chapter, we will return to the story of the rich, young ruler. We must first, however, complete what we have begun regarding the true nature of salvation. Once we understand the roles of repentance and obedience, we are much better suited to understand what Jesus said to the rich, young ruler.

---

[7] For a more in-depth discussion of this passage of Scripture, see my book, *The Great Gospel Deception*, pp. 79-84.

THREE

One Thing You Still Lack
Mark 10:17-30

Before we can return to our study of Jesus' encounter with the rich ruler, we must finish what we've begun in the previous chapter. We've already considered what Jesus taught about the roles of repentance and obedience in regard to salvation. He wanted obedient disciples, not crowds of people who ignored His commandments while professing to believe in Him. That is precisely why He commissioned the apostles to go and make disciples, baptizing them and teaching them to obey everything He commanded (see Matt. 28:19-20). Jesus gave no indication that He thought, as do so many modern theologians, that there were two categories of heaven-bound people—the believers and the disciples—disciples being more committed believers. To Jesus, only committed disciples were true believers. Jesus once even challenged a crowd of newly-professing believers to consider if they were truly His disciples. Only if they would abide in His word were they truly His disciples, and as they learned His truth, they would be set free from sin (see John 8:30-36).[1]

If preaching that obedience is necessary for salvation nullifies God's grace, then Jesus nullified God's grace by His preaching.

The Apostles Followed Jesus' Example in
Preaching the Necessity of Repentance

Now let's consider the gospel of the apostles. If the preaching of repentance nullifies the gospel of God's grace, then Peter and Paul's preaching also nullified God's grace, because they preached that no one could be saved without repentance. Had they not, they would have been disobedient to Jesus' explicit command that "repentance for forgiveness of sins should be proclaimed in His name" (Luke 24:47). But having received His

---

[1] For further proof that only Christ's disciples are true believers, see my book *The Great Gospel Deception*, pp. 85-89.

grace, they didn't consider themselves relieved of the responsibility to obey Him. They preached that people must repent if their sins were to be forgiven.

On the day of Pentecost, when his convicted audience asked what they should do, Peter responded, "Repent, and let each of you be baptized in the name of Jesus Christ for the forgiveness of your sins; and you shall receive the gift of the Holy Spirit" (Acts 2:38). Didn't Peter know that people are saved by faith? Why then didn't he mention faith or believing to his audience? Simply because those who believed would repent.

During his second sermon at the portico of Solomon, Peter declared, "Repent therefore and return, that your sins may be wiped away" (Acts 3:19). Now that is preaching *"repentance for forgiveness of sins"* (Luke 24:47, emphasis added).

Peter realized that the opportunity God gave people to repent was an act of His grace. Before the Sanhedrin, he proclaimed of Jesus,

> He is the one whom God exalted to His right hand as a Prince and a Savior, *to grant repentance* to Israel, and forgiveness of sins (Acts 5:31, emphasis added).

Repentance was something that was granted, that is, given by grace. Obviously, Peter didn't mean that God sovereignly granted certain persons the *ability* to repent. Peter declared that God granted repentance to *Israel*, that is, every Israelite was granted the opportunity to repent. Peter would later write, "The Lord is not slow about His promise, as some count slowness, but is patient toward you, *not wishing for any to perish but for all to come to repentance* (2 Pet. 3:9, emphasis added).

No one earns the opportunity to repent. It is granted by God's grace. All of the Jerusalem elders acknowledged this same truth after Peter reported the salvation of the Gentiles:

> And when they heard this, they quieted down, and glorified God, saying, "Well then, God has granted to the Gentiles also *the repentance that leads to life*" (Acts 11:18, emphasis added).

Notice that the repentance God granted to all the Gentiles was a repentance that *led to life*. Clearly, the Jerusalem elders meant "eternal life," and their statement again confirms their belief that repentance was essential for salvation.

Paul believed that "the sorrow that is according to the will of God produces a *repentance* without regret, leading to salvation" (2 Cor. 7:10, emphasis added). Thus, on Mars Hill in Athens, he proclaimed,

> Therefore having overlooked the times of ignorance, God is now declaring to men that *all everywhere should repent,*

because He has fixed a day in which He will judge the world in righteousness through a Man whom He has appointed, having furnished proof to all men by raising Him from the dead (Acts 17:30-31, emphasis added).

Unrepentant people are not ready for that judgment. Paul believed that repentance is absolutely necessary for salvation. And he also obviously saw no contradiction between preaching repentance and God's wonderful grace. For example, in his farewell address to the elders of the church at Ephesus, Paul recounted his several years of ministry among them:

I did not shrink from declaring to you anything that was profitable, and teaching you publicly and from house to house, *solemnly testifying to both Jews and Greeks of repentance toward God and faith in our Lord Jesus Christ*....But I do not consider my life of any account as dear to myself, in order that I may finish my course, and the ministry which I received from the Lord Jesus, to *testify solemnly of the gospel of the grace of God* (Acts 20:20-21, 24, emphasis added).

Did you notice that Paul solemnly testified of both repentance and God's grace? (If not, read the italicized portions in the above scripture.) Although those things are contradictory in the minds of many modern theologians, to Paul, they harmonized without problem.

Before King Agrippa, Paul summarized many years of his ministry by telling him,

Consequently, King Agrippa, I did not prove disobedient to the heavenly vision, but kept declaring both to those of Damascus first, and also at Jerusalem and then throughout all the region of Judea, and even to the Gentiles, that they should *repent and turn to God, performing deeds appropriate to repentance* (Acts 26:19-20, emphasis added).

How many modern preachers would similarly summarize their ministries? Again, if preaching repentance nullifies God's grace, then Peter and Paul nullified God's grace by their preaching.

The Apostles Followed Jesus' Example in Preaching the Necessity of Obedience

The apostles also followed Jesus' example in proclaiming the necessity of obedience for salvation. If preaching the necessity of obedience for salvation nullifies God's grace, then the apostles nullified God's grace by their preaching.

Paul, who wrote, "by grace you have been saved through faith; and that not of yourselves, it is the gift of God" (Eph. 2:8), also made some very strong statements about the necessity of obedience in his letters:

> Or do you not know that the unrighteous shall not inherit the kingdom of God? Do not be deceived; neither fornicators, nor idolaters, nor adulterers, nor effeminate, nor homosexuals, nor thieves, nor the covetous, nor drunkards, nor revilers, nor swindlers, shall inherit the kingdom of God (1 Cor. 6:9-10).

> Now the deeds of the flesh are evident, which are: immorality, impurity, sensuality, idolatry, sorcery, enmities, strife, jealousy, outbursts of anger, disputes, dissensions, factions, envying, drunkenness, carousing, and things like these, of which I forewarn you just as I have forewarned you that those who practice such things shall not inherit the kingdom of God (Gal. 5:19-21).

> But do not let immorality or any impurity or greed even be named among you, as is proper among saints; and there must be no filthiness and silly talk, or coarse jesting, which are not fitting, but rather giving of thanks. For this you know with certainty, that no immoral or impure person or covetous man, who is an idolater, has an inheritance in the kingdom of Christ and God. Let no one deceive you with empty words, for because of these things the wrath of God comes upon the sons of disobedience (Eph. 5:3-6).[2]

Paul did not believe that faith and obedience could be separated, but wrote of "the obedience of faith" on two occasions (see Rom. 1:5; 16:26). Saving faith is manifested by unselfish love (see Gal. 5:6). The gospel is not only something to believe, but also something to obey (see 2 Thes. 1:7-9). False Christians "profess to know God, but by their deeds they deny Him" (Tit. 1:16). This was all Paul's doctrine.

Paul believed that eternal life waits those "who by perseverance in doing good seek for glory and honor and immortality" (Rom. 2:7), and that "glory and honor and peace" would be experienced by every person who "does good" (Rom. 2:10). However, "wrath and indignation" await those "who are selfishly ambitious and do not obey the truth, but obey unrigh-

---

[2] Some who teach a false grace claim that there is a difference between *inheriting* the kingdom of God and *entering* heaven. "Inheriting the kingdom" is only equivalent to walking in God's blessings while here on earth, they say. This absurd theory is easily disproved, however, by reading Paul's usage of the same phrase in 1 Cor. 15:50: "Now I say this, brethren, that flesh and blood cannot *inherit the kingdom of God*; nor does the perishable inherit the imperishable" (emphasis added). Paul was obviously talking about entering into heaven, and the impossibility of doing that in a perishable physical body. No doubt Paul borrowed the expression, *inherit the kingdom*, from Jesus Himself, who foretold of the time when the righteous would enter heaven: "Then the King will say to those on His right, 'Come, you who are blessed of My Father, *inherit the kingdom* prepared for you from the foundation of the world'" (Matt. 25:34, emphasis added).

teousness" (Rom. 2:8). "There will be tribulation and distress for every soul of man who does evil" (Rom. 2:9).

Paul warned Christian believers,

> So then, brethren, we are under obligation, not to the flesh, to live according to the flesh—for if you are living according to the flesh, you must die; but if by the Spirit you are putting to death the deeds of the body, you will live (Rom. 8:12-13).

The author of the book of Hebrews also believed that obedience is essential for salvation. He wrote that Jesus "became to all those who *obey Him* the source of eternal *salvation*" (Heb. 5:9, emphasis added). He declared that,

> For if we go on sinning willfully after receiving the knowledge of the truth, there no longer remains a sacrifice for sins, but a certain terrifying expectation of judgment, and the fury of a fire which will consume the adversaries (Heb. 10:26-27).

He admonished his readers to "Pursue peace with all men, and the sanctification without which no one will see the Lord" (Heb. 12:14).

James, Peter, John and Jude say "Amen"

The apostle James wrote about God's grace (see Jas. 4:6), but also wrote that a person's "religion is worthless" if he doesn't bridle his tongue (Jas. 1:26), and that "judgment will be merciless to one who has shown no mercy" (Jas. 2:13).

He also wrote at length about how faith without works is dead, useless, and cannot save anyone (see Jas. 2:14-26). He declared, "whoever wishes to be a friend of the world makes himself an enemy of God" (Jas. 4:4).

Peter, who mentioned God's grace ten times in his two epistles, also preached that God gives the Holy Spirit "to those who obey Him" (Acts 5:32) and that "in every nation the man who fears [God] and does what is right, is welcome to Him" (Acts 10:35). He, like Paul, believed that the gospel was something to be obeyed (see 1 Pet. 4:17). He wrote of the increase of Christian virtues in the lives of believers, saying, "As long as you *practice* these things, you will never stumble; for *in this way the entrance into the eternal kingdom of our Lord and Savior Jesus Christ will be abundantly supplied to you*" (2 Pet. 1:10-11, emphasis added). He warned believers of the eternal consequences of returning to a life of sin:

> For if after they have escaped the defilements of the world by the knowledge of the Lord and Savior Jesus Christ, they are again entangled in them and are overcome, the

last state has become worse for them than the first. For it would be better for them not to have known the way of righteousness, than having known it, to turn away from the holy commandment delivered to them. It has happened to them according to the true proverb, "A dog returns to its own vomit," and, "A sow, after washing, returns to wallowing in the mire" (2 Pet. 2:20-22).

The apostle John, who believed that "grace and truth were realized through Jesus" (John 1:17) and that all believers have received "grace upon grace" (John 1:16), also believed that obedience is essential for salvation. His first epistle is primarily about the identifying marks of authentic Christians. John made it clear that true believers do more than believe— they love and obey.

John declared that only those who keep Christ's commandments know Him (see 1 John 2:3-4). Those who love the world or its things do not have "the love of the Father" in them (1 John 2:15). It is the one who does the will of God who "abides forever" (1 John 2:17). The one who "practices righteousness" is born of God (1 John 2:29). Everyone who has the hope of seeing Jesus "purifies himself, just as He is pure" (1 John 3:3). We can only be assured of our salvation if we demonstrate practical love for fellow believers (see 1 John 3:14-20).

John also wrote:

> Little children, let no one deceive you; the one who practices righteousness is righteous, just as He is righteous; the one who practices sin is of the devil; for the devil has sinned from the beginning. The Son of God appeared for this purpose, that He might destroy the works of the devil. No one who is born of God practices sin, because His seed abides in him; and he cannot sin, because he is born of God. By this the children of God and the children of the devil are obvious: anyone who does not practice righteousness is not of God, nor the one who does not love his brother (1 John 3:7-10, emphasis added).

Finally, the apostle Jude warned his readers against a heresy that divorced obedience from God's grace:

> Beloved, while I was making every effort to write you about our common salvation, I felt the necessity to write to you appealing that you contend earnestly for the faith which was once for all delivered to the saints. For certain persons have crept in unnoticed, those who were long beforehand marked out for this condemnation, ungodly

persons who *turn the grace of our God into licentiousness and deny our only Master and Lord, Jesus Christ* (Jude 3-4, emphasis added).

If preaching that obedience is necessary for salvation nullifies God's grace, then Paul, Peter, James, John, Jude, and the author of Hebrews all nullified God's grace. But obviously, they haven't, and so it is our understanding of God's grace that needs adjustment. Any preacher, pastor, or theologian who says that repentance and obedience are not required for salvation are contradicting what the entire Bible teaches. They are guilty of a damnable heresy and have made themselves enemies of Christ, Paul, Peter, James, John and Jude.

The Twisting of Paul

Regrettably, the biblical doctrine of salvation by faith has been taught in such a way that it has nullified the doctrine of the necessity of holiness for salvation. Paul's teaching in particular, which so often emphasizes God's grace in salvation, has been ripped from its context and twisted. Paul clearly believed that holiness is essential for gaining eternal life:

> Now the deeds of the flesh are evident, which are: immorality, impurity, sensuality, idolatry, sorcery, enmities, strife, jealousy, outbursts of anger, disputes, dissensions, factions, envying, drunkenness, carousing, and things like these, of which I forewarn you just as I have forewarned you that those who practice such things shall not inherit the kingdom of God (Gal. 5:19-21).

Paul did not believe that the unholy would inherit God's kingdom. So how could he also teach that salvation was gained by grace through faith?

A closer study of Paul's letters reveals the reason why he so frequently emphasized that salvation is by grace and not by works. It is apparent that Jewish teachers were his chief antagonists as he worked to bring about the "obedience of faith among all the Gentiles" (Rom. 1:5). Those Jewish teachers sought to undermine his God-given gospel to Gentiles with a message that salvation was not based on believing in Jesus, but on a pathetic standard of works, most often circumcision and keeping some ceremonial aspects of the Mosaic Law (see, for example, Gal. 4:10-11; 5:2-3, 6, 11, 6:12-15).

Paul fought their teaching tooth and nail in many of his letters. He also differentiated between the works that the Jewish legalists were emphasizing so much and true holiness. For example, he wrote to the Corinthian Christians:

> Circumcision is nothing, and uncircumcision is nothing, but what matters is the keeping of the commandments of God (1 Cor. 7:19).

This single verse speaks volumes about the true nature of Paul's battle with legalists. Yet by many contemporary definitions of legalism, this one verse would make Paul a legalist himself!

Understanding this background, we can better grasp why Paul wrote statements such as those found in Ephesians 2:8-9, addressed primarily to *Gentile* believers (see Eph. 2:11-3:6):

> For by grace you have been saved through faith; and that not of yourselves, it is the gift of God; not as a result of works, so that no one may boast (Eph. 2:8-9).

Did Paul write those words because he was concerned that the Ephesian believers were becoming overly-zealous about obeying Christ's commandments? No, he wrote them because he didn't want them to be deceived by Jewish legalists who were trying to convince his Gentile converts that they needed to be circumcised and keep other ceremonial aspects of the Mosaic Law to be saved.

Moreover, did Paul mean that because salvation is by grace and not a result of works, that one can gain heaven without holiness? As we read at little bit further in his letter, the answer is plain:

> For this you know with certainty, that no immoral or impure person or covetous man, who is an idolater, has an inheritance in the kingdom of Christ and God. Let no one deceive you with empty words, for because of these things the wrath of God comes upon the sons of disobedience (Eph. 5:5-6).

These two sentences from the same letter prove beyond any shadow of doubt that Paul did not mean in 2:8-9 that, because salvation is a gift of grace not based on works, holiness is of no consequence. And there are other similar scriptures in Paul's writings that affirm this (as we have already seen, for example 1 Cor. 6:9-10, Gal. 5:19-21). Clearly, Paul believed that no one who is immoral, impure or covetous (which are all forms of idolatry according to Paul) will inherit God's kingdom, exactly what Jesus taught in His Sermon on the Mount. Paul believed that although salvation is not the result of works, works (good works, that is) are the result of salvation. In fact, had we only read one verse beyond 2:8-9, we would have immediately realized that fact:

> For we are His workmanship, created in Christ Jesus for good works, which God prepared beforehand, that we should walk in them (Eph. 2:10).

We are not saved *by* good works but *unto* good works. The gracious salvation that God offers provides more than forgiveness. It also provides transformation.

Jesus Harmonized With Paul

Jesus, too, solemnly warned those who proudly trust in their own works for salvation, while He encouraged sinners to humble themselves, repent, and rely on God's grace for salvation. For example, we read His words in Luke 18:

> And [Jesus] also told this parable to certain ones who trusted in themselves that they were righteous, and viewed others with contempt: "Two men went up into the temple to pray, one a Pharisee, and the other a tax-gatherer. The Pharisee stood and was praying thus to himself, 'God, I thank Thee that I am not like other people: swindlers, unjust, adulterers, or even like this tax-gatherer. I fast twice a week; I pay tithes of all that I get.' But the tax-gatherer, standing some distance away, was even unwilling to lift up his eyes to heaven, but was beating his breast, saying, 'God, be merciful to me, the sinner!' I tell you, this man went down to his house justified [righteous in God's eyes] rather than the other; for everyone who exalts himself shall be humbled, but he who humbles himself shall be exalted" (Luke 18:9-14).

This parable is often abused by those who are pushing a twisted concept of God's grace. But let's consider it honestly. Notice the primary difference between the Pharisee and the tax-gatherer was this: The tax-gatherer realized he was a sinner who needed God's grace to be saved, while the Pharisee saw no such need. That is what a true "legalist" is—*someone who is blind to his own sinfulness and his need for God's grace to be saved.* He sees salvation as something purely to be earned, and usually by means of his own pathetic standards of righteousness. In this case, the Pharisee actually believed that his weekly fasts and scrupulous tithing, along with a few other virtues, made him righteous in God's eyes. Jesus taught, however, that tithing is a very minor commandment in comparison to what God considers important (see Luke 11:42). Neither was fasting high on Jesus' list (see Matt. 9:14-15). The truth is, those who truly believe in Jesus are born again (in reality and not just in theory) and are radically transformed by the indwelling Holy Spirit (another evidence of God's grace in salvation), and their righteousness so far exceeds that of the scribes and Pharisees that there is no comparison.

In spite of what some folks try to tell us, as Jesus related the attitude of the Pharisee in this parable, He was not thinking of sincere believers who have realized their sinfulness and their need for God's grace, who have believed in Him and repented, and who are now "working out their salvation with fear and trembling" (Phil. 2:12) as they "strive to enter the narrow gate" (Luke 13:24) as He commanded them! Rather, Jesus was thinking of the proud scribes and Pharisees who were blind to their sin, who saw no need for God's grace if they were to be saved (and consequently saw no need for a Savior who would die for their sins), who didn't come close to attaining God's standards of righteousness, and who, on top of all this, "viewed others with contempt" (a direct quote from Jesus' preface to the parable). And let us not add more to the parable than what was said. Let us not imagine that Jesus wanted us to think that the tax-gatherer left the temple to return to his greedy and dishonest lifestyle on his sure way to heaven!

What are the differences between the "works" of a legalist and the "works" of a true believer in Jesus? There are many.

The works of a legalist fall far, far short of God's righteous standards. They are an outward façade, and the inward motivation is often the love of people's approval. The works of the legalist are more likely to be religious and ceremonial than moral and self-denying (see Mark 12:33), things such as church attendance and tithing, which produce pride. The works of the legalist are an insult to God, because they nullify His grace and Christ's sacrifice (see Gal. 2:21). Legalists in essence say to God, "I can save myself...I don't need Jesus or His sacrifice." Legalists don't understand their own sinfulness or the righteousness of God. They are comparable to people who think they should be granted the Nobel Prize because they let their dog sleep inside.

In contrast, the works of a truly born-again believer are of a much higher standard. They stem from a pure and thankful heart that loves God and wants to please Him. They have their origin in Christ Himself who lives within the believer by the Holy Spirit, as Jesus said, they are "wrought in God" (John 3:21). The works of the born-again believer are more likely to be moral and self-denying than religious and ceremonial. True believers who were formerly religious have repented of their "dead works" (see Heb. 6:1), the works of the legalist.

Back to Our Story...

Hopefully we can now return to Jesus' encounter with the rich ruler with a more biblical understanding of salvation.

When the rich ruler asked Jesus which commandments he needed to keep in order to inherit eternal life, Jesus enumerated six of the Ten Commandments (see Mark 10:19), those that deal with our relationships with others. All six could be summarized by the commandment, "You shall love your neighbor as yourself," which was the seventh commandment

Jesus listed in His response (see Matt. 19:19).

The rich ruler declared that he, from his youth, had kept all the commandments Jesus listed, and then asked what he still lacked. He apparently believed that he had loved his neighbor as himself since his youth! He was perhaps sincere, yet certainly deceived about his own unrighteousness, as Jesus would soon reveal to him. He had lived in disobedience to the second greatest commandment for some time.

How representative this rich ruler is of so many of us. We have no idea how far short we fall of keeping God's commandments. Although our lives are characterized by greed and we are nowhere close to loving our neighbors as ourselves, we aren't aware of it. And even more tragically, some of us who are aware of it think that our dead faith serves as a substitute for obedience, and so we have no need to strive to conform our lives to God's will. Having "received Christ as Savior," we think it is safe to continue rejecting Him as Lord.

Jesus' Sincere Love

Scripture says that at this point, Jesus felt a love for the young man (see Mark 10:21). Jesus' love, of course, was a genuine love, so He spoke truth at the risk of offending. Looking at the rich man with compassion, Jesus pointedly said, "One thing you lack: go and sell all you possess, and give to the poor, and you shall have treasure in heaven; and come, follow Me" (Mark 10:21).[3]

Jesus was simply informing the rich man that he lacked one thing in obeying the commandment to love his neighbor as himself, which happens to be the second greatest commandment. He lacked one *very* important thing in obeying one *very* important commandment. How could he claim to love his neighbor as himself if he held on to his great wealth knowing full well the plight of needy people? His sin was brought to light.

Now came the moment of crisis. Jesus hoped that the man would repent of his greed and become His follower. That is what He commanded the man to do. Jesus would have forgiven him, and he would have tasted

---

[3] Grasping at straws, some interpreters point out that Matthew, unlike Mark and Luke, records Jesus as saying to the rich man, "If you wish to be complete [or *perfect* as the NASB marginal note says], go and sell your possessions." Elevating Matthew's gospel above Mark and Luke's, they attempt to convince us that the subject changes at this point from salvation to sanctification, that is, becoming more holy, or *complete*, on the road to perfection. However, neither logic nor the context supports such an interpretation. If that is what Jesus meant and what the rich man thought Jesus meant, why did he walk away so grieved? And why did Jesus then make His statement about how hard it is for a rich man to enter the kingdom of heaven? Why did the disciples ask, "Then who can be saved?" And why did Peter remind Jesus that he and the other disciples had left everything to follow Him, then asking, "What then will there be for us?" Clearly, Jesus did not change the subject from what is required for salvation to what might be an optional step in the process of sanctification. Therefore, Jesus' words as rendered by Matthew, "If you wish to be complete," can only be intelligently interpreted if they are harmonized with what Mark and Luke quoted Jesus as saying. The phrase, "if you wish to be complete" must be synonymous with the phrase, "one thing you still lack." Combining and harmonizing the three Gospel accounts would give us something like, "One thing you still lack (to inherit eternal life), and if you wish to be complete, not lacking that one thing, go and sell all you possess..."

of Jesus' amazing grace. But in order to follow Jesus, making Jesus his Master, he first had to turn away from his old master, money. He needed to repent of greed, because it would be impossible for him to serve God and mammon (see Matt. 6:24).

The Eternal Decision

As you know, the man decided to cling to his old master. Not only had he been unwilling to love his neighbor as himself for a long time, he also decided to remain unwilling. Even though Jesus told him that he would be repaid in heaven for liquidating his assets, those earthly assets meant too much to him. They were holding his heart. Thus "he went away grieved; for he was one who owned much property" (Mark 10:22).

It was then that Jesus made His famous statement that has been twisted, softened, and misinterpreted perhaps more than any other words of His:

> Truly I say to you, it is hard for a rich man to enter the kingdom of heaven. And again I say to you, it is easier for a camel to go through the eye of a needle, than for a rich man to enter the kingdom of God (Matt. 19:23-24).

If we take Jesus' words at face value, we must admit that they have application to any and all wealthy people. It is very hard for them to enter the kingdom of heaven—as hard as it is for a camel to go through the eye of a needle. And why is it so hard for them? It is hard for all wealthy people for the same reason it was hard for the rich, young ruler. God requires wealthy people to repent of greed, just like the rich young ruler, and they find it difficult to turn from their old master. They love money too much. Scripture unequivocally states that no greedy/covetous person will inherit the kingdom of God (see 1 Cor. 6:9-10, Eph. 5:3-6). Thus, greedy and covetous people must repent of greed in order to inherit God's kingdom. Regardless of what anyone says, that is what Jesus said and what the New Testament affirms.

Jesus' disciples were astonished at His statement about the camel and needle and asked, "Then who can be saved?" (Mark 10:26). Obviously, they interpreted Jesus' words to be applicable to all wealthy people, not just one man. And they wondered if *anyone* could make it into heaven if the requirements were so stringent.

Jesus responded, "With men it is impossible, but not with God; for all things are possible with God" (Mark 10:27). Jesus did not mean that God would, in the case of some wealthy people, eliminate His requirement that they turn from their old master. Neither did He mean that God would violate His own word and allow greedy people who have never repented of greed into heaven. That, of course, would annul everything Jesus had just said, and would have been grossly unfair to the rich man who just walked away sadly. In fact, it would have made Jesus a liar in relationship to him.

Rather, Jesus' statement was a revelation of the transforming grace of God that is available to greedy people. God gives grace to the humble, and as greedy people humble themselves, confess their guilt and cry out for God to change them, His power will deliver them from their greed. As I said in the introduction to this book, God's power and grace can get camels through needles. God's grace is available to forgive and transform.

A Very Common Objection Answered

It is often stated that Jesus told only one person to sell his possessions and give to the poor. Based on that assumption, it is then argued that it is wrong to apply to anyone else what Jesus said to only one person two-thousand years ago.

Is it not true, however, that it would be unfair of Jesus to require something of one person to be saved that He does not require of every other person? Imagine a wealthy man standing before Christ's judgment throne who on earth "accepted Jesus." Imagine Jesus telling the man that he is welcome to enter heaven, even though he held on to his many earthly possessions during his life. Now imagine the rich, young ruler viewing this scene. Would he not have a valid objection? He would have had the right to say, "Jesus, you required of me what you did not require of that man!" "I will go to hell for not doing what he did not do either!"

As the rich ruler sadly walked away, Jesus knew he was making a damning decision. Are we really to think that Jesus was making it harder for him to escape eternal damnation than He would for every other wealthy person in the world? No, Jesus requires that every person repent. All greedy people must repent of greed, regardless of how much money they have. If they truly do repent of greed, it will begin to manifest itself in their actions.

But even more important, as I have already pointed out, as the rich ruler walked away sadly, Jesus plainly declared that what He said to him was applicable to all wealthy people for all time. He said, "It is easier for a camel to go through the eye of a needle than for a rich man to enter the kingdom of God" (Mark 10:25). He didn't say, "that rich man," but "a rich man." And it is obvious from the apostles' response that they believed what He said had application to them and everyone else.

Moreover, Jesus repeatedly reinforced the same message at other times using different words. Did He not say that no one can be His disciple "who does not give up all his own possessions"? (Luke 14:33). Did He not say that anyone who wants to come after Him must "deny himself, and take up his cross daily"? (Luke 9:23). Does daily denial have anything to do with material things? Did Jesus not warn, "For what will a man be profited, if he gains the whole world, and forfeits his soul?" (Matt. 16:26). Does that not indicate a correlation between gaining and keeping wealth and ultimate damnation? Did not Jesus once compare the kingdom of heaven to "a treasure hidden in the field, which a man found and hid; and from joy over it he goes and sells all that he has, and buys that field"? (Matt. 13:44). Did He not forbid all of His followers to lay up treasures on earth (see Matt. 6:19) and warn them that no one could serve God and mammon, because they would love one and hate the other? (see Matt. 6:24). Did He not command all His followers to sell their possessions and give to charity, making for themselves "purses which do not wear out, an unfailing treasure in heaven"? (Luke 12:33). Did He not proclaim, "Woe to you who are rich, for you are receiving your comfort in full"? (Luke 6:24). Did He not state that loving one's neighbor as oneself is the second greatest commandment? (see Matt. 22:39). Did He not command us to love one another even as He loved us and treat others just as we want to be treated? (see John 13:34-35; Matt. 7:12). Did He not warn His followers to beware of greed and then illustrate greed's eternal danger with the Parable of the Rich Fool? (as we studied in a previous chapter; see Luke 12:13-21). Did He not warn of the final fate of those who live in self-indulgence, ignoring the plight of the poor, in the story of the Rich Man and Lazarus? (which we will study in a later chapter; see Luke 16:19-31). Did He not warn everyone of a future judgment at which those who ignored the plight of His very poor brethren will be cast into hell? (see Matt. 25:31-46). How then can anyone say that Jesus told only one man to sell all his possessions and give to charity? *Jesus commanded all of His followers to sell their possessions and give to charity* (see Luke 12:33).

So we see the great error in assuming that Jesus does not require anyone today to give up his possessions for Him because He only supposedly required that of one man during His earthly ministry. We might as well claim that Jesus does not require anyone today to repent of adultery because He only ever told one woman who was caught in the act to go and sin no more.

Of course, it certainly seems reasonable to conclude that Jesus was not requiring the rich ruler to literally sell every single thing that he owned so that he would be homeless, naked and without any food, ultimately poorer than the people he helped by his charity. He was, according to Luke, "extremely rich" (Luke 18:23), and was being required to scale down dramatically, giving up what he didn't need. But he wasn't being required to do what Jesus Himself didn't do. It is also true that it would have taken some time for the rich ruler to liquidate his assets, although he could have immediately begun taking some steps in that direction.

A Tax Collector Repents of Greed and is Saved

The story of Zaccheus, a rich tax collector, helps us understand biblical salvation and what it means to repent of greed. As he was perched in a sycamore tree alongside a street in Jericho, Jesus said to him, "Zaccheus, hurry and come down, for today I must stay at your house" (Luke 19:5).

Who has the right to command someone whom he has never met to stop immediately what he is doing and proceed home, and then tell him, "I'm coming with you, because I'll be staying at your house today"? If anyone but God made such a request, we would consider him to be unbelievably presumptuous. But God has such a right, and Jesus' directive to Zaccheus demonstrated that He believed He was entitled to rule Zaccheus' time and possessions.

Zaccheus apparently also believed Jesus had that right. He immediately obeyed Him, not offended in the least. On the way to his house, Zaccheus further demonstrated his faith by publicly pledging to his new Lord, "Behold, Lord, half of my possessions I will give to the poor, and if I have defrauded anyone of anything, I will give back four times as much" (Luke 19:8).

Zaccheus apparently knew that Jesus was preaching a repentance that included repentance from greed. And obviously, Zaccheus knew he was guilty of greed in at least two ways. First, he neglected the poor, living in self-indulgence. Second, he gained his wealth, at least in part, by defrauding others, not an uncommon sin among tax collectors in Jesus' day. Both forms of his greed were violations of the second greatest commandment. When Zaccheus repented of both forms of greed, however, salvation came. Jesus immediately responded to Zaccheus' pledge by saying, "Today salvation has come to this house, because he, too, is a son of Abraham" (Luke 19:9). Zaccheus' heart-felt repentance was immediate and so was his salvation, although the working out of his repentance would have taken some time.

Zaccheus was not saved by his works, but by grace through faith, the only way any sinner can be saved. Grace offered him the opportunity to repent and be forgiven, and his faith was a true, living faith. When he believed in Jesus, he repented and began obeying Jesus. How would Jesus have responded if Zaccheus had said, "Lord, I am going to continue living in self-indulgence, ignoring the plight of the poor and defrauding people, but I do accept you as my Savior!"?

Did Zaccheus liquidate all of his assets? It seems very unlikely that he relinquished his daily food and clothing or any other essentials. Perhaps he scaled down to a smaller house if the one he owned was more than he needed. We know with certainty that he pledged to give half of his possessions to the poor. He also pledged to pay back four times what he had defrauded from anyone. Obviously, Zaccheus had been guilty of that very sin or he would never have mentioned it. If only one-eighth of his net worth had been gained by defrauding people, it would have cost him half of all he had in order to repay them all fourfold. Thus the real possibility exists that Zaccheus was ultimately left with only a small fraction of his original wealth.[4]

So in the story of Zaccheus, we see a clear example of a wealthy person who repented of greed when he was saved. He didn't just change his attitude about his wealth, but he changed his actions, the very thing Jesus expected of the rich ruler.

The Similarities Between the Rich Ruler and Ourselves

"But I am not like the rich, young ruler!" so many claim. "He obviously had a real problem with greed. The reason Jesus made such a difficult demand of him is because his disease could only be healed by radical surgery. Since we don't have his sickness, we don't need his cure."

But what makes us think we don't have the same sickness as the rich ruler, and thus don't need his cure? Our resistance to everything I've written so far reveals our sickness. The only reason we have so much difficulty with what Jesus plainly taught is because we can't imagine giving up any of our possessions. Our possessions have our hearts. We're every bit as greedy and covetous as the rich, young ruler. In fact, it is quite likely that the rich ruler tithed all his life, something that the majority of professing Christians have never done. Moreover, the majority of things we own *could not* have been owned by the rich ruler. Our lives may well be overflowing with much more *stuff*.

Moreover, we have the responsibility to spread the gospel all over the world, something the rich ruler was never expected to do. Beyond that, we, unlike the rich ruler, have access to information about suffering Christians and non-Christians around the globe and have means of supplying relief even though we live thousands of miles away. This being so, our greed may be even greater than his. The fundamental difference between so many of us and the rich young ruler is this: He believed what Jesus said was required of him to inherit eternal life and walked away sadly, while we don't believe what Jesus said is required of us to inherit eternal life and walk away rejoicing in our self-deception. If the rich ruler had said, "Jesus, I won't repent of greed and give up my possessions, but I do accept You as my Savior," and walked away praising God for his salvation, what would have been Christ's commentary?

The Rationalizations of Self-Deception

"I may have many possessions, but my possessions don't have me!" is a defense frequently heard. What would Jesus have said to the rich ruler if he had proffered such an excuse? Do you suppose He would have said,

---

[4] Why did Zaccheus promise to pay back four times what he had gained by defrauding others? Probably because that is what the Law of Moses required of those who stole their neighbor's sheep (see Ex. 22:1; 2 Sam. 12:6).

"Oh! Now that makes a *real* difference! I'm sorry that I misjudged you! Since that's the case, you don't need to sell any of your property"?

As I've previously mentioned, we've somehow convinced ourselves that greed is just an attitude about what we possess, and therefore it has nothing to do with how much we possess and what we do with our possessions. Applying this logic, however, one could be the richest person in the world, share none of his wealth, and not be guilty of greed. It makes no difference how many people starve while he collects mansions, jets, and diamonds, as long as he maintains the right attitude about his possessions! How absurd!

Jesus didn't require the rich ruler to change only his attitude (if such a thing were even possible). He didn't say, "How hard it is for those with *greedy attitudes* to enter the kingdom of heaven." He said it would be hard for those who are *wealthy* to enter the kingdom of heaven. And the reason it is hard for them is because they must repent of their greed, which means financial adjustments in line with God's will. If all they needed to do was change their attitudes but not their actions, it wouldn't be hard for them at all.

A similar twisted logic is found in the common excuse, "It doesn't matter how much you have. It only depends on what is in your heart. All that Jesus requires is that we inwardly give up all we possess, because greed is a sin of the heart." Again, what would Jesus have said to the rich ruler if he had made such a statement to Him? "Lord, I'll inwardly obey You, but outwardly I'll ignore You."

Greed is indeed a sin of the heart. However, it is one that is revealed by our actions. Outwardly clinging to our possessions reveals inward clinging. Jesus said, "For where your treasure is [outward clinging], there will your heart be also [inward clinging]" (Matt. 6:21). It is that simple.

What should we think of a man who is drunk every day and who says, "Alcohol doesn't have me! Inwardly, I'm sober!"? What should we think of a murderer, who, as he drives a knife into the heart of his victim says, "I don't actually hate this person. Inwardly, I'm full of love!"? What should we think of a man whose house has pornographic magazines stacked to the ceilings and who says, "These magazines mean absolutely nothing to me. Inwardly, I'm pure!"? We would think that every one of those people was self-deceived. That being so, then why do we go on fooling ourselves with similar statements about our possessions and our supposed freedom from greed?

The list of our smokescreens is almost endless, and all are proved equally foolish when considered in the light of simple logic. For example, I've heard it said, "Poor people can be just as greedy as rich people!"

Perhaps that is true. But does that make it right for anyone to be greedy?

I've heard it said, "You can give up all your possessions to feed the poor and still not have love! Isn't that what Paul wrote in 1 Corinthians 13:3?"

Yes, Paul did write that. But does that prove that everyone who gives up his possessions to feed the poor does not have love? Does that mean that none of us should give up any of our possessions to feed the poor? The answers are obvious. *One may give without loving, but one cannot love without giving.*

"I read in one Bible commentary where the author explained how Jesus was not literally speaking of a needle when He spoke of the camel and needle's eye. Jesus had in mind a certain gate in Jerusalem called "the Needle Gate," through which camels could pass only if their load was removed and they knelt."

This particular idea of a needle gate has no archeological or historical evidence to support it. It is only a myth. And even if Jesus were referring to a so-called "Needle Gate," His illustration would still convey the idea of getting rid of one's possessions in humble obedience to Him in order to enter heaven. So this interpretation doesn't really soften what He said. I must also point out that Jesus didn't say, "Needle Gate," but "a needle." He didn't say "gate" or "opening" but "eye."

Repentance from Greed Harmonizes with Apostolic Teaching

Repentance from greed was certainly something that the apostles emphasized in their teaching. They obeyed Jesus' commandment to teach their disciples to obey all that He had commanded them (see Matt. 28:18-20).[5] Thus, everything He taught the apostles about money, possessions and stewardship, they passed on to their disciples. For example, during His earthly ministry, Jesus instructed all His followers to sell their possessions and give to charity (as we have already seen in Luke 12:33), and that is, no doubt, what the apostles taught their disciples. For that reason we read in the book of Acts,

> And they were continually devoting themselves to the apostles' teaching….And all those who had believed were together, and had all things in common; and they began selling their property and possessions, and were sharing them with all, as anyone might have need….And abundant grace was upon them all. For there was not a needy person among them, for all who were owners of land or houses[6] would sell them and bring the proceeds of the

[5] Incidentally, the words of Jesus found in Matthew 28:18-20 clearly disprove the theory that Jesus' words during His earthly ministry have application only to those who lived before His death and resurrection. Jesus commanded His apostles to teach their converts to obey all that He had commanded them, which would have obviously been a perpetual commandment binding upon every future Christian

[6] We will see later in our study that many early Christians continued to own their homes. Thus it seems reasonable to conclude that Luke was reporting how those individuals who owned *houses* (plural) sold those they didn't need in order to give to charity and lay up heavenly treasures. People need a place to live.

sales, and lay them at the apostles' feet; and they would
be distributed to each, as any had need (Acts 2:42, 44-45;
4:33-35).[7]

In other places in the New Testament, we find examples of sacrificial giving by the early Christians. Once the Holy Spirit revealed to a prophet named Agabus that there would soon be a great famine. Luke tells us that, "in the proportion that any of the disciples had means, each of them determined to send a contribution for the relief of the brethren living in Judea. And this they did" (Acts 11:29-30). Note that any follower of Christ who had any means to help, did help.

While encouraging the Corinthian Christians to participate in an offering for poor Christians in Judea, Paul reported to them how the Macedonian Christians had given sacrificially, motivated by God's transforming grace:

> Now, brethren, we wish to make known to you the grace
> of God which has been given in the churches of Macedo-
> nia, that in a great ordeal of affliction their abundance of
> joy and their deep poverty overflowed in the wealth of
> their liberality. For I testify that according to their ability,
> and beyond their ability they gave of their own accord,
> begging us with much entreaty for the favor of participa-
> tion in the support of the saints (2 Cor. 8:1-4).

Talk about cheerful givers!

Such offerings for the poor are mentioned in other places in Acts and the New Testament epistles (see Acts 11:27-30; 24:17; Rom. 15:25-28; 1 Cor. 16:1-4; 2 Cor. 8-9). Paul considered giving to the poor to be a very important part of what it meant to follow Christ. In fact, so did Peter, James and John. When Paul first visited them to compare his gospel with theirs, they gave him their full endorsement, and Paul later recounted, "They only asked us to remember the poor—the very thing I also was eager to do" (Gal. 2:10). Assisting the poor was secondary only to the preaching of the gospel.

Paul taught that greed is a characteristic of those whose minds are depraved (see Rom. 1:28-29). He also taught that no greedy or covetous person will inherit the kingdom of God (see 1 Cor. 6:9-10, Eph. 5:3-5). He equated greed with idolatry (see Eph. 5:5; Col. 3:5), which is another way of saying just what Jesus said, that one can't serve God and mammon, two masters.

Paul instructed the Corinthian Christians not to associate or eat with any covetous person who claimed to be a Christian, because that person's profession of faith is obviously bogus (see 1 Cor. 5:9-13). How would the

---

[7] We will later consider the modern explanations that are used to prove that the unselfish sharing of the early Christians is not a good example for modern Christians to follow.

early church have determined if any of their members were guilty of covetousness? There could be only one way—by looking at their lifestyles.

Paul also instructed Timothy to tell rich people to "do good, that they be rich in good works, ready to distribute, willing to communicate; laying up in store for themselves a good foundation against the time to come, *that they may lay hold on eternal life* (1 Tim. 6:18-19, KJV, emphasis added). If Paul had written, "Tell them to believe in Jesus that they may lay hold on eternal life," we would have interpreted his words to mean that rich people need to believe in Jesus in order to receive eternal life. So why not interpret what he did actually write as meaning that rich people must be just as rich in good works of giving if they want to inherit eternal life?

John wrote that we know we are saved by our love for our brethren in Christ (see 1 John 3:14). John, however, wasn't talking only about warm, sentimental feelings of love, but of a practical love that gives whenever it sees a need and whatever it is able to give. This was the only way one could have true assurance of salvation:

> We know love by this, that He laid down His life for us; and we ought to lay down our lives for the brethren. But whoever has the world's goods, and beholds his brother in need and closes his heart against him, how does the love of God abide in him? [The obvious answer to that rhetorical question is, "It doesn't." If one does not love his neighbor, he does not love God either, as he disobeys God's second greatest commandment.] Little children, let us not love with word or with tongue, but in deed and truth. We shall know by this that we are of the truth, and shall assure our heart before Him (1 John 3:16-19).

As I have previously mentioned, James, in illustrating the truth that faith without works is dead, used the example of a professing Christian who showed no love for a fellow impoverished believer. Although he knew of fellow believers who were "without clothing and in need of daily food" (Jas. 2:15), he did not "give them what is necessary for their body," but only said, "Go in peace, be warmed and be filled" (Jas. 2:16). James comments: "What use is that? Even so faith, if it has no works, is dead, being by itself" (Jas. 2:17).

James also wrote the following scathing condemnation of rich people:

> Come now, you rich, weep and howl for your miseries which are coming upon you. Your riches have rotted and your garments have become moth-eaten. Your gold and your silver have rusted; and their rust will be a witness against you and will consume your flesh like fire. It is

in the last days that you have stored up your treasure! Behold, the pay of the laborers who mowed your fields, and which has been withheld by you, cries out against you; and the outcry of those who did the harvesting has reached the ears of the Lord of Sabaoth. You have lived luxuriously on the earth and led a life of wanton pleasure; you have fattened your hearts in a day of slaughter. You have condemned and put to death the righteous man; he does not resist you (Jas. 5:1-6).

Obviously, James was not writing about heaven-bound people. But was there any hope for these greedy people whom James condemned? Certainly—if they believed in Jesus, repented of defrauding fellow human beings and ceased laying up treasures on earth, ignoring the plight of the poor. Do you suppose James would have assured them of their salvation otherwise? Of course not. The apostles universally believed that no greedy person was saved unless he repented in heart and action.

I have by no means exhausted the biblical evidence to prove that the teaching of the apostles harmonizes perfectly with what Jesus told the rich, young ruler. The evidence is overwhelming. Yet the majority of the church today is ignoring this clear message from Christ and His apostles.

Another Objection Considered

Some teach that Jesus' words in the story of the rich ruler have application only to "those who trust in wealth." They supposedly have no application to those who simply have wealth but don't "trust in it," because that is what some later manuscripts add to Mark's rendition of Jesus' encounter with the rich ruler, recorded in Mark 10:24. (None of the other Gospel accounts include this phrase.)

If the later manuscripts of Mark's Gospel are a more accurate rendition of what Jesus actually said, then "trusting in wealth" must have been the sin of which the rich ruler was guilty, because his refusal to sell all was the basis of Christ's statement. How was the rich ruler "trusting in wealth"? He could have been trusting in his wealth as a means of security for the future, as revealed by his unwillingness to liquidate it in order to benefit those who were suffering pressing needs. Wealthy people often cling to their money out of fear. Not trusting God to take care of them, they trust in their money. *Only those who have wealth can trust in it, and the only way to stop trusting it is to liquidate it.* One who trusts in God and not in wealth has no need to lay up wealth on the earth.

Beyond that, the rich ruler, "trusting in wealth," had made it his trusted master, and he served it, giving to it what rightfully belonged only to God—his heart's devotion. So in that sense as well, all who refuse to repent of greed are also trusting in wealth.

What else could the phrase, "trusting in wealth" mean, other than these two possibilities I have suggested? Thus, even if the later manuscripts of Mark's Gospel are to be trusted above the early manuscripts, and if they are to be trusted above what Matthew and Luke recorded about the same story, Jesus' message and meaning are not altered in the least.

Yet Another Objection Considered

One well-known prosperity preacher would like us to believe that, although the rich ruler came looking for eternal life, Jesus offered him apostleship, thus the reason for the difficult requirements. This absurd theory illustrates how far some go to justify their greed.

This flimsy theory is partially built on the statement that Jesus told the rich ruler to *follow* Him, just as He asked other certain people to follow Him who became apostles. However, a study of Jesus' "follow Me" expressions quickly reveals that Jesus extended the invitation to everyone to follow Him, and to become His follower was equivalent to believing in Him and doing His will (see Matt. 10:38; 16:24; John 10:27; 12:26). Even when Jesus called certain specific individuals to follow Him, it wasn't until they began following Him that He appointed some of them as apostles.

Additionally, if Jesus was offering the rich ruler apostleship, why didn't He say so? Why did He let him sadly wander away thinking that he had to sell his possessions in order to inherit eternal life, when that was only required of him if he wanted to meet the requirements for apostleship? Why did Jesus make His statement about the camel and the needle and entering the kingdom of heaven? Why didn't Jesus clear up the apostles' misunderstanding, as revealed by their question about salvation? Many other similar questions could easily be asked that expose the fallacies of this poor theory.

Back to Our Story Again...

Peter's response to Jesus, "Behold, we have left everything and followed You; what then will there be for us?" (Matt. 19:27), reveals, as I've already stated, that he believed Jesus' previous words had application to more than just one man. Clearly, Peter realized that what Jesus had just said had application to him and the rest of the apostles. We, unfortunately, know nothing about the details of their personal wealth. We do know, however, that they left all they had to follow Jesus. He, in turn, assured all of them that their sacrifices would be worth it. They would be rewarded in this life and the next, as would all who make similar sacrifices. And, yes, all such people will inherit eternal life. Below I combine Matthew and Mark's Gospels to include all that Jesus said in response to Peter:

Truly I say to you, that you who have followed Me, in the

regeneration when the Son of Man will sit on His glorious throne, you also shall sit upon twelve thrones, judging the twelve tribes of Israel....There is no one who has left house or brothers or sisters or mother or father or children or farms, for My sake and for the gospel's sake, but that he shall receive a hundred times as much now in the present age, houses and brothers and sisters and mothers and children and farms, along with persecutions; and in the age to come, *eternal life*[8] (Matt. 19:28; Mark 10:29-30, emphasis added).

Some modern prosperity preachers, in a masterful manipulation of all that Christ said in this passage, tell us that if the rich ruler had only stayed a few minutes longer, he would have learned that Jesus really wasn't asking him to give up anything! Rather, Jesus wanted to make him one hundred times wealthier, and all he had to do was "sow a seed" that would reap a hundred-fold harvest.

Interestingly, I've never heard any of those prosperity preachers try to claim the hundred-fold return on children, or for that matter on brothers, sisters, mothers and fathers. They only claim the hundred-fold return on the houses and farms. This shows the fatal flaw of their misinterpretation of Jesus' promise.

Jesus was not promising lavish material wealth to those who sacrificed for His sake. Rather, He was promising that those who leave their families, homes and farms for the sake of the gospel will enjoy the blessing of winning many people to Christ. Those new believers will become their spiritual family, and those new brothers, sisters, mothers and fathers will open their homes to share everything they have with those who left everything for the sake of the gospel. As we have already read, of the early Christians Luke recorded, "Not one of them claimed that anything belonging to him was his own; but all things were common property to them" (Acts 4:32). Of course, this kind of sharing only occurs among real Christians, not those who imagine that they can serve God and mammon.

Had the rich ruler obeyed Jesus, he would have actually experienced greater economic security. At present, his wealth stood the chance of "[making] itself wings, like an eagle that flies toward the heavens" (Prov. 23:5). Through a bad decision, change of fortune, or even judgment from God, he could find himself destitute. His wealth was "like a high wall in his own imagination" (Prov. 18:11), and Scripture warns that "riches do not profit in the day of wrath" (Prov. 11 :4). However, if the rich ruler had disposed of his wealth as Jesus commanded, he would have been guaranteed that his true needs would have been met all of his life and throughout

---

[8] Notice that the topic is still eternal life, as it was at the beginning of the story.

eternity. He would have been joining a family that loved him.

What Then Shall We Do?

Have you perhaps discovered that you are a greedy person and that money, rather than Jesus, is your master? Then you are at the same point as the rich ruler just before he walked away sadly from Jesus. What a fool he was, esteeming earthly wealth more valuable than heavenly riches and a relationship with God. Don't make his mistake.

You can repent right now and begin to know the joy of true faith in Christ, the kind of faith that makes Jesus, and not mammon, Lord and Master. What joy you will experience as you break free from greed and begin liquidating your assets to feed the hungry, clothe the naked, and send the gospel to the lost millions of this world! Think of how much good you will be able to do with your future earnings as you scale down and live more simply! Think of how much you will glorify God as you imitate Christ, no longer living for self-indulgence, but living to love God and your neighbor as yourself! Your heart will be in heaven, where your Lord and Savior is, and where your eternal treasure waits.

> Teach me Your way, O Lord;
> I will walk in Your truth;
> Unite my heart to fear Your name (Ps. 86:11).

FOUR

A Steward, A Rich Man and a Beggar
Luke 16:1-31

If you have made it this far that is a very good sign. Be encouraged. God must be helping you in answer to your prayers.

Although we've laid a foundation, there is still more that Jesus wants us to learn about stewardship. Many questions still loom, but we must take our time. We have been so "brain-dirtied" that the plain biblical truth is difficult to swallow. This chapter, like the last three, is guaranteed to make you examine your lifestyle in light of what Jesus commanded. Perhaps it seems as if I'm overdoing it. Keep in mind, however, that so far we've only covered two passages of Jesus' words about stewardship, and in this chapter we'll study a third. So if I'm overdoing it, it could be said that Jesus did as well. I would prefer, however, to think that Jesus knew what He was doing. So please begin with another prayer for God's grace and help as we continue through the needle's eye. Remember that on the other side of the needle is unspeakable joy on earth and in heaven.

A Forgotten Word

Our present state in this world is perhaps best described by a word that has practically disappeared from the English language, the word *steward*. A steward is one who is entrusted with what belongs to another. He is thus faithfully expected to use, according to the owner's wishes, what has been committed to him, and therefore he must periodically give account of his stewardship.

Every person, saved and unsaved, is in some sense a steward of God.[1] All of us have been entrusted with a God-given life, and God expects that we will live our lives according to His will. We're also given opportunities, talents and treasures, for which all of us must one day give a full account.

---

[1] See Matt. 25:14-30, a story Jesus told about three stewards. At the end of the story, two stewards are rewarded and one steward is cast into hell. Thus, God considered the unsaved person to be a steward.

Those who prove themselves unfaithful will forfeit their stewardship eternally. Those who are found faithful will hear their Lord say, "Well done, good and faithful slave; you were faithful with a few things, I will put you in charge of many things, enter into the joy of your master" (Matt. 25:21). *Only those who have been faithful to their Master will enter His joy.*

In Jesus' day, wealthy people often employed stewards to look after their financial affairs. If a steward was entrusted with a sum of money, his responsibility was to invest it wisely in order to reap profits for his master. Unprofitable stewards enjoyed little job security.

Jesus once told a story of an unfaithful steward who found himself suddenly unemployed. The story served to illustrate several truths of eternal significance regarding our financial stewardship before God. We would be wise to listen to and heed what Jesus taught:

> Now [Jesus] was also saying to the disciples, "There was a certain rich man who had a steward, and this steward was reported to him as squandering his possessions. And he called him and said to him, 'What is this I hear about you? Give an account of your stewardship, for you can no longer be steward.' And the steward said to himself, 'What shall I do, since my master is taking the stewardship away from me? I am not strong enough to dig; I am ashamed to beg. I know what I shall do, so that when I am removed from the stewardship, they will receive me into their homes.' And he summoned each one of his master's debtors, and he began saying to the first, 'How much do you owe my master?' And he said, 'A hundred measures of oil.' And he said to him, 'Take your bill, and sit down quickly and write fifty.' Then he said to another, 'And how much do you owe?' And he said, 'A hundred measures of wheat.' He said to him, 'Take your bill, and write eighty.' And his master praised the unrighteous steward because he had acted shrewdly; for the sons of this age are more shrewd in relation to their own kind than the sons of light" (Luke 16:1-8).

We don't know the exact details, but somehow it was discovered that this particular steward had been unfaithful, "squandering" his master's possessions. Because he could no longer be trusted, his master understandably terminated his employment. At the same time, however, he requested an accounting from his steward so that he would know what only the steward knew: Exactly how much did his various debtors owe him?

The Plan

Armed with this knowledge, the unfaithful steward realized that he had a short window of opportunity to do something dishonest that could benefit him in the future: He could fudge the figures of his accounting and decrease the debts of each of his master's debtors. They, in turn, hopefully feeling obligated to repay his favor, would open their homes to him in his unemployment.

So he called his master's debtors together. Amazingly, the steward knew little more than his master did concerning the amounts that each one owed. He had to ask them for the amounts! That, of course, is something he should have known, and it gives us some insight as to why he was dismissed.

The steward then significantly reduced the debts of each of his former master's debtors with their full cooperation. All of them were knowingly stealing from the master. After presenting the falsified accounting to the master, the unemployed steward went whistling on his way.[2]

When the master eventually discovered how shrewdly his former steward had acted, he praised him, being a shrewd fellow himself. He had been beaten at his own game, but his losses weren't significant so he took it all in stride. Jesus commented: "The sons of this age [the unsaved] are more shrewd in relation to their own kind [other unsaved people] than the sons of light [the saved]" (Luke 16:8). Thank God for that!

The Application of the Story

After relating the story, Jesus then supplied the application to His audience. His application included at least three points. Here is the first one:

> And I say to you, make friends for yourselves by means of
> the mammon of unrighteousness; that when it fails, they
> may receive you into the eternal dwellings (Luke 16:9).

Because this first point is puzzling, it is often ignored. Jesus, however, must have meant *something* by it, and so we would be wise to give some thought to its meaning. When we do, we soon see that there is only one possible interpretation that makes sense.

Jesus was not, of course, endorsing the sinful deeds of the unfaithful steward and his friends. He was not encouraging us to lie, buy favors with someone else's money, or cheat our employers. That should be obvious. However, there is one sense, and only one sense, in which Christ's followers should imitate the steward in Jesus' story.

Just as the unfaithful steward wisely (albeit shrewdly and sinfully) prepared for his future by making friends by the means of money, so should

---

[2] It has been suggested by some that the steward only reduced the debts of his friends by his own commission, which he now realized he would never be paid by his master. This is of course speculative, but it is so, the steward and his debtors did not consequently conspire to steal from the master, and the master's praise of his steward's shrewdness could have been quite sincere. Regardless, the steward had been reported as squandering his masters' possessions, and it seems odd that he apparently didn't know how much his master's debtors owed.

Christ's followers. We've all been entrusted with some "mammon of un-righteousness" (so-called because money is so intrinsically linked to the world's evil). We, too, should "make friends" with it, that is, use it for the good of others, particularly to relieve and assist believers. That way, when "it fails," as will all our money on the day we die, "they," that is, those whom we have assisted and who have gone to heaven before us, "may receive [us] into the eternal dwellings."[3]

Incidentally, if God is going to call the entire populations of ancient cities to testify against certain groups of people at their judgment (see Matt. 12:41), wouldn't it be good to have some fellow believers at your judgment, those whom you assisted on earth to stand as witnesses on your behalf? That is, those who could say of you, "I was hungry, and he fed me," "I was naked, and she clothed me," and so on?

The Second Point

Jesus continued:

> He who is faithful in a very little thing is faithful also in much; and he who is unrighteous in a very little thing is unrighteous also in much. If therefore you have not been faithful in the use of unrighteous mammon, who will entrust the true riches to you? And if you have not been faithful in the use of that which is another's, who will give you that which is your own? (Luke 16:10-12).

Trust is something that generally must be earned. Parents observe how their children handle small responsibilities before entrusting them with larger responsibilities. Single people, as they fall in love, risk less at the beginning of their relationship, until they are certain they can trust their beloved with their whole heart. Employers read résumés and references to determine if a potential employee can be trusted. Before banks lend money, they check a person's credit history. They've all learned that they can predict someone's future by studying his past.

In Jesus' story, the steward was discovered to be unfaithful. He thus lost the trust of his master, who realized that if he continued to employ his steward, he would only suffer greater losses. And he was correct in his assumption. His steward proved himself to be even more unfaithful after he lost his job, shrewdly stealing from him even more. The steward's character didn't change.

"He who is unrighteous in a very little thing is unrighteous also in much" (Luke 16:10). Although we all know and apply this most basic

---

[3] There are only two "eternal dwellings" of which Scripture speaks: heaven and hell. Since Jesus was speaking to His followers, telling them to make friends with money so that those friends would receive them into the eternal dwellings, this seems to be the most reasonable interpretation of this passage.

truth in our dealings with others, we often forget that God is at least as smart as we are. *If we are unfaithful to God on earth, whatever makes us think we would be faithful to Him in heaven?* We might fool ourselves, but God is not fooled.

If we love and serve mammon on earth, He knows we wouldn't love and serve Him in heaven. If we don't obey Him in the use of "unrighteous mammon," He will not entrust us with "true riches" (Luke 16:11), just as He said. What else could "true riches" be but ultimate salvation and eternal life?[4]

Jesus went on to say, "If you have not been faithful in the use of that which is another's, who will give you that which is your own?" (Luke 16:12). "That which is another's" corresponds to the master's money, and "that which is your own" corresponds to the steward's continued employment. Once the master found out that the steward was squandering *his* money, he certainly wasn't about to continue giving the steward *his* paycheck. If we squander God's money that He has entrusted to us, we will forfeit our opportunity to be His stewards as well.[5]

The Final Summary of the Parable

Finally, with one phrase, Jesus summarized everything that He was trying to convey about His followers' stewardship of money, something He had said at another time:

> No servant can serve two masters; for either he will hate the one, and love the other, or else he will hold to one, and despise the other. You cannot serve God and mammon (Luke 16:13).

This famous phrase summarizes what Jesus has already more specifically said. We are either serving God or mammon, loving one and hating the other. Our actions reveal who has our allegiance. Most of us claim to be serving and loving God, but our lifestyles often reveal that we actually love mammon. We aren't serving God in one of the most fundamental ways He requires, thus proving that we really don't love Him. We can't imagine sacrificially sharing our wealth with the poor or giving up our

---

[4] Naturally, some interpreters attempt to soften Jesus' warning so that it is heavenly rewards, not heaven itself, that unfaithful people risk forfeiting. However, when we read Jesus' statement in the entire context of Luke 16, particularly considering His warning about the impossibility of serving two masters just two verses later, as well as His story about the fates of the rich man and Lazarus (which we are about to read), we must question the validity of such a softening. Are we to believe that one who is untrustworthy with his money, not using it according to God's will, who thus "serves mammon," making it his true master, proving his love for it and hatred for God (as Jesus said), will be a citizen of heaven, where the God whom he hates reigns? Is all that he forfeits certain heavenly rewards? Is that what Jesus is teaching in this chapter?

[5] Jesus taught this very same stewardship principle in the Parable of the Talents, which concludes with the warning, "For to everyone who has shall more be given, and he shall have an abundance; but from the one who does not have, even what he does have shall be taken away. And cast out the worthless slave into the outer darkness; in that place there shall be weeping and gnashing of teeth" (see Matt. 25:14-30).

possessions, because we love what we have, and we want more. Money is really our master, and as Jesus declared, no one can serve two masters. Either we will love one and hate the other or vice versa.

The Pharisees who heard Jesus' parable and its application scoffed (see Luke 16:14), and Luke tells us why: They were "lovers of money" (Luke 16:14). They were the very ones who needed to hear what Jesus was saying! *But what do you suppose they would have answered if you asked them if they loved God?* Certainly they would have answered in the affirmative. Like so many who profess to love God today, they were completely self-deceived, thinking they loved God, while actually loving money.

Jesus then told them, "You are those who justify yourselves in the sight of men, but God knows your hearts" (Luke 16:15a). How appropriate are Jesus' words to scoffers in the church today! Many are the ways that we justify our greed in the sight of others! The list seems endless. Here is a sample of a few of the justifications I've heard, many of them from pastors:

"If those heathen countries would turn to Christ, God would bless them with prosperity just like He's blessed our nation!"

How do you suppose the hundreds of millions of poor, yet devout Christians in developing countries would feel about such a remark? And is wealth always an indication of God's blessing? Are drug smugglers wealthy because God is blessing them? Are we really to think that America is so wealthy because God is rewarding us for our righteousness? Do we not lead the world in sin and export our filth everywhere? Could part of the reason for our great prosperity be our great greed? Could it be due, in part, to the exploitation of cheap foreign labor by American companies? Chances are, the clothes you are wearing right now were manufactured overseas in a garment factory where the employees are happy to work for what we would consider slaves' wages. Have you ever considered the reason that so many products are so inexpensive for us is because others pay for it by giving their time so cheaply to manufacture it?

"If those lazy people in those poorer countries would work hard like I do, they'd have plenty too!"

That is a gross misconception. How about those hundreds of thousands of "lazy" Mexicans who labor in the fields of America as migrant workers? Why aren't most U.S. citizens willing to take those jobs? Or how would you like to sit under the hot sun, six or seven days a week, ten to twelve hours a day, in a granite quarry in India with a hammer in your hand, breaking large rocks into pieces in order to make road gravel? And when the sun goes down, you have barely enough money to buy your single meal for the day before you lay your head on a dirt floor in your tin shanty. Not only that, but your pre-teen children must all toil twelve-hour days rolling cigarettes on a factory floor, due to the fact that you had to borrow money to pay for emergency medical expenses. Most Americans have little idea of how hard people in many poorer countries work.

"God wants us to be blessed with abundance! He wants us to enjoy all our material blessings and be happy."

As those indwelled by Christ, how could we possibly find enjoyment in selfish indulgence while 34,000 children die every day of preventable diseases and malnutrition, and while at least one-third of the world has yet to hear the name of Jesus? Why isn't our longing to see the gospel spread to unreached peoples greater than our longing to indulge ourselves with more material things? Is it possible that we have equated happiness with temporarily-satisfied greed?

"God wants me to live in an exclusive neighborhood so I can reach my wealthy neighbors."

May I ask, *How many have you reached so far?* Is that how Jesus reached the wealthy? And how can you explain to your unsaved neighbors, as you encourage them to follow Christ, that your own lifestyle stands in opposition to what Christ practiced and preached? How do you tell them that it is easier for a camel to go through the eye of a needle than for a rich person to enter the kingdom of God?

"I must buy a new car every year because I need reliable transportation."

Are you saying that every used car on the road is unreliable?

"Solomon was wealthy and God didn't condemn him! In fact, the Bible says God made him rich!"

How can we rightfully justify amassing wealth like Solomon in light of Jesus' command to sell our possessions and give to charity, not laying up treasures on earth (see Luke 12:33)? Are we permitted to annul everything Jesus said on the subject of wealth because of the practice of one biblical figure? And even if we ignore what Jesus said, why don't we likewise justify amassing wives like Solomon?

I might add that God specifically told Solomon that He would make him rich because he *didn't* ask for wealth, but rather requested wisdom to serve God's people (see 2 Chron. 1:11-12). God wanted Solomon to use his divinely-given wealth to serve Him and others, as any wise person would. Thus He commanded Solomon to build a great temple and forbade him to multiply horses, wives, gold or silver for himself, all of which he ultimately did (see Deut. 17:14-20; 1 Kin. 4:26; 10:26-27; 11:1-3). His seven hundred wives (and three hundred concubines) ultimately turned his heart away from God so that he became an idolater, just as God had warned (see 1 Kin. 11:4-10). Solomon couldn't have supported so many wives if he had not been so rich, and so it can be said that his wealth was his downfall. He didn't use his wealth to love his neighbor as himself. Rather, he loved himself and effectively robbed one thousand men of the joy of marriage. The world's wisest man became the world's greatest fool. Is he to be our role model?

More Common Justifications

"The tenth commandment only forbids me to covet my neighbor's goods. I'm not coveting what belongs to anyone else; I only enjoy what is mine."

The Bible not only forbids us from coveting what is our neighbor's, it also commands us to love our neighbor as ourselves, which means God wants us to share our wealth with the hungry and naked. If we don't, we may not be coveting, but we are guilty of greed, keeping in our possession what God says should be in our neighbor's possession. It could even be called stealing.

"You sound like a communist, trying to redistribute everyone's wealth and remove all incentive to work!"

First, if our sole incentive to work hard is to enrich only ourselves, then our incentive is pure selfishness. No matter what we do, Christians are supposed to do their work heartily, "as for the Lord rather than for men" (Col. 3:23), and should labor "in order that [we] may have something to share with him who has need" (Eph. 4:28; see also Acts 20:35). Communism always fails because unregenerate people don't do their work as unto the Lord; they are selfish, and thus they don't work motivated by a desire to share with others.

Second, I am not advocating subsidizing the lazy, sinful lifestyles of other people, or enabling them to continue in their immorality or irresponsibility. Scripture says, "If anyone will not work, neither let him eat" (2 Thes. 3:10). Many people should be left to go hungry so they will be motivated to repent. The book of Proverbs has plenty to say to sluggards.

Third, I am not advocating the "forced charity" of communism, but the free-will generosity of those who are now indwelled by Christ.

Fourth, I *am* advocating helping truly needy people, those defined in Scripture as not having food or covering, not those who can't afford brand new cars or furniture. I'm also advocating using our God-given resources to spread the gospel to the third of the world that has never yet had a chance to hear it once. *Which true follower of Christ could find fault with such a goal?* This doesn't even remotely resemble communism.

"Shall we all live in grass huts?"

This comment is usually a smokescreen used by those who are unwilling to scale down or sacrifice in the least. They aren't concerned about having to live in a grass hut; they are concerned about relinquishing any of their luxuries.

"When we drive new cars and have houses full of nice furniture, it is a testimony before the world of how our God loves us and supplies our needs! If we drive old cars and have worn-out furniture, it sends a message to the world that our God is poor, or that He doesn't care about His children."

This is just another smokescreen to justify our greed, an attempt to make selfishness virtuous.

How many unsaved people, upon seeing your new car or nice furniture, have said, "Wow! God really loves and takes care of you! Can you tell me how I can be saved?" Why do we fool ourselves that unsaved people, upon seeing our nice possessions, which many other people own who make no profession of faith, have even a fleeting thought about God? They simply assume that we have a good-paying job or that we are deep in debt like everyone else who believes the American lie and is thus pursuing the American dream. Might we not make a greater impact upon the unsaved if we stood out from the world, demonstrating contentment, repenting of greed, and giving generously? Jesus did command us, by the way, to let our lights shine so that men might see our good works (not our great greed) and by so doing, we would glorify our God (see Matt. 5:16). What would be the impression upon your neighbor who asked you why your big house was for sale, and you told him, "I've become a follower of Christ and repented of my greed. I'm no longer living to impress other people of my success by what I own, plus I want to have more to share with the poor. So I'm scaling down to a smaller, but fully adequate house"?

Incidentally, why is the church growing in so much of the developing world, where poor Christians can't show off their new cars and furniture to prove to their neighbors how much God loves them, yet the church isn't growing at all in the wealthy West?

"I tithe! That is all God requires!"

Are we to believe that an old covenant commandment to tithe nullifies Christ's new covenant commandments, for example, His commandment that forbids the laying up of earthly treasures? Is it possible to tithe and still lay up treasures on earth? Obviously, yes. The New Testament reveals that although the Pharisees scrupulously tithed and even gave alms to the poor, they were still lovers of money (see Matt. 5:20 with 6:2; 23:23; Luke 16:14). Incidentally, those under the old covenant were commanded not only to tithe, but to provide for the poor (see Deut. 15:11). Just because one tithed did not mean he had obeyed the second greatest commandment. The tithe was little more than a tax, primarily for the support of the priests.

"The important thing is that we are thankful for all that God has given us. That is what is important."

Certainly being thankful is important, but did Jesus say that the second greatest commandment was to be thankful? By being thankful, does that release us from our responsibility to love our neighbors as ourselves, as well as obey all the rest of the commandments?

"It doesn't matter how much you have, just as long as you hold it loosely."

This "Christian cliché" is the epitome of twisted logic and self-deception. It means that we can keep whatever we want, as long as we are willing to give it away! An unwilling willingness! Doesn't the fact that we keep most of what we have clearly indicate our unwillingness to give it away? We've deceived ourselves if we think that we're holding loosely what we never give. Willingness to obey God is revealed by actual obedience. Disobedience to God reveals unwillingness to obey Him. What could be more obvious than that?

"All that I possess means nothing to me."

If it means nothing, why is your life devoted to it? Why do you work so hard to own it, maintain it, protect it and insure it? If it means nothing to you, then why don't you sell it and use the proceeds to provide what will mean everything to your beneficiary? To a starving person, food means everything. To a hell-bound person, salvation could mean everything.

"There are other sins that are just as bad as greed!"

Does that make greed acceptable?

"We are all at different levels of spiritual growth, you know. I'm just not at the same level as you are concerning my wealth."

Such a statement proves that one is not a disciple of Jesus Christ who declared, "No one of you can be My disciple who does not give up all his own possessions" (Luke 14:33). If one is not a disciple of Christ, neither is he a Christian. The modern notion that one can be saved without being Christ's disciple has no basis at all in Scripture.[6]

Moreover, when do you suppose that you actually will achieve that level to which you currently have not attained? If you don't achieve it now, adjusting your heart and repenting, you are only fooling yourself if you think you will do so in the future. You won't. By hardening your heart to the clear commands of Christ now, you are only strengthening greed's grip on your heart and increasing the darkness that clouds your mind. Jesus didn't say to the rich ruler, "Don't concern yourself with your greed, selfishness and disobedience to the second greatest commandment. Perhaps in the future you will arrive at a higher level of spiritual growth."

"It was God who has blessed me with my job and my wealth. If He didn't want me to enjoy my wealth, then why did He give it to me?"

Isn't it possible that God has given you more than you need so that you can share with those who have needs? One day you, like the Rich Fool of Luke 12, will have to give an account to Him.

"I tithed back in the days when I had nothing."

That is certainly praiseworthy. However, if you are resting on the laurels of your former self-denial, and your current tithe requires no real sacrifice because of your prosperity, you are making a grave mistake. Does your former obedience give you the right to currently disobey God? Does

---

[6] See chapter 4 of my book, *The Great Gospel Deception*, for a thorough discussion of this subject.

your previous self-denial hide your current self-indulgence from God's eyes? (If you don't know the answer, read Ezekiel 18:21-32.)

Jesus Continues...

Jesus had still more to say that day on the subject of money and possessions. Still speaking to the scoffing Pharisees about wealth, He continued, "That which is highly esteemed among men is detestable in the sight of God" (Luke 16:15). Why the disparity between divine and human perspectives?

The unregenerate world admires those who "make it to the top," gawking at their luxurious possessions and expensive lifestyles. They congratulate their friends when they "move up" or exhibit their latest acquisition. Position, power, prestige and wealth—these are what the world highly esteems, but God sees things in a vastly different light. He beholds all the selfishness, pride, envy, greed and ambition. People see a mansion, and He sees a pig sty. The masses adore a beautifully adorned woman wearing clothing and jewelry worth thousands of dollars, and He pities a poor woman who is dressed in spiritual rags. Folks gape at a man driving his shiny new luxury automobile, and God weeps for a proud peacock on parade.

But before we condemn the ultra-rich, how much of what we do with our money is motivated by the same sins of selfishness, pride, envy and greed? If everyone in the world were blind except myself, what would I own? The difference between what I would own and what I do own is what I own to impress others. Revivalist Charles Finney used to ask Victorian-era congregations, "Why do you spend so much time preparing your outward appearance to attend church on Sunday and so little time in preparing your spirit before God? You say that you go to worship, but do you really go to be worshipped?"

Take a look around your church's parking lot next Sunday when you leave. Which cars would you be ashamed to drive? Why would you be ashamed? Is it not because you want to convey by your car how successful you are?

Drive around some less affluent neighborhoods. Which houses would you never think of living in? Why not? Is not your pride a primary reason?

Another Story with an Unmistakable Meaning

Jesus' mercy is so great. In a desperate attempt to provoke the thinking of the hard-hearted, money-loving Pharisees who were scoffing at His message about money, Jesus next related a story about a rich man who went to hell. It is so simple to understand that only a theologian or prosperity preacher could miss its meaning:

Now there was a certain rich man, and he habitually dressed in purple and fine linen, gaily living in splendor every day. And a certain poor man named Lazarus was laid at his gate, covered with sores, and longing to be fed with the crumbs which were falling from the rich man's table; besides, even the dogs were coming and licking his sores. Now it came about that the poor man died and he was carried away by the angels to Abraham's bosom; and the rich man also died and was buried. And in Hades he lifted up his eyes, being in torment, and saw Abraham far away, and Lazarus in his bosom. And he cried out and said, "Father Abraham, have mercy on me, and send Lazarus, that he may dip the tip of his finger in water and cool off my tongue; for I am in agony in this flame." But Abraham said, "Child, remember that during your life you received your good things, and likewise Lazarus bad things; but now he is being comforted here, and you are in agony. And besides all this, between us and you there is a great chasm fixed, in order that those who wish to come over from here to you may not be able, and that none may cross over from there to us." And he said, "Then I beg you, Father, that you send him to my father's house—for I have five brothers—that he may warn them, lest they also come to this place of torment." But Abraham said, "They have Moses and the Prophets; let them hear them." But he said, "No, Father Abraham, but if someone goes to them from the dead, they will repent!" But he said to him, "If they do not listen to Moses and the Prophets, neither will they be persuaded if someone rises from the dead" (Luke 16:19-31).

Why did this rich man go to hell? He himself knew *exactly why*. It was because he never repented. He stated that he knew his brothers had to repent if they were to escape his fate (see Luke 16:30).

Specifically, as the details of the story make so clear, the rich man went to hell because he never repented of greed.[7] *All greedy people go to hell*. And Jesus couldn't have illustrated what greed is any better than He did, by juxtaposing the rich man and Lazarus. Greed is the selfish use of one's money and possessions. The rich man had an expensive wardrobe and "gaily lived in splendor every day" (Luke 16:19). With his abundance, he could have easily relieved some of the distress of sick and starving Laza-

---

[7] I heard a famous evangelist, speaking about this story, say, "The rich man didn't go to hell because he was rich any more than Lazarus went to Abraham's bosom because he was poor!" That sounds so logical, but it is so misleading. Lazarus' poverty was not the reason he went to Abraham's bosom, but the rich man's wealth had a lot to do with his going to hell. He went to hell because he was rich and didn't share his wealth.

rus whom he must have seen at his own gate. But because he was selfish, he didn't have compassion. He preferred to spend his money on continued vanity and selfish indulgence rather than keep a starving man alive.

What is the sin of a man who ignores the plight of a starving man and has the means to help him? By withholding what could have helped a starving man to live, has he not made a decision that will cause the man to die? When people are starved to death in concentration camps, do we not consider their captors to be murderers also? When people starve *outside* of concentration camps, are not those who knew of their plight and had the resources to have kept them alive responsible for their deaths? God will hold them accountable. Was not the greedy man in Jesus' parable guilty of murder? How does he differ from any greedy person?

> Deliver those who are being taken away to death, and those who are staggering to slaughter, O hold them back. If you say, "See, we did not know this," does He not consider it who weighs the hearts? And does He not know it who keeps your soul? And will He not render to man according to his work? (Prov. 24:11-12).

Hell for the Greedy

Hoping to arouse the minds of the scoffing Pharisees and everyone else who would hear His story, Jesus revealed something of what hell will be like for the greedy.

The rich man was "in torment" and "in agony in [the] flame" (Luke 16:23-24). He knew he was being punished for his sins and had no hope of escape. Any visions he had previously possessed on earth of a God so loving that He need not be feared had vanished from his mind. Now he understood the true nature of God's love—a universal love from which justice flows.

The rich man didn't have the courage to ask for even a cup of cold water (realizing that was a vain hope), and asked only for the smallest bit of mercy—just a single drop of water to cool his tongue. But even that miniscule request was denied. Justice now triumphed over mercy.

We can only speculate on why the rich man specifically requested for Lazarus to perform that small act of relief. You would think he would be ashamed to ask for any alleviation from Lazarus, of all people, in light of how he ignored Lazarus' plight on the earth. What could have motivated him? Could it have been because God allowed him to see only Lazarus in Abraham's bosom, in keeping with the divine promise that everyone will reap what he sows (see Gal. 6:7)? Was not the rich man now in a position of longing for help from Lazarus, just as Lazarus was once in a position of longing for help from him? Abraham even said to the rich man, "Remember that during your life you received your good things, and likewise

Lazarus bad things; but now he is being comforted here, and you are in agony" (Luke 16:25). Their circumstances had been exactly reversed.

Giving up all hope of even the slightest relief, the rich man began thinking of his five brothers who were still alive and just like him. He knew they would join him in hell unless they repented, and so he attempted to intercede on their behalf. *Some of the most earnest evangelists are in hell.* But his request was denied, not because Abraham didn't care, but because he knew how hard-hearted the rich man's five brothers were. If they would ignore what God said through Moses and all the prophets, they wouldn't be persuaded to repent even if someone rose from the dead. Since Jesus spoke those words, Someone has risen from the dead, and His resurrection is not enough to convince many who profess to believe in Him that they need to heed His words about greed and repent!

Finally, take note that nothing is said about how the rich man gained his money. Not a word is said about his gaining it illegitimately. He may well have gained it by inheritance or by running some kind of business. But he was guilty of greed because of what he did with his wealth. He didn't use it to love his neighbor as himself, just like millions of wealthy people who live in luxury and profess to be Christians. They think they aren't guilty of greed because they gained their money honestly. (We will later consider just how difficult it is to gain wealth without breaking the second greatest commandment.)

How We Might Be Like the Rich Man

What do you suppose would have been the fate of the rich man if Lazarus had been laid, not at his gate, but on the street corner a hundred yards away, so that the rich man didn't see him quite as often? What if Lazarus had been on the other side of town, and the rich man only saw him occasionally on his journeys? Was the rich man's responsibility to relieve Lazarus changed by his proximity or number of encounters?

Clearly, the rich man's responsibility to assist Lazarus was based on his knowledge of Lazarus' plight and his available resources. John mentioned both aspects of our responsibility to relieve suffering brethren when he said, "But whoever has the world's goods [available resources], and beholds [has knowledge of] his brother in need and closes his heart against him, how does the love of God abide in Him?" (1 John 3:17).

I might use the excuse, "If suffering people were laid at my doorstep like Lazarus was laid at the rich man's doorstep, I would do something to help them." But what difference does it make if they are at my doorstep or on the other side of the world? If I know of their distress and have the means to help them, what valid excuse do I have not to help them? If I ignore their plight, am I not just like the rich man in Jesus' story? How am I any different than the man who wished to justify his disobedience to the second greatest commandment by asking Jesus, "And who is my neighbor?" (Luke 10:29). And if I only help those who are laid at my doorstep, does that not reveal that my motivation is likely to be evil? If I didn't assist those on my doorstep it would make me look bad in the eyes of my neighbors. Better keep up the "Christian" image, you know.

Likewise, how often do we attempt to salve our consciences by sharing small portions of our abundance? Again, our motives are often selfish. We want to feel good about ourselves, and so our giving is like taking a drug that numbs us. As we throw a little money to the poor we deceive ourselves into thinking that we really are good people after all, and then go right back to living in self-indulgence. Is that really loving our neighbor as ourselves?

Do you recall the time that Jesus and His disciples were sitting opposite the treasury, observing the people who were putting money into it? Scripture tells us, "many rich people were putting in large sums" (Mark 12:41). It is interesting that the whole contribution process was set up so observers would know what every contributor was giving.

A poor widow came and put in two small copper coins, which was equal in Christ's day to about 1/64th of a day's wages. (What do you make in seven and a half minutes?) Jesus then commented to His disciples:

> Truly I say to you, this poor widow put in more than all
> the contributors to the treasury; for they all put in out of
> their surplus, but she, out of her poverty, put in all she
> owned, all she had to live on (Mark 12:43-44).

Jesus was not impressed with those who gave out of their surplus. Their giving required little, if any true selfless love or self-denial. But isn't that the picture of so much of the giving that is done by professing Christians today? We give only what is easy to give.

Amazingly, so many of us claim we can't afford even to tithe (an old covenant standard), yet our self-deception is exposed by all we can afford. We can afford to spend thousands of dollars a year on non-essentials, vanities, interest payments and self-indulgence, all the time claiming to follow the One who once asked, "Why do you call Me, 'Lord, Lord,' and do not do what I say?" (Luke 6:46).

Guilty Again

So you should be feeling quite guilty by now. Don't become angry with me! All I've done is read the Bible honestly. God's Word has produced the guilt you feel. That means *God* is making you feel guilty. His goal is to make you holy, like Jesus, perfectly obedient to His will. Once our excuses are all stripped away, there stands our greed, naked and exposed. Then there is nothing to do but repent.

If you've made it this far you must keep reading. In the next chapter we will begin to consider the practical working out of our obedience to Christ's words regarding stewardship. That is where joy begins!

For His anger is but for a moment,
His favor is for a lifetime;
Weeping may last for the night,
But a shout of joy comes in the morning (Ps. 30:5).

FIVE

Lay Not Up For Yourselves Treasures
Matthew 6:2-4, 19-34

When therefore you give alms, do not sound a trumpet before you, as the hypocrites do in the synagogues and in the streets, that they may be honored by men. Truly I say to you, they have their reward in full. But when you give alms, do not let your left hand know what your right hand is doing that your alms may be in secret; and your Father who sees in secret will repay you....

Do not lay up for yourselves treasures upon earth, where moth and rust destroy, and where thieves break in and steal. But lay up for yourselves treasures in heaven, where neither moth nor rust destroys, and where thieves do not break in or steal; for where your treasure is, there will your heart be also. The lamp of the body is the eye; if therefore your eye is clear, your whole body will be full of light. But if your eye is bad, your whole body will be full of darkness. If therefore the light that is in you is darkness, how great is the darkness! No one can serve two masters; for either he will hate the one and love the other, or he will hold to one and despise the other. You cannot serve God and mammon. For this reason I say to you, do not be anxious for your life, as to what you shall eat, or what you shall drink; nor for your body, as to what you shall put on. Is not life more than food, and the body than clothing? Look at the birds of the air, that they do not sow, neither do they reap, nor gather into barns, and yet your heavenly Father feeds them. Are you not worth much more than they? And which of you by being anxious can add a single cubit to his life's span? And why are you anxious about clothing? Observe how the lilies of the field grow; they do not toil nor do they spin, yet I say to you that even Solomon in all his glory did not clothe himself like one of these. But if God so arrays the grass of the field, which is alive today and tomorrow is thrown into the furnace, will He not much more do so for you, O men of little faith? Do not be anxious then, saying, 'What shall we eat?' or 'What shall we drink?' or 'With what shall we clothe ourselves?' For all these things the Gentiles eagerly seek; for your heavenly Father knows that you need all these things. But seek first His kingdom and His righteousness; and all these things shall be added to you. Therefore do not be anxious for tomorrow; for tomorrow will care for itself. Each day has enough trouble of its own" (Matt. 6:2-4, 19-34).

Jesus' most famous sermon, the Sermon on the Mount, was evangelistic in nature. That is, by reading it, one learns something about how to avoid eternal damnation and receive salvation. Allow me to briefly prove this.

In the introduction, in what are commonly called the Beatitudes, Jesus enumerated wonderful blessings that certain blessed people can anticipate (see Matt. 5:1-12). The blessed will (1) inherit the kingdom of heaven, (2) be comforted, (3) inherit the earth, (4) be satisfied in righteousness, (5) receive mercy, (6) see God, (7) be called sons of God and (8) enjoy great heavenly rewards. The blessed are obviously those who are saved. Certainly, we would be wrong to think that Jesus was describing eight different groups of people. Otherwise we would have to conclude that some people who will see God might not inherit the kingdom of heaven, or that some people might inherit the kingdom of heaven but not receive mercy.

What are the character traits of the saved? They are poor in spirit, mourning, gentle, hungering for righteousness, merciful, pure in heart, peacemaking and persecuted. Their faith is not dead, but alive with fruit. Those who don't manifest such fruit are not among the blessed, and they are therefore not going to experience the blessings. Thus, any person could read the Beatitudes, examine his life, and determine if he is saved or not. We also see that from the very beginning, the Sermon on the Mount can be considered evangelistic in nature.

After the Beatitudes, we read four verses that set the stage for everything else Jesus intended to communicate in His sermon:

Do not think that I came to abolish the Law or the Prophets; I did not come to abolish, but to fulfill. For truly I say to you, until heaven and earth pass away, not the smallest letter or stroke shall pass away from the Law, until all is accomplished. Whoever then annuls one of the least of these commandments, and so teaches others, shall be called least in the kingdom of heaven; but whoever keeps and teaches them, he shall be called great in the kingdom of heaven. For I say to you, that unless your righteousness surpasses that of the scribes and Pharisees, you shall not enter the kingdom of heaven (Matt. 5:17-20).

Jesus plainly stated that He had not come to abolish the commandments and teachings found in the Law and the Prophets. On the contrary, He had come to fulfill them (see Matt. 5:17). That is, He would "fill to the full" all that God had previously revealed.

Some of the commandments of the Law, particularly the ceremonial and symbolic ones, Jesus "filled to the full" by His sacrificial death and present-day ministry. We no longer are required to sacrifice animals, as Jesus was the Lamb of God, our Passover. We no longer need an earthly high priest, as Jesus now fulfills that role, and so on.

The moral requirements of the Law and Prophets, however, Jesus "filled to the full" by fully endorsing, fully explaining, and fully expecting His followers to obey them. Jesus declared that not the smallest part of the Law would pass away "until heaven and earth pass away" and "all is accomplished" (Matt. 5:18). Have heaven and earth passed away yet? Thus the theory that the Mosaic Law has absolutely no relevance since Christ died is proved fallacious.

How important is it to obey the Law, as it is now "filled to the full" by Christ? It is so important that one's status in heaven is determined by it. Jesus said that anyone who annulled "one of the least of" the commandments and taught others the same, would "be called least in the kingdom of heaven," but whoever kept and taught the least of the commandments would "be called great in the kingdom of heaven" (Matt. 5:19). Additionally, one's practical righteousness, that is, his obedience to the Law, must surpass that of the scribes and Pharisees, or he will "not enter the kingdom of heaven" (Matt. 5:20).[1] This is another proof that the Sermon on the Mount was evangelistic in nature.[2]

More Proof

Within the majority of the remainder of the Sermon on the Mount, Jesus specifically taught His followers what to do to make sure their righteousness exceeded that of the scribes and Pharisees. It was important

---

[1] The theory that Jesus was making reference here to the *imputed* righteousness of Christ that all believers enjoy is certainly not supported by contextual evidence. Rather, the context supports the fact that Jesus was referring to *practical* righteousness.

[2] Jesus was, of course, speaking to Jews under the Law of Moses. All those under the new covenant are under the law of Christ (see 1 Cor. 9:21). We must keep in mind, however, that a large percentage of the Law of Moses is included in Christ's law. Everything found in the Sermon on the Mount is part of the law of Christ, yet the entire sermon is based on the Law of Moses.

for His followers not only to obey the letter of the law (as did the scribes and Pharisees to some degree), but also the spirit of it. For example, the scribes and Pharisees considered themselves obedient to the sixth commandment as long as they didn't physically murder someone. Jesus, however, revealed that God has higher standards than that. Murderous hatred in one's heart is just as damning as murder. Jesus stated that a person who exhibits hatred for his brother by calling him a fool "shall be guilty enough to go into the hell of fire" (Matt. 5:22). If that isn't a call for hate-filled people to repent or perish, what is?

The scribes and Pharisees also considered themselves obedient to the seventh commandment if they didn't physically commit adultery. Jesus, however, revealed to His followers what is obvious to any honest person: If it is wrong to have a sexual relationship with your neighbor's wife, then it is also obviously wrong to undress her mentally. The tenth commandment warns against this—coveting another's wife. Jesus warned those who are lustful that hell is their destiny (see Matt. 5:29-30), a wake-up call for lustful people to repent or perish.

Jesus mentioned heaven and hell at other times during the Sermon on the Mount. He admonished all of His audience to "enter by the narrow gate; for the gate is wide that leads to destruction," but said that "the gate is small, and the way is narrow that leads to life, and few are those who find it" (Matt. 7:13-14). He warned that those who don't produce good fruit will be "thrown into the fire" (Matt. 7:19), and declared that not everyone who calls Him Lord will enter heaven, but only those who do God's will (see Matt. 7:21). He foretold that many who expect to enter heaven will be turned away because of their unrighteousness (see Matt. 7:22-23). Finally, He concluded His entire sermon by comparing two men, one who obeyed Him and one who didn't. Jesus compared the one who didn't obey Him to a foolish man who built his house on the sand. When the floods came, his house was completely destroyed, illustrating the fate of the unrepentant (see Matt. 7:24-27).

All of this plainly proves that the Sermon on the Mount was very evangelistic, revealing the way of salvation according to Jesus.

Some, who don't understand the correlation between faith and works, have difficulty reconciling what Jesus taught about salvation with scriptures that declare salvation is received by grace through faith and not works. The simple explanation, however, which I've already elaborated upon in the second and third chapters, is that there is an inseparable correlation between one's belief and his behavior. If one believes, he acts as if he believes. If one does not act like he believes, he does not believe. If one believes in Jesus, he obeys Jesus. If one does not obey Jesus, he does not really believe in Jesus. Obedience validates faith. It's just that simple.

All of this being so, we must not look at Jesus' sermon as a great piece of advice, or as a collection of "helpful hints from heaven." Our obedience to His commandments within the Sermon on the Mount reveals if we believe in Him or not. All of us will be judged by and repaid according to our deeds (see Matt. 12:36-37; 16:27; 25:31-46; John 5:28-29; Rom. 2:6; 2 Cor. 5:10; Rev. 2:23; 20:12-13). We are either building on rock or sand, and our destiny is either God's eternal kingdom or eternal damnation.

What Jesus Said About Money

Almost one-fourth of the entire content of Jesus' most famous sermon (25 out of 109 verses) has something to do with money and possessions. For example, Jesus instructed all of His followers to "give to him who asks of you, and do not turn away from him who wants to borrow from you" (Matt. 5:42). If this commandment were obeyed most of us would soon find ourselves owning considerably less. Christ's followers should be characterized by their willingness to help those facing pressing needs by means of their money, either by giving or lending it. (I don't think, however, that Jesus was talking about helping people make their monthly payments on luxury items bought with credit.)

Jesus also commanded His followers to make certain that their motives were pure when they gave alms to the poor, unlike the hypocritical scribes and Pharisees who sounded trumpets to announce their public distributions (see Matt. 6:1-4). We should give secretly.

Note that Jesus didn't say, "*if* you give alms," but "*when* you give alms." He expected His followers to give to the poor. Many professing Christians, however, have no need to examine their motives for giving to the poor, because they don't give anything to the poor. Does their righteousness surpass that of the scribes and Pharisees?

Jesus had more to say to His followers about their possessions:

> Do not lay up for yourselves treasures upon earth, where moth and rust destroy, and where thieves break in and steal. But lay up for yourselves treasures in heaven, where neither moth nor rust destroys, and where thieves do not break in or steal; for where your treasure is, there will your heart be also (Matt. 6:19-21).

A few years ago, as a citizen of one of the world's wealthiest nations, I asked myself how my obedience to this commandment was being exhibited in my life. What if I were asked to stand in front of everyone at my church next Sunday in order to share with them how I obeyed Jesus' commandment not to lay up treasures on the earth? What would I say? *What would you say?*

"Treasures" Defined

Some of us suppose that Jesus' words have application only to those who own literal treasures, chests full of gold and diamonds. But Jesus was not speaking to an affluent crowd. The treasures that He had in mind are those that potentially can be stolen by thieves, destroyed by moths or consumed by rust. Thieves might steal anything of value. Rust eats just about all that is metallic. Moths consume clothing. When we considered the Parable of the Rich Fool, Jesus said the foolish man had laid up "*treasure* for himself" (Luke 12:21, emphasis added), and his treasure consisted primarily of an abundance of stored crops that he didn't need.

We also gain some idea of what Jesus meant by the word *treasures* when we consider that He wants us to sell them and give the money to charity in order to lay up *treasure* in heaven (see Luke 12:33). Thus, anything we own that potentially could serve a higher spiritual and eternal purpose than it presently does could conceivably be a "treasure." Specifically, treasures would be those possessions that reveal our love for ourselves rather than our love for God and neighbor.

Taking all of what Jesus said into consideration, the treasures of which he spoke could be *anything that one doesn't need, any non-essential item that one might possess, the ownership of which reveals love for ourselves and the selling of which reveals our love for God and neighbor. They are those things that keep our hearts focused on earth rather than heaven, our eternal home where our Father resides.*

Like more literal treasures, our 'treasures" testify of our disregard of the second greatest commandment. The reason Jesus probably calls them "treasures" is because they are owned for the same reason that more literal treasures are owned—selfishness. Our treasures are of lesser value than chests of diamonds, and perhaps are less obvious to the undiscerning, but they are still our little treasures. They are cherished every bit as much as a king's treasure.

The treasures of which Jesus spoke also all have one thing in common—temporality. They are either perishing or in danger of perishing and are guaranteed to ultimately perish. Contemporary readers sometimes miss the point of Jesus' examples of perishing treasures, because our fabrics aren't appetizing to moths, our modern metals don't always rust, and thieves are a rare problem. Had Jesus been speaking to today's culture, He may have used different examples: "Don't lay up treasures on earth, where the stock market can lose fifty percent of its value in a few months, styles constantly change, computer chips are soon outdated, and planned obsolescence is engineered into appliances." Jesus wants us to see the foolishness in owning depreciating assets when we have the wonderful opportunity to invest in eternal assets. Why waste money on nonessential temporal things that will ultimately be worthless when we can lay up imperishable treasures in heaven? That makes perfect sense.

So let's take a look at everything we own. Everything besides basic food and basic covering is actually nonessential in the strictest sense. (When I say "covering," I mean clothing and shelter.) Anything beyond those could conceivably be a treasure. I realize such a view is radical in the fantasyland we call America, but do you suppose that the three billion people in the world who live on less than two dollars per day have much more than food and covering? The Bible that we profess to believe tells us,

> But godliness actually is a means of great gain, when accompanied by contentment. For we have brought nothing into the world, so we cannot take anything out of it either. And *if we have food and covering, with these we shall be content*. But those who want to get rich fall into temptation and a snare and many foolish and harmful desires which plunge men into ruin and destruction. For the love of money is a root of all sorts of evil, and some by longing for it have wandered away from the faith, and pierced themselves with many a pang (1 Tim. 6:6-10, emphasis added).

The *Christian* Bible says to all *Christians* that we shall be content with food and covering. That is all we really need. Would you be content if all you had was food and covering? If you are not content with what you currently possess, you are fooling yourself if you think you could be content with only food and covering.

Paul also stated that discontentment is an indication of the love of money, agreeing perfectly with Hebrews 13:5: "Make sure that your character is free from the love of money, being content with what you have." *Discontentment reveals love of money.* There is no escaping this if we simply accept Hebrews 13:5 at face value. But discontentment so dominates our culture that we see nothing wrong with it. I encourage you to pause a moment and re-read the two scriptures I've just quoted (1 Tim. 6:6-10 and Heb. 13:5) and allow them to sink in. They are shocking.

Taking Inventory

As Jesus Himself declared, if we are His true disciples, we must give up all our possessions (see Luke 14:33). Taking the most liberal interpretation of His words, we must, at the very least, put all we own under His lordship, using everything just as He directs. Nobody can argue against that.

But let us not fool ourselves in this matter as so many do. Jesus has already directed all of His followers not to lay up earthly treasures, so none of us need to pray about what to do with our earthly treasures. God's will is perfectly clear. Yet, so many times professing Christians claim, "If God told me to get rid of any of my possessions, I would do it in a second. But God hasn't directed me to do that." The truth is, they only imagine that God hasn't directed them to give up any of their possessions, and the reason they imagine such a thing is because those possessions are their treasures. They are doing the very thing Jesus commanded them not to do—they are laying up treasures on earth.

This being so, all of us who consider Jesus to be our Lord must, of course, take inventory of every item we possesses. Are we laying up earthly treasures? Our goal should be to live as simply as possible. We should begin by asking, *Is it a necessity, a convenience, or a nonessential luxury?*

Necessities are of course lawful.[3] You and your family need clothing. But how much clothing do you need? John the Baptist told everyone who had two tunics to share with him who had none. Apparently he thought that only one tunic was really necessary. Wearing a garment of camel's hair (see Matt. 3:4), John practiced what he preached. And you can be certain that Jesus owned only one tunic, otherwise He would have needed to repent at the preaching of John the Baptist.

Jesus was perfect in love. He denied Himself daily in service to others, loving His neighbor as Himself. Our goal is to become like Him. How much clothing do we need? Additionally, do we need expensive designer clothing? As I have previously asked, what motivates us to have elaborate and expensive clothing? Is it not a desire to be accepted and admired by others? What would your wardrobe look like if everyone in the world were blind?

A second necessity is food. But how much food do you and your family need? Only what sustains health and stamina. Do not our diets and waistlines (or is it *waste* lines?) testify to our regular self-indulgence? I personally know Christians in developing nations who live in deep poverty, yet who fast one day a week in order to have food to give to the "poor." Where will we stand in the judgment with them?

A third necessity is shelter. But how elaborate of a shelter do you and your family need? Do you really need more than one place in your house to eat your meals? How many rooms do you need that have no other purpose than as a place to sit? Does every child need his or her own bedroom? How many bathrooms do you really need? Many other questions could be asked in this regard. Scripture doesn't always give us exact answers, but God did give us brains and consciences.

The World in Your Cul-De-Sac

Here is a sobering analogy: Imagine a neighborhood of six homes on a cul-de-sac that is representative of the entire world. Imagine your resi-

---

[3] I hesitate using the word *lawful* as so many professing Christians are so adverse to any mention of law. "We're not under the Law," they say. However, Paul declared that we are "under the law of Christ" (1 Cor. 9:21; Gal. 6:2), which would include everything Jesus commanded, just like the Law of Moses includes everything God commanded through Moses. One of Christ's laws is that we don't lay up earthly treasures. Jesus commanded His apostles to go and make disciples, and to teach those disciples to obey everything He had commanded them (see Matt. 28:19-20). So we are all under the law of Christ. Jesus also declared that those who "practice lawlessness" will be cast into hell (Matt. 7:23). There are many other positive references to law in the New Testament that could be cited. For an in-depth explanation, see my book, *The Great Gospel Deception*.

dence as one of the six. Of the other five families in your neighborhood, three live on less than two dollars a day. Their homes are one or two rooms, constructed out of crude boards, plastic tarps, corrugated aluminum, cardboard, dried mud or dung, or a combination of those materials, with dirt, concrete or rough wooden floors. They have no running water, no indoor toilet, and no electricity. At night, you might see an old kerosene lantern hanging from a rafter. They have no lawns to fertilize and mow, and no ornamental shrubbery. They generally eat one or two simple meals a day, and their diet consists primarily of rice, beans and other basic fare. They cook outside on a fire. Their children have no shoes, one ragged set of clothes, and nothing you would call a toy. The parents wear shoes that you would have thrown in the garbage. Their water is stored in a large pot outside the house. It is filled with rainwater that runs off their roof or by water carried from a nearby stream or pond. At least two of your poor neighbors have never heard anything about Jesus. They have never even heard His name.

Now, imagine yourself arriving home from church on Sunday afternoon after you've enjoyed lunch at the local buffet. On that one meal you spent more than a month's income for each of your three poor neighbors. As you pull into your driveway, you momentarily think about how your lawn needs watered, but convince yourself that it can wait until after you've watched the game on your big-screen TV in your "game room" (just think about the name of that room for a moment). As you look across the street at some of your neighbors' houses, you are secretly glad that so many of them are illiterate. Otherwise they might question what the bumper sticker on the back of your car means. How would you explain, "Honk if you love Jesus!"?

The only difference between the neighborhood I've just described and how things really are is this: The real neighborhood is one billion times larger, but the proportions are the same. And wealthy people generally don't live next door to poor people.

I warned you it was a sobering analogy. When we begin to realize how poor so many people are, we begin to realize that we are incredibly rich. Maybe there *is* a way that we can live on less.

Other "Necessities"

It seems to me, although I would respect anyone who might think otherwise, there are other things that could be considered to be legitimate necessities for most of us who live in developed, industrialized countries. We must each individually determine before God, and be ready to give an account to Him, what our necessities are beyond food and covering. For example, unless you are retired, you need some means of earning money in a modern economy so that you may have food and covering. If you were a subsistence farmer in America, the local government would soon take your land from you because you would not be able to pay your property taxes. So you must either have a job, or you must produce some cash crop in order to pay your property taxes.

One of the great advantages that we who live in developed countries have is the potential to earn an income that supercedes our needs, thus enabling us to give away so much more than a subsistence farmer can in the developing world. The problem is, however, that we are so tempted by greed, and our giving, even if we share much, requires much less sacrifice than the subsistence farmer who shares his food. So let us not congratulate ourselves too much for the relatively small sacrifices we make, even if they appear large to others.

In any case, it seems that I could also consider the following to be necessities, perhaps among others: (1) the required tools of my trade, (2) business capital (if I own my own business or am self-employed), and (3) a means of transportation to my workplace. Let's consider all three, beginning with tools of one's trade.

Prior to the years of His ministry, Jesus was a carpenter (see Mark 6:3).[4] Thus, He must have either owned or used someone else's carpentry tools. They were necessities for His earning a living. Fishermen in His day needed a boat and a net. Shepherds needed sheep and grazing land.

Our modern tools are often much more sophisticated, but are just as necessary. A mechanic needs tools to earn his living. A Christian mechanic, however, should consider if he must have new tools or if it would be better stewardship to purchase used tools so that he has more money to share. An accountant might require a laptop computer, but the Christian disciple must consider if owning the latest and fastest model is the best stewardship. Job training or an education to prepare for a vocation can be considered tools of one's future trade. The follower of Christ, however, must consider if going deeply into debt to attend a prestigious college or living at home while first attending the local community college would be more pleasing to His Master.

In order to earn a living, some business capital is often necessary. A farmer needs land as well as money to purchase seed, fertilizer and farm equipment. But his business expenses are separate from his personal earnings, which he takes from his business profits. The same is true for any person whose business requires working capital. One who is saving some of his earnings for future business capital could conceivably consider that money to be a necessity, as long as his life is devoted to God's will, thus insuring his future business profits will not be used to lay up earthly treasures. But one could easily fool himself into giving very little under the guise of saving everything for future business capital.

---

[4] It is thought by some that Jesus the word translated "carpenter" in Mark 6:3 is better translated "builder." If so, that could indicate that Jesus was simply a laborer who helped build structures of clay bricks, rocks and mortar that were common in His day. If so, Jesus may not have needed any of His own tools.

Finally, another necessity for many is transportation to their workplace. Perhaps the only way you can get to your job is by automobile. Do you, however, need a new car? Probably not, and the Christian disciple who makes wise choices regarding auto purchases can save tens of thousands of dollars in his lifetime, enabling him to give all of that to charity. But most of us don't purchase cars to get us from Point A to Point B. We purchase them to make a statement about ourselves as we drive from Point A to Point B.

Conveniences and Luxuries

Is it wrong to have more than life's necessities? What about conveniences?[5] Are they earthly treasures?

Those are good questions, and opinions will surely differ. Jesus obviously didn't give us an itemized breakdown of what does and does not constitute a treasure. I've tried to form my opinion by considering the two greatest commandments. If our conveniences allow us to love God and others better, if they give us more time to serve and do good, then I think that there is nothing wrong with them. The problem is that the more conveniences most of us have, the more we live in self-indulgence. A washing machine, for example, doesn't give us more time to pray or visit the sick, it gives us more time to watch TV, an activity that often fuels greed and lust. (The average American reportedly watches about fifty hours of TV per week. Every commercial is designed to create discontentment.) A phone can become a tool to serve God by making it possible to "visit" many more sick people or encourage those who are far away, or it can become a means of spreading gossip and wasting time in idle conversation.

We must decide individually, before God, if any convenience we own helps or hinders us in loving Him and neighbor. Jesus said, "From everyone who has been given much shall much be required" (Luke 12:48). If you are privileged to own conveniences, be prepared to give an account. It is certainly debatable whether or not all so-called conveniences better enable us to love God and our neighbor when we consider how much money some conveniences cost, how little time they actually save us, and how much time is spent in maintaining them.

One convenience that I happen to own is a dishwasher. I recently read that one study indicated that owning a dishwasher saves the average person only one minute per day. The reason? Because most people spend time thoroughly rinsing their dishes before placing them in the dishwasher, and those who own dishwashers typically use more dishes than those

---

[5] Take indoor plumbing, for example, a wonderful convenience. We all need water to sustain our lives. If we lived in some remote place, perhaps we could drink pure water from a nearby spring or stream. Or a well could be dug, but some expense would be incurred in digging it and in the apparatus used to regularly draw out the water. In modern urban and suburban areas, however, having sufficient pure water requires additional expense by the population. Our water will come from local water companies through pipes, a modern "necessity" that is also quite convenient. A good steward can find ways to conserve water to have more money to lay up heavenly treasures.

who don't own dishwashers since they "won't have to wash them."

Luxuries are, of course, in the category of self-indulgence. We purchase them only because we love ourselves, and by owning them we testify of our lack of love for God, ignoring His second greatest commandment. Certainly all luxuries are "treasures laid up on earth." How can they not be? How can one who owns any luxury claim to be obeying Jesus' prohibition against laying up treasures on earth?

As I've already stated in other words, by upgrading our possessions, many necessities can easily become luxuries. This is true of cars, houses, clothing and even food. Blessed and wise is the person who can be honest with himself in this regard. (And blessed is the believer who sets a high standard for himself but who doesn't condemn others who don't quite attain his personal standard, and who gives them the same time to grow that God gave him.)

Laying Up Treasures in Heaven

Note that Jesus' command was twofold. We are not to lay up treasures for ourselves on earth, but we are to lay them up in heaven. There is no virtue in being frugal unless we serve others with what we save.

Treasures are laid up in heaven as we give to earthly charities, as Jesus told us (see Luke 12:33). This would include giving to any worthy cause that magnifies Jesus Christ, whether it be feeding the hungry, sheltering refugees, supporting a missionary or assisting any biblical ministry. We need to let the Holy Spirit lead us in this matter and use wisdom as good stewards.

Jesus' two-fold commandment is obeyed by His disciples in a two-step process. Once they initially know His will, they should inventory their possessions and obey His clear command recorded in Luke 12:33: "Sell your possessions and give to charity; make yourselves purses which do not wear out, an unfailing treasure in heaven, where no thief comes near, nor moth destroys." This commandment is simple to understand and applies to anyone who has more than he needs: Sell what you don't need, and use the proceeds for God's glory. Every earthly treasure should be sold. In some cases it could be a matter of downsizing, for example, to a more modest home or less expensive car.

Perhaps someone might ask, "My home is much larger than I need, but I regularly open it to house refugees who are fleeing religious persecution and who seek asylum in the United States. Other times I take in people who have met with hard times. Must I sell it just because it is more than I personally need?"

Certainly not. You are already using your house for charity, just as you would use the money from its sale. We have effectively "given up all our possessions" if we use them all for Christ's kingdom. If you own a small home, but want to take in refugees to show them Christ's love, it might be

God's will for you to buy a larger home.[6]

The second step for the Christian disciple is to adopt new spending habits. Every spending decision should be preceded by one or more of the following questions: Do I really need what I am considering purchasing? If so, is there a way to purchase it less expensively? Why do I really desire it? Will its purchase strengthen any sin in my life, such as pride? Will this purchase glorify God? Since I'm about to spend some of God's money of which I am a steward, what is His will in this matter? Will this purchase better help me serve Him?

Why do we make purchases all the time without considering God's will in the matter, but when we're asked to consider giving to a charity, we often respond, "I'll pray about that and see how the Lord leads me"? Whom are we fooling?

True Happiness

"But if I do what you advocate, I'll be so unhappy!" some readers might be thinking.

That all depends on whether we love money or God. If we love money, we won't do what Jesus commanded. Rather, we'll find an excuse for our continued greed and selfishness, taking our chances that Jesus didn't really mean what He said. If we love God, however, we'll discover true happiness in doing His will. That is what Jesus was talking about when He said, "For whoever wishes to save his life shall lose it; but whoever loses his life for My sake shall find it" (Matt. 15:25). We were created to live for God, finding our happiness in knowing, loving and serving Him. What the world calls "happiness" is usually nothing more than selfishness temporarily satisfied.

If you do what Jesus commanded, you'll have all you really need. You won't be living in poverty, but you will no longer be entangled by those possessions that presently own you. No more worship of material gods. No more giving your life for things that are destined to perish. You'll have much more time to do all the things God wants you to do.

Moreover, you'll enjoy a clear conscience, something that very few people ever experience. Think of all the joy that you'll possess as you serve others and truly obey God. Imagine people thanking you in heaven for denying yourself in order to support missionaries who led them to Christ. You will be truly rich, "rich toward God" (Luke 12:21), laying up treasure in heaven where it will never perish.

A Strange Bird

What would you think if you saw a bird building a three-nest addition to her nest? Would you not think that there was something wrong

---

[6] But be cautious that you don't fool yourself by acquiring a larger home for *future* ministry to the poor that never occurs.

with her? If you could communicate, would you not say something like, "You're just a bird! Be content with one nest! That's all you need!"?

What if that bird was practically killing herself trying to get those extra three nests built, working herself to exhaustion, gathering and placing twigs and straw from sunup to sundown, weighed down with anxiety, losing sleep and neglecting her three chicks? What if she had no time to sing at sunrise? Would you not consider that bird to be even more foolish?

What if you heard that bird say, "I absolutely must have my nests lined with silk"? And so she journeys far and wide in search of silk scraps, flying in storms, dodging cats and fighting vultures, scavenging in city dumps and risking her health and life in the process. She is away for days at a time, and when she returns, exhausted and discouraged, she finds a brood of disgruntled chicks who have been fighting continually in her absence. Would she not be the source of her own woe?

Finally, what if you noted that because this one bird was so aggressive in gathering building materials for her expansive project, that other nest-building birds were unable to find what they needed to complete their single nests? Would you not consider her guilty of greed? Would you not think that she could be much happier if she were content with what she had, and if she used her spare time to help other birds build their nests? Then why do you imagine that you would not be happier if you lived as simply as possible and devoted more time to serving others? Why would you think that a life that is not centered on acquiring more and more material things would be a life of unhappiness? An absurd thought indeed!

Since the Garden of Eden the problem has been the same—we are not content with what God has given us. We seek happiness in gaining more. The result of our discontentment has also been the same—misery for us and others.

The Evil Eye

Let's return now to Jesus' Sermon on the Mount to consider more of what He said regarding the ownership of possessions. We'll read something I've previously quoted but then add some context to give us a better understanding:

> Do not lay up for yourselves treasures upon earth, where moth and rust destroy, and where thieves break in and steal. But lay up for yourselves treasures in heaven, where neither moth nor rust destroys, and where thieves do not break in or steal; for where your treasure is, there will your heart be also. The lamp of the body is the eye; if therefore your eye is clear, your whole body will be full of light. But if your eye is bad, your whole body will be full of darkness. If therefore the light that is in you is darkness, how

great is the darkness! No one can serve two masters; for
either he will hate the one and love the other, or he will
hold to one and despise the other. You cannot serve God
and mammon (Matt. 6:19-24).

What was Jesus trying to convey in His statement about the lamp of
the body being the eye? The context is the key to our understanding. Before and after His words about the eye being the body's lamp, Jesus was
speaking of money and possessions. So it is safe to assume that His words
about the eye and body have something to do with the same.

Note that the first two sentences in this passage contrast laying up treasures on earth with laying them up in heaven. Likewise, the two sentences
that follow Jesus' words about the clear eye and bad eye contrast two
people, one who serves God and one who serves mammon. Clearly, the
one who is laying up treasures on earth is also serving mammon, and the
one who is laying up treasures in heaven is also serving God.

Also note that the sentences about the eye being the body's lamp contrast a person with a bad eye whose body is full of darkness and a person
with a clear eye whose body is full of light. It is easy to see that all three of
these contrasts in this passage are related. On one side is the person who
is laying up treasures on earth with a bad eye and a body full of darkness,
serving mammon. On the other side is a person who is laying up treasures
in heaven with a clear eye and a body full of light, serving God.

Was Jesus speaking of actual light literally coming through a person's
eye and into his body? Obviously not. Light, in this and in many other
places in Scripture, is symbolic of truth. The person whose body is full of
light is a person who is full of the truth. The person whose body is full of
darkness is a person who has no truth within him.

In Jesus' Parable of the Laborers in the Vineyard, we also find Him
using "the bad eye" expression, which was a common idiom in His day.
There we read of a landowner telling some disgruntled workers, "Is your
eye envious [or 'evil' as the marginal note in the NASB says] because I
am generous?" (Matt. 20:15). The Greek word here translated "envious"
(*poneros*) is the same word translated "bad" in the passage in the Sermon
on the Mount that we are presently considering. Thus a "bad eye" is an
"envious eye." Obviously, physical eyes can't be envious, so an "envious
eye" means an "envious desire" or "envious/greedy heart."[7]

One who possesses a bad, evil or envious eye—a heart that is focused
on material things—is the same person who is laying up earthly treasures,
serving mammon and full of darkness. Sadly, so many people who fit that
description perfectly are professing Christians. They think they are full
of light, yet are full of darkness, and as Jesus warned, "If therefore the

---

[7] This "evil eye" idiom is also found in Proverbs 28:22, where an evil eye is equated with greed: "A man
with an evil eye hastens after wealth, and does not know that want will come upon him." See also the NASB
marginal note for Proverbs 23:6.

light that is in you is darkness [that is, you think your darkness is actually light], how great is the darkness!" (Matt. 7:23). If one knows he is full of darkness, there is hope that he might receive the light. But if one thinks he is already full of light when he is actually full of darkness, his darkness is the greatest. There is little hope of his escaping his deception. He is fully blinded by Satan's lies while convinced that he believes God's truth. He is certain that he is saved while he lays up earthly treasures and serves mammon every day of his life. He thinks he loves God, but he actually proves that he hates God because his love of money is so evident.

What it Means to Serve Mammon

Consider once again Jesus' words in this passage about the impossibility of serving two masters:

> No one can serve two masters; for either he will hate the one and love the other, or he will hold to one and despise the other. You cannot serve God and mammon (Matt. 6:24).

"Serving mammon" is a sin committed by anyone who is primarily focused on material things rather than on God. Those who are laying up treasures on earth, those whose primary pursuit is the acquiring and selfish enjoyment of money, their god is mammon. Money, not God, is directing their lives.

How many professing Christians have I just described? Quite a few. Our non-stop pursuit of gaining and enjoying wealth can only be described as religious devotion. Why won't we do for God what we will do to gain money, dedicating ourselves in a daily sacrifice of time and energy? Why will we rise early, sit in traffic jams, endure pressure and stress all day, and work long hours in devotion to money, but can't find time to pray or worship God? Why do we have so much time to spend and enjoy our wealth, but have no time for good works? Why do we who have so much money share so little? Simply because money is directing our lives. It is our true god. Our primary pursuit is the acquiring and selfish spending of money. When we aren't earning it, we're using what we've earned for personal indulgence. Meanwhile, 34,000 children die every day of preventable diseases and malnutrition, 1.3 billion hungry people live in grinding poverty, at least one-third the world has never heard about Jesus. And we keep right on ignoring or explaining away what Jesus clearly taught.

Speaking of Explaining Away What Jesus Taught...

I recently read some comments by one of America's most well-known evangelical leaders concerning Christ's warnings against laying up earthly treasures and the impossibility of serving God and mammon—the same scriptural passages that we are now considering. He wrote, "If we regard those possessions as our treasures, the affections of our hearts will be directed toward material, temporal, things. As a result, *our relationship with God will be hindered*" (emphasis mine). To support his teaching, he then immediately quoted Matthew 6:24 ("No one can serve two masters").

This is a classic example of the way Jesus' sayings are so often skillfully stripped of their meaning. Can you see the subtle hazard in what this man wrote? Supposedly, our possessions are dangerous only if we *regard* them as treasures. We can have as many things as our greedy hearts desire, just as long as we don't treasure them!

This is just another version of defining greed as nothing more than an attitude toward possessions. In so many people's minds, greed has nothing to do with what they possess, but only with how they view those possessions. But that is completely illogical. Ownership cannot be separated from attitude. Every possession owned reveals a heart attitude by the owner toward himself, God and others. Whom do you love? Your possessions reveal the answer. *Every possession is a revelation.*

Moreover, this well-known evangelical leader stated that if we *do* regard our possessions as treasures, our relationship with God is only *hindered*. That stands in direct contradiction to what Jesus stated. Jesus emphatically declared that there is no middle ground. If we serve God, we cannot serve mammon. If we serve mammon, we cannot serve God. One can't serve a little bit of both. If you love one, you will hate the other. Yet this man claims that you can have a relationship with God and serve mammon; you will just have a hindered relationship!

How easy it is to be deceived in this regard. How many think that they love God, and at the same time think they are neutral about money, possessing no hatred toward it in any sense? Jesus said that is impossible. If you love one master, you'll despise the other. One who loves God hates money as a master. He hates even the thought of a life in bondage to its lordship. Everywhere he goes, the sight of money's enslavement of people troubles him, primarily because money requires people's devotion, a devotion that rightfully should belong to God. Greed is idolatry, and God is a jealous God (see Ex. 34:14; Eph. 5:5; Col. 3:5). The sight of money's enslavement of people also troubles the lover of God because he thinks of all the good that could be done with the money that is selfishly being wasted by those who love it. The lover of God strives to eradicate anything that even smells like greed in his own life. That is why Paul wrote so solemnly that we should not allow greed even to be named among us (see Eph. 5:3).

By the same token, one who loves money hates the thought of a life truly devoted to God. He couldn't imagine giving up any of his pleasures or anything he owns. In fact, he longs for more of both. He'll ignore or twist God's word to justify his lifestyle. He despises the thoughts of self-sacrificing love for fellow man and costly obedience to Christ, proving that he actually despises God. Jesus plainly said, "If you love Me, you will keep My commandments" (John 14:15). He wasn't talking about all His commandments except the ones that have something to do with money and possessions. If we love Jesus, we won't lay up treasures on earth. If we do lay up earthly treasures, we prove that we don't love Jesus. It is just that simple.

More About the Meaning of Serving Mammon

Directly after Jesus spoke of the impossibility of serving God and mammon, He gave specific examples to clarify what He meant. His very next sentence begins with, "For this reason I say to you" (Matt. 6:25), clearly connecting what He just said with what He was about to say:

> For this reason I say to you, do not be anxious for your life, as to what you shall eat, or what you shall drink; nor for your body, as to what you shall put on. Is not life more than food, and the body than clothing? Look at the birds of the air, that they do not sow, neither do they reap, nor gather into barns, and yet your heavenly Father feeds them. Are you not worth much more than they? And which of you by being anxious can add a single cubit to his life's span? And why are you anxious about clothing? Observe how the lilies of the field grow; they do not toil nor do they spin, yet I say to you that even Solomon in all his glory did not clothe himself like one of these. But if God so arrays the grass of the field, which is alive today and tomorrow is thrown into the furnace, will He not much more do so for you, O men of little faith? Do not be anxious then, saying, 'What shall we eat?' or 'What shall we drink?' or 'With what shall we clothe ourselves?' For all these things the Gentiles eagerly seek; for your heavenly Father knows that you need all these things. But seek first His kingdom and His righteousness; and all these things shall be added to you. Therefore do not be anxious for tomorrow; for tomorrow will care for itself. Each day has enough trouble of its own (Matt. 6:25-34).

Once again Jesus obviously was not speaking to a wealthy audience. Just as obvious is the fact that money can be master over those who have very little if they become preoccupied with acquiring life's most basic necessities, as we have previously read. When their lives consist primarily of worrying about and seeking food and clothing, they are serving mammon. God wants our lives to be focused on doing His will, seeking first His kingdom and righteousness. If we'll do that, He'll supply our true needs.

Most importantly, if one who is preoccupied with gaining life's necessities is guilty of serving money as his master, how much more is one guilty of the same sin if he is preoccupied with gaining life's conveniences, pleasures and luxuries? Can you honestly say that you are seeking first God's kingdom and righteousness?

James Adds His Commentary

Many Bible students have noticed similarities between the epistle of James and Jesus' Sermon on the Mount. It seems apparent that as James wrote his letter, Jesus' most famous sermon was very near to his thoughts. His epistle can rightly be used as a commentary that helps us better understand Jesus' words.

First, notice how James borrows several expressions from the Sermon on the Mount in the following short passage:

> Come now, you rich, weep and howl for your miseries which are coming upon you. *Your riches have rotted and your garments have become moth-eaten.* Your gold and your silver have rusted; and their rust will be a witness against you and will consume your flesh like fire. It is in the last days that *you have stored up your treasure*! Behold, the pay of the laborers who mowed your fields, and which has been withheld by you, cries out against you; and the outcry of those who did the harvesting has reached the ears of the Lord of Sabaoth. You have lived luxuriously on the earth and led a life of wanton pleasure; you have fattened your hearts in a day of slaughter. You have condemned and put to death the righteous man; he does not resist you (Jas. 5:1-6; emphasis added).

Notice that James condemned the rich for a number of things, including storing up treasures (5:3), something Jesus said shouldn't be done. Those treasures could be abundant food that might rot (5:2), just as Jesus taught in the Parable of the Rich Fool (see Luke 12:16-21). They could be excessive clothing (5:2), just as Jesus said in the Sermon on the Mount (see Matt. 6:19-20). They could be silver and gold (5:3), representative of any luxury or selfish excess. Those treasures will testify in the court of heaven of people's love of money and lack of love for God and neighbor. And they will burn around them in hell as God repays them according to their deeds, just as He has repeatedly warned.

An Objection Answered

But wasn't James only condemning the "unrighteous rich," people who gained their wealth by not paying the laborers who harvested their fields, and who "condemned and put to death the righteous man"? (Jas. 5:6). No, not entirely. Note that James condemned the rich on two counts, either of which is sinful by itself: (1) how they obtained their wealth and (2) what they did with their wealth.

Even though we may have come by our wealth honestly, that doesn't automatically exempt us from wrongdoing in God's eyes. We may still be violating the second greatest commandment by what we do with our honestly-acquired wealth. We may be laying up earthly treasures. *We should not consider ourselves automatically free of greed simply because we've earned our money honestly any more than a Mafia boss should consider himself free of greed simply because he gives a portion of his "earnings" to the poor.* There is more than one way to violate the second greatest commandment.

But have we come by our wealth honestly? James condemned the rich of his day for how they gained their wealth, by "withholding the pay of the laborers." That is, they took advantage of common laborers. They weren't treating those laborers as they themselves would want to be treated. They weren't loving those laborers as themselves. *Their riches were gained at the expense of others, and for that, James condemned them.* That should disturb many of us as well, because we're gaining our wealth, at least in part, very similarly.

Think about this for a moment: How is it possible for one person to gain wealth that far exceeds what others possess? There is only one way, by profiting from the labor of others. Can any wealthy person say otherwise?[8] Even if wealth is gained by inheritance, that wealth was originally gained by profiting from the labor of others. Or if one earns a large amount of wealth through one business transaction, the money that was given to him for his service was earned by another person who profited from the labor of others. Or if one is a highly-skilled person, the law of supply and demand makes it possible for him to charge very high fees for his services. The many people who pay his high fees, however, must gain them either by (1) working many more hours than were required of him to provide his service to them or (2) by profiting themselves from the labor of others. Even if you are a high-paid government employee who has become wealthy, you are profiting from the labor of many others by means of the taxes they pay. Again, the only way to grow wealthy is to find a way to profit directly or indirectly from the labor of other people.

The Disproportionate Share

Here is a common example of this principle: Imagine the person at the top of the corporation who makes much more money than those at the bottom and middle. Why is he so rich? Because he profits from the labor of the lower employees. Without them, he wouldn't be wealthy. It is just that simple. Does the CEO actually believe that his hourly wage is worth four

---

[8] Perhaps this is why billionaire John Paul Getty said: "I would rather have 1% of one hundred peoples' efforts than 100% of my own."

hundred times as much as the average worker in his company?[9] All the company's laborers are working together to produce wealth, and he takes a disproportionate share. It could be said that he is exploiting thousands of people under him to enrich himself. He may justify his disproportionate share by some means, but is he loving his neighbor as himself? If he loved them as himself he would share more equitably the profits they are *all* creating. Why doesn't he take his ten million dollar bonus this year and give each of the ten thousand employees a $1,000 bonus?

The difficulty for the follower of Christ who profits from the labors of others is how to do it without *exploiting* them. He should have his laborers' interests in mind, treating them just as he would want to be treated if he were in their shoes, a great challenge. But this is not just a challenge for business owners and CEOs. This is an ethical problem for all of us who live in North America.

I've previously mentioned the fact that the large majority of our clothing is manufactured overseas by people who work for what we would consider a slave's wage. If they were paid more, our clothing would cost us more. They would be wealthier and we would be less wealthy. Do we believe that we deserve to be wealthier than they? Can we truthfully say that we work harder, or that our jobs are more difficult than sewing in a sweatshop all day?

Imagine going to a local department store to purchase some clothing. You expect to pay seventy-five dollars for what you've selected, but as you stand at the cash register, the store manager drags before you a foreign woman dressed in tattered clothes. She is then forced to open her shabby purse and hand you fifty dollars, which the manager explains is the store's courtesy-discount on your purchase. Would you feel good about your purchase?

That is an unfair example, some readers may be thinking, because no one is forcing anyone to work in foreign factories. Those cheap foreign laborers are happy to work for what we would consider very low wages, because it provides them with more income than they would otherwise have.

That is often true, but it is possible to justify slavery the same way: "These former savages are so much better off picking cotton on my plantation than they were in the African jungles." Even if they are, does that make it right for the plantation owner to make himself fabulously rich by exploiting someone's lot in life, pulling them out of hell and placing them in purgatory? Is that loving our neighbors as ourselves? Is the real motive behind finding cheap foreign labor to lift people out of poverty or to increase our own wealth?

Indeed, those foreign factory workers can now afford a slightly higher

---

[9] This was the average ratio for large companies at the time of this writing in 2004. The ratio was even higher in the 1990s.

standard of living. As things continue to improve for them they can soon purchase things that we export and market to them, often things like cigarettes, cosmetics, pornography, baby formula and MTV. Are they really better off? And as we bombard these developing markets with advertisements to persuade them of all they need to enjoy our good life, we create desires for things they previously never realized they needed, evangelizing them to join us in a deeper consecration to mammon. The entire system is dependent upon lower tiers of poorer people who are continually chasing after the carrot of wealth, hoping to become more like us.

Who benefits from the labor of those very poor people? We do. If through my retirement plan for example, I own stock in a company that employs low-wage foreign workers, I benefit. As the company profits, I profit. My comfortable retirement will be made possible, in part, by the hard work of people who live in shacks. Additionally, every time I purchase a product from that company, it was paid for in part by a poor citizen in the developing world who was willing to work for low wages. If you want to know how often you benefit from cheap overseas labor, just look at the labels on your possessions that reveal the place of manufacture and assembly.

Life on a Cruise Ship

Here is an example that is easy to understand, involving an industry that brings cheap foreign laborers face to face with wealthy Americans by the hundreds of thousands: If you have ever been on a cruise ship, you know that the cruise lines essentially employ only foreign workers. The reason is because they are less expensive to employ, and cruise lines don't have to abide by U.S. labor laws. So that means they can charge American tourists a smaller fee for their cruises. Consequently, many American tourists enjoy something quite luxurious, which they otherwise couldn't afford, because other people are willing to work for a wage for which those Americans would personally never work (unless they *were* those workers from those countries). That is a microcosm of everyday life all over North America. We are on one big cruise ship, only the foreign laborers aren't on the ship with us. They're in rowboats all around us.

Even if you refuse to take cruises or invest in or purchase the products of multinational companies that employ cheap foreign laborers (a virtual impossibility), you can't avoid benefiting from those exploited workers if you live in North America. Those multinational companies pay taxes from their profits that benefit everyone in the commonwealth. Our very roads are paved, in part, with the human misery of poor people in other countries. There isn't any way that citizens of wealthy nations like ours can escape benefiting materially from the structural evil that exists in the world.

Are you beginning to understand why Jesus referred to money as "the mammon of unrighteousness"? (Luke 16:9). Greed—personal and corporate, historic and contemporary, hidden and manifest—is responsible for much of the evil in the world and much of the wealth we enjoy.

Surge-Up Economics

And there are other factors to consider besides those already mentioned. Foreign factories do help lift foreign workers economically. But again, who is profiting the most? Why is it that in 1960, the income of the wealthiest 20 percent of the world's countries was 30 times the income of the poorest 20 percent, and in 1995, the ratio had increased to 74 to 1?[10] Is globalization really benefiting everyone, as we are often told? And what happens when a multi-national company employing foreign laborers finds cheaper laborers? Case in point:

> Nike is the number one maker of sport shoes in the world...
>
> Virtually 100 percent of Nike's shoe assembly is in Asia. In the last five years the company has closed down twenty production sites in South Korea and Taiwan as wages have risen and opened up thirty-five new ones in China, Indonesia, and Thailand, where wages are rock bottom. The company has a global payroll of over 8,000, virtually all in management, sales, promotion, and advertising. The actual production is in the hands of about 75,000 Asian subcontractors.
>
> ...Nikes made in Indonesia cost $5.60 to produce, and sell on the average in North America and Europe for $73 and as much as $135. The Indonesian girls who sew them can earn as little as fifteen cents an hour. (A 1991 survey of Nike-licensed plants reported in *Indonesia Today* put the average wage for an experienced female worker at $.82 a day.) Overtime is often mandatory, and after an eleven-hour day that begins at 7:30 A.M., the girls return to the company barracks at 9:15 P.M. to collapse into bed, having earned as much as $2.00 if they are lucky.[11]

That report was from 1994. As I write eleven years later, little has changed. I read today in a newspaper article that Nike has finally responded to the continual criticism of its overseas labor practices by disclosing, for the first time, the names and locations of more than 700 factories that produce its products:

---

[10] United Nations. *Human Development Report* (New York: United Nations, 1999).

[11] Richard Barnett and John Cavanagh, *Global Dreams: Imperial Corporations and the New World Order* (New York: Simon & Shuster, 1994)

According to the report, Nike audited 569 factories in 2003 and 2004 and found abuses it has previously identified. Monitors found cases of "abusive treatment"—either physical or verbal—in more than a quarter of its South Asian factories, and between 25 percent and 50 percent of the contract factories in the region restrict access to toilets and drinking water during the work day.

The monitors found that in more than half the South Asian factories, and in over 25 percent of factories overall, the normal course of business led to work hours in excess of 60 hours per week. In more than one-tenth of all the plants surveyed, refusal to work overtime led to a penalty of some kind, the report said.[12]

Keep in mind this is based on Nike's own report. And this is just one of hundreds of such huge multinational companies who employ low-wage foreign workers. John Perkins, who worked for several decades exploiting the developing nations that he now is trying to protect from corporate and governmental greed, writes,

Today, men and women are going into Thailand, the Philippines, Botswana, Bolivia, and every other country where they hope to find people desperate for work. They go to these places with the express purpose of exploiting wretched people—people whose children are severely malnourished, even starving, people who live in shanty-towns and have lost all hope of a better life, people who have ceased to even dream of another day. These men and women leave their plush offices in Manhattan or San Francisco or Chicago, streak across continents and oceans in luxurious jetliners, check into first-class hotels, and dine at the finest restaurants the country has to offer. Then they go searching for desperate people.

Today, we still have slave traders. They no longer find it necessary to march into the forests of Africa looking for prime specimens who will bring top dollar on the auction blocks of Charleston, Cartagena, and Havana. They simply recruit desperate people and build a factory to produce jackets, blue jeans, tennis shoes, automobile parts, computer components, and thousands of other items they can sell in the markets of their choosing. Or they may elect not even to own the factory themselves; instead, they hire a local businessman to do all their dirty work for them.

---

[12] Rukmini Callimachi, *Nike Reveals Info on Overseas Factories* (Associated Press, April 12, 2005)

These men and women think of themselves as upright. They return to their homes with photographs of quaint sites and ancient ruins to show to their children. They attend seminars where they pat each other on the back and exchange tidbits of advice about dealing with the eccentricities of customs in far-off lands. Their bosses hire lawyers who assure them that what they are doing is perfectly legal. They have a cadre of psychotherapists and other human resource experts at their disposal to convince them that they are helping those desperate people.

The old-fashioned slave trader told himself that he was dealing with a species that was not entirely human, and that he was offering them the opportunity to become Christianized. He also understood that slaves were fundamental to the survival of his own society, that they were the foundation of the economy. The modern slave trader assures himself (or herself) that the desperate people are better off earning one dollar a day than no dollars at all, and that they are receiving the opportunity to become integrated into a larger world community. She also understands that these desperate people are fundamental to the survival of her company, that they are the foundation of her own lifestyle. She never stops to think about the larger implications of what she, her lifestyle, and the economic system behind them are doing to the world—or of how they may ultimately impact her children's future.[13]

Murderous Greed

Is it not likely that we have corporately "put to death the righteous man" (Jas. 5:6) as James decried? Only God knows how many people have died because of corporate North American greed. How many people are in the grave because of American toxic waste? How many have suffered the slow death of lung cancer due to smoking American cigarettes, aggressively marketed to them by companies whose profits flow into millions of American retirement funds? How many exploited foreign laborers are dead because they worked under unsafe conditions and were denied basic health care? How many people around the world have been slaughtered by weapons purchased from the United States, by far and away the world's leading arms dealer?[14] And did we not profit by those arms sales? How many people are dead because our wealthy country has "protected its national interests" (that means corporate financial interests) at the ex-

---

[13] John Perkins, *Confessions of an Economic Hit Man* (San Francisco: Berrett-Koehler, 2004) pp 180-181.

[14] See http://www.cdi.org/adm/Transcripts/637/

pense of the lives of innocent soldiers and civilians? How many babies, in the name of family planning or population control, have been murdered in their mothers' wombs, here and abroad, subsidized by the tax dollars of wealthy America?[15] How many are dead because of money-motivated foreign policies initiated by American Big Business?[16] How many are dead due to our trade embargoes that primarily hurt the poor? How many are dead because of pressure that wealthy nations put on developing nations to repay their huge debts, loans that were often made to corrupt and now-defunct governments? According to UNICEF's *The State of the World's Children 1989*, "Hundreds of thousands of the developing world's children have given their lives to pay their countries debts, and many millions more are still paying the interest with their malnourished minds and bodies." UNICEF estimates that about 500,000 children die annually from austerity measures mandated due to national debt. In Tanzania, for example, where 40 percent of the population dies before age 35, the government currently spends nine times more on foreign debt payments than on health care.[17] Greed kills.

We can wax eloquent about the great benefits of the global economy and the ever-increasing size of the proverbial pie, but the fact remains that at any given moment, the pie is one size, and the pieces are divided very unequally among the people of the world. "The United Nations estimates that the richest 20 percent of the world's persons are at least 150 times richer than the poorest 20 percent."[18] Twenty percent of the world's population holds eighty percent of its wealth. And their wealth is due, in part, to poor people who are willing to work for a wage that the wealthy would consider obscene if offered to them.

What can be done to right this great wrong? Can we ever hope that

---

[15] See "Depopulation Bomb" by Matt Kaufman in *Citizen* magazine, May, 1998, Vol. 12, No. 5, published by Focus on the Family. Or visit the website of the Population Research Institute at upuw.pop.org.

[16] Former two-time recipient of the Congressional Medal of Honor, General Smedley Butler of the Marine Corps wrote in 1935, "As a soldier, I long suspected that war was a racket; not until I retired to civilian life did I fully realize it. It may seem odd for me, a military man, to adopt such a comparison. Truthfulness compels me to. I spent 33 years and 4 months in active service as a member of our country's most agile military force—the Marine Corps...And during that period I spent most of my time being a high-class muscle man for Big Business, for Wall Street and for the bankers. In short, I was a racketeer for capitalism...Thus I helped make Mexico...safe for American oil interests in 1914. I helped make Haiti and Cuba a decent place for the National City Bank boys to collect revenues in. I helped in the raping of half a dozen Central American republics for the benefit of Wall Street. The record of racketeering is long. I helped purify Nicaragua for the international banking house of Brown Brothers in 1909-12. I brought light to the Dominican Republic for American sugar interests in 1916. I helped make Honduras 'right' for American fruit companies in 1903. In China in 1927 I helped see to it that Standard Oil went its way unmolested. During those years, I had, as the boys in the back room would say, a swell racket. I was rewarded with honors, medals, promotion. Looking back on it, I feel I might have given Al Capone a few hints. The best he could do was to operate his racket in three city districts. We Marines operated on three continents." (Major General Smedley D. Butler, "America's Armed Forces, Part 1, "Military Boondoggling, " Common Sense, October 1935, pp. 6,7,10. Bulter, Part 2, "In Time of Peace: The Army," p. 8. Italics in the original.)

[17] As this book goes to print, I am happy to report that the consciences of many wealthy nations are motivating them to cancel debts of poor nations.

[18] Ron Sider, *Rich Christians in an Age of Hunger* (Dallas: Word, 1997), p. 25.

money will not be the world's master, served with a passion? Will greed ever cease to be a root of all sorts of evil? Will the people of the world ever learn to be content with what they have? Will the forces of supply and demand ever change in this age? No, not at least until Jesus rules the world. One thing, however, can change before then: individuals can repent of greed and begin loving God with all their heart, mind, soul and strength and loving their neighbors as themselves. If they do, they will speak out and work for justice as God gives them opportunity, because injustice is a violation of the second greatest commandment. And they will live without greed, resisting the temptation to lay up treasures on earth, obeying Christ's commandment to lay them up in heaven.

For the Lord is righteous;
He loves righteousness;
The upright will behold His face (Ps. 11:7).

SIX

The Deceitfulness of Riches
Mark 4:3-10, 13-20

There is yet still more to all that Jesus taught about material steward-ship. In light of all that He said on this subject, it is amazing how little of it is mentioned in Christian circles. When it is, it is all too often softened to the point of being made meaningless.

As we continue our squeeze through the needle's eye, our own eyes are opened more and more, and we ultimately wonder how we remained so blind for so long. But it is quite easy to gradually slip back into the dark-ness again, because the world around us is feverishly worshipping at the altar of mammon and continually tempts us to join in her rituals. In this chapter, we will consider Jesus' warning about the danger of that very deception. Start with a prayer and let us begin.

There was a day when Jesus was teaching along the shore of the Sea of Galilee. Mark tells us that the crowd grew so large that Jesus "got into a boat in the sea and sat down; and the whole multitude was by the sea on the land" (Mark 4:1). He then told the crowd a parable, which He later explained to His disciples:

> "Listen to this! Behold, the sower went out to sow; and it came about that as he was sowing, some seed fell beside the road, and the birds came and ate it up. And other seed fell on the rocky ground where it did not have much soil; and immediately it sprang up because it had no depth of soil. And after the sun had risen, it was scorched; and be-cause it had no root, it withered away. And other seed fell among the thorns, and the thorns came up and choked it, and it yielded no crop. And other seeds fell into the good soil and as they grew up and increased, they yielded a crop and produced thirty, sixty, and a hundredfold." And

He was saying, "He who has ears to hear, let him hear."

And as soon as He was alone, His followers, along with the twelve, began asking Him about the parables....And He said to them, "Do you not understand this parable? And how will you understand all the parables? The sower sows the word. And these are the ones who are beside the road where the word is sown; and when they hear, immediately Satan comes and takes away the word which has been sown in them. And in a similar way these are the ones on whom seed was sown on the rocky places, who, when they hear the word, immediately receive it with joy; and they have no firm root in themselves, but are only temporary; then, when affliction or persecution arises because of the word, immediately they fall away. And others are the ones on whom seed was sown among the thorns; these are the ones who have heard the word, and the worries of the world, and *the deceitfulness of riches, and the desires for other things enter in and choke the word,* and it becomes unfruitful. And those are the ones on whom seed was sown on the good soil; and they hear the word and accept it, and bear fruit, thirty, sixty, and a hundredfold" (Mark 4:3-10, 13-20; emphasis added).

There is no doubt that this parable has application to salvation. In Matthew's rendition of the same parable, Jesus explained that the seed is "the word of the kingdom" (Matt. 13:19), which was the gospel Jesus preached (see Matt 4:23; 9:35; Luke 16:16). Also, according to Luke, Jesus revealed the significance of the first soil by stating, "And those beside the road are those who have heard; then the devil comes and takes away the word from their heart, so that they may not *believe and be saved*" (Luke 8:12, emphasis added). Information about salvation was what Jesus had in mind in the Parable of the Sower and Soils. As the gospel is proclaimed, people of varying receptivity hear it. Consequently, some people are saved and some are not.

The Meanings of the Soils

Note that seed in the parable was sown in four different types of soil, but in only three of the soils did the seeds germinate and begin to grow. Additionally, in only one of the soils did the seeds ultimately produce fruit. The question is, *Which soils represent people who are saved?*

Clearly, the first soil represents those who were never saved, rejecting the gospel as they heard it.[1] And obviously, the fourth soil represents truly saved people. But what about the second and third soils?

---

[1] Amazingly, one of American's most popular radio and television preachers says otherwise. This first soil,

One's position on "eternal security" is a primary factor in how he answers that question. To those who believe that true Christians can never forfeit their salvation,[2] the second and third types of soil can only represent either (1) fruitless believers or (2) phony believers who were never actually saved.

To those who believe that true Christians *can* forfeit their salvation,[3] the second and third soils may represent true believers who fell away and forfeited their salvation. (The fourth soil then represents those who don't fall away, but who persevere in faith and bear much fruit.)

So who is correct?

It is impossible for me to believe that the second and third soils represent "fruitless believers," because the New Testament repeatedly teaches that there is no such thing. A "fruitless believer" is an oxymoron, because faith without works is dead, useless, and cannot save, according to James 2:14-26. Jesus warned over and over again against the false idea that one could be saved without obedience, and so did Paul, Peter, John and Jude, as I've shown in Chapters 2 and 3. The second and third soils cannot represent what the entire New Testament says does not exist.

Thus we've now narrowed down three possibilities to two. The second and third soils represent either (1) false believers who never truly believed or (2) true believers who fell away and forfeited their salvation. Which is the correct interpretation?

How is it possible that the second and third soils could represent phony believers who were never saved? In both cases there was *true* germination, *true* new life and *true* growth that was sustained for a while.

Added to this is the fact that in Luke's version of the parable, Jesus explained that the second soil represented those who *"believe for a while, and in time of temptation fall away"* (Luke 8:13, emphasis added). Jesus declared that they believed. Jesus also taught that if one believes, he is saved (see John 3:16), thus, unless Jesus was lying, those represented by the second type of soil were truly saved. Jesus said, however, that they were only temporary and fell away. The plant withered and died.

All this being so, the second soil can only represent one who truly believes, is truly saved, but who abandons his faith under persecution and dies spiritually, forfeiting his salvation.

This is not difficult to accept in light of the fact that it agrees perfectly

he claims, represents a believer who resists God's word, and thus never grows spiritually or bears fruit. Yet Jesus plainly said, "And those beside the road are those who have heard; then the devil comes and takes away the word from their heart, so that they may not *believe and be saved*" (Luke 8:12; emphasis added).

[2] This view is known as the doctrine of unconditional eternal security or *once saved always saved*. Calvinists prefer a slightly different version of unconditional eternal security known as the doctrine of "the perseverance of the saints."

[3] This view is known as the doctrine of conditional eternal security. Adherents of this view do not necessarily believe that one loses his salvation if he commits a sin. More likely, adherents to this view believe that one forfeits his salvation if he abandons faith in Christ and/or returns to the practice of sin, ignoring the discipline of the Lord over a period of time.

with what so many passages of the New Testament teach.[4] Christians can forfeit their salvation if they abandon their faith in Jesus. Salvation is received and maintained by faith. That is why Christians are repeatedly admonished in the New Testament to persevere in faith lest they lose what they've gained (see Acts 14:22; Rom. 11:22; 1 Cor. 15:2; Col. 1:21-23; Heb. 3:6, 14). Are we to think that Jesus will cast into hell people who never believed in Him, and then welcome into heaven those who had faith in Him when they were children, but who were serial rapists and murderers when they died?[5] And what will those sinners do once they're in heaven? Will they invent new ways to show God how much they hate Him?

Does True Faith Always Endure?

In contradiction to those scriptures that admonish believers to persevere in faith,[6] some maintain that true faith always endures. Supposedly, if one receives salvation from God by faith, his salvation could never be forfeited because his faith will persevere to the end. If one dies unsaved, it proves that he never possessed true faith during his lifetime, even if he apparently manifested spiritual fruit. His fruit was not genuine fruit of the Spirit.[7] He was never actually saved.

Scripture teaches, however, that true faith may not persevere. Did Peter have *true* faith when he walked on the water toward Jesus? Was Peter receiving a *true* miracle from God then, or was his walking on water a false miracle? The answers to those questions are obvious. Peter possessed true faith and received a true miracle.

Did Peter's true faith endure? No. Did Peter forfeit his true miracle? Yes. Peter lost by unbelief what he had gained by faith just a few moments before. True faith does not necessarily endure.

All this being so, the third soil, in which the implanted seed sprouts and grows until the plant is choked by thorns, may also, like the second soil, represent a true believer who ultimately forfeits his salvation. And what causes his demise? "The worries of the world... the deceitfulness of riches, and the desires for other things...choke the word" so that "it

[4] See, for example, Matt. 18:21-35; 24:4-5, 11-13, 23-26, 42-51; 25:1-30; Luke 12:42-46; John 6:66-71; 8:31-32, 51; 15:1-6; Acts 11:21-23; 14:21-22; Rom. 6:11-23; 8:12-14, 17; 11:20-22; 1 Cor. 9:23-27; 10:1-21; 15:1-2; 2 Cor. 1:24; 11:2-4; 12:21-13:5; Gal. 5:1-4; 6:7-9; Phil. 2:12-16; 3:17-4:1; Col. 1:21-23; 2:4-8, 1 Thes. 3:1-8; 1 Tim. 1:18-21; 4:1-16; 5:11-15; 6:9-12, 17-19, 20-21; 2 Tim. 2:11-18; Heb. 2:1-3; 3:6-14; 4:1-14; 5:8-9; 6:4-20; 10:23-39; 12:9, 14-17; Jas. 1:12-16; 4:4; 5:19-20; 2 Pet. 1:5-11; 2:20-22; 3:16-17; 1 John 2:15-17, 24, 28; 5:16; 2 John 8-9; Jude 20-21; Rev. 2:7, 10-11, 17, 20, 26-28; 3:4-5, 8-12, 14-22; 21:7-8; 22:18-19.

[5] Calvinists respond to this question by claiming that such a scenario is impossible, since true faith (supposedly) will always persevere. Thus, one who possesses true faith as a child will continue to have faith all his life. Yet true faith doesn't always persevere, as I will soon prove from Scripture.

[6] If all true believers automatically persevered in faith, there would have been no reason for the authors of the epistles to admonish believers to persevere. Their admonition proves the possibility that believers might not persevere.

[7] If this theory were true, it would be impossible for any person to have assurance of his salvation until his final breath, because only then could he be certain that his faith is genuine, having persevered. He could not trust any fruitfulness that was manifest in his life, as it might prove to be false if he later falls away.

becomes unfruitful" (Mark 4:19).

If you can't concede that Jesus' explanation of the third soil is a revelation of what might cause a believer to forfeit his salvation, there are only two alternative interpretations. You must believe that Jesus was either warning about (1) what could rob a believer of *all* fruitfulness,[8] or (2) what could keep a person from ever being saved.[9] In any case, Jesus was warning about some very serious issues. The worries of the world, the deceitfulness of riches, and the desires for other things are a terrible triplet—eternally damning at worst and capable of destroying all the Spirit's fruit in believers at best.

All three of these potential pitfalls seem to share some relationship to money, the "deceitfulness of riches" being the most obvious of the three. Consider also, however, "the worries of this world." Jesus specifically counseled against those worries at other times when He warned against laying up earthly treasures and about the impossibility of serving God and mammon (see Matt. 6:24-34; Luke 12:22-34). Thirdly, "the desires for other things" could certainly include material things. Luke translates the third pitfall as being the "pleasures of this life" (Luke 8:14), which, if he was talking about the kind of pleasures that the world seeks, normally require money.

A Serious Warning to Believers

For reasons I've already stated, I'm convinced that the second and third soils represent true believers who ultimately fall away and forfeit their salvation. If I'm correct, then every true believer needs to beware of the worries of the world, the deceitfulness of riches and the desires for other things. Failure to do so could have very sobering eternal consequences.

Unlike the second soil scenario where the believer faces persecution and, as Jesus said, "immediately" (Mark 4:17) falls away, the third soil scenario is more gradual. As the good seeds sprout and grow, so do the thorn seeds. Slowly, almost imperceptibly, the thorns began to intertwine with the good plants, robbing them of sunlight, moisture and nutrients from the ground, eventually dominating and crowding them so that the plant is "choked" (Mark 4:7). It was a sad ending to a promising beginning.

Is this not the picture of many professing Christians? Having received the gospel, they begin by following Jesus closely, passionately devoted to Him. He fills their thoughts and lives. They live to do His will, and evaluate everything in light of His Word, which they study diligently.

But then something happens. First they begin to notice that older Christians don't seem nearly as zealous as they are; in fact, some of those older Christians even warned them that their initial zeal would cool. Then they

---

[8] Which would, of course, be an indication of the absence of saving faith.

[9] This, again, is difficult for me to accept, because the seed in the third soil did germinate, sprout and grow for a while.

allow themselves to become distracted. There are temporal things to worry about. Temptations that begin to capture their attention present themselves. Although they resist scandalous sins, they find themselves distracted by things that seem harmless—career, innocent pleasures and new responsibilities. They don't realize it, but thorns are beginning to wrap around their legs. Imperceptibly, they are being entangled with worldly, temporal cares and pursuits.

Soon they find themselves less involved in their church and regular devotions. No longer do they attend prayer gatherings or participate in outreach. Witnessing is a thing of the past because it hinders certain financial prospects and invites persecution. Next they begin noticing the faults of other Christians who seem to be more zealous. It makes them feel better.

The thorns grow higher, wrapping around their arms and hands, restricting them further. Now there are so many things that occupy their time and energy. As they prosper, they have more money to spend, and so leisure activities and hobbies take more and more precedence. Before long, their devotional life is non-existent. Private prayer and Bible reading are things of the past. The thought of visiting someone who is sick or in prison, or of denying themselves in order to feed the hungry or support a missionary never enters their minds. They're too busy. Making money and spending it dominates their days. Money is now directing their lives. It has become their god.

Finally the thorns weave themselves around their heads, covering their eyes and ears. Darkness has set in. Their religion consists of going to church on Sunday—unless there is something that is more important to do—and avoiding what is openly scandalous. They prefer the early service. Otherwise, as they say, "the whole day is killed." Sunday becomes a day to enjoy the fruits of their labor. They have no real concern for the lost or for missionary work; thus they give only what costs them little or nothing. If they happen to be in church when a convicting sermon is preached, they are much more apt to criticize the pastor during lunch at the local cafeteria than shed a tear for their own pathetic spiritual state. They would much prefer to hear about how all who profess to believe in Jesus are unconditionally eternally secure, and soon decide that it may be time to start looking for a new church where they feel more comfortable. *They've been completely deceived by riches.* Thinking that they are safe and secure in God's grace, they are unconcerned that their lives reveal no fruit beyond that of decent heathen, even in spite of Jesus' repeated warnings about their condition. They are lovers of money, even though they think they love God. Because they are deceived, they don't know it, and all attempts to persuade them otherwise are futile. "The light that is in [them] is darkness," and "how great is the darkness!" (Matt. 6:23), just as Jesus said.

Ultimately they die and stand before Jesus at a judgment that they knew was coming, but for some reason their darkened minds never seemed to worry about it:

> And all the nations will be gathered before Him; and He will separate them from one another, as the shepherd separates the sheep from the goats; and He will put the sheep on His right, and the goats on the left. Then the King will say to those on His right, "Come, you who are blessed of My Father, inherit the kingdom prepared for you from the foundation of the world. For I was hungry, and you gave Me something to eat; I was thirsty, and you gave Me drink; I was a stranger, and you invited Me in; naked, and you clothed Me; I was sick, and you visited Me; I was in prison, and you came to Me." Then the righteous will answer Him, saying, "Lord, when did we see You hungry, and feed You, or thirsty, and give You drink? And when did we see You a stranger, and invite You in, or naked, and clothe You? And when did we see You sick, or in prison, and come to You?" And the King will answer and say to them, "Truly I say to you, to the extent that you did it to one of these brothers of Mine, even the least of them, you did it to Me." Then He will also say to those on His left, "Depart from Me, accursed ones, into the eternal fire which has been prepared for the devil and his angels; for I was hungry, and you gave Me nothing to eat; I was thirsty, and you gave Me nothing to drink; I was a stranger, and you did not invite Me in; naked, and you did not clothe Me; sick, and in prison, and you did not visit Me." Then they themselves also will answer, saying, "Lord, when did we see You hungry, or thirsty, or a stranger, or naked, or sick, or in prison, and did not take care of You?" Then He will answer them, saying, "Truly I say to you, to the extent that you did not do it to one of the least of these, you did not do it to Me." And these will go away into eternal punishment, but the righteous into eternal life (Matt. 25:32-46).[10]

They will be shocked as the truth sinks into their hearts. How foolish they had been to base the security of their salvation on a sinner's prayer once prayed. They died with a religion that consisted of calling Jesus their Lord while ignoring His commandments.

---

[10] If this passage of Scripture does not teach that there is a relationship between salvation and what one does with his time and money, then what does it teach?

Take note that Jesus told of the future judgment of the sheep and goats in order to forewarn those who think they are ready to face His judgment but are not. We may call Jesus our Lord when we stand before him. Yet He has forewarned us that calling Him Lord is not enough. Our faith must be proved genuine by devoted obedience:

> Not everyone who says to Me, "Lord, Lord," will enter the kingdom of heaven; but he who does the will of My Father who is in heaven. Many will say to Me on that day, "Lord, Lord, did we not prophesy in Your name, and in Your name cast out demons, and in Your name perform many miracles?" And then I will declare to them, "I never knew you; depart from Me, you who practice lawlessness"(Matt. 7:21-23).

It will be too late to repent. Deceived by riches, focused on the worries and pleasures of earthly life, having laid up treasures on earth rather than in heaven, they will be cast into eternal flames. As Jesus said, this will be the fate of all those who "practice lawlessness," which will certainly include those who make a practice of not loving their neighbors as themselves, ignoring the second greatest commandment.

An Old Testament Warning of the Same

The Old Testament also warns against the deceitfulness of riches and the potential danger of falling away from God in the pursuit of wealth. Moses believed that it was actually very possible for those who served God to forget Him while enjoying His many blessings. Before entering the Promised Land, Moses warned the descendants of those who had perished in the wilderness:

> Therefore, you shall keep the commandments of the Lord your God, to walk in His ways and to fear Him. For the Lord your God is bringing you into a good land, a land of brooks of water, of fountains and springs, flowing forth in valleys and hills; a land of wheat and barley, of vines and fig trees and pomegranates, a land of olive oil and honey; a land where you shall eat food without scarcity, in which you shall not lack anything; a land whose stones are iron, and out of whose hills you can dig copper. When you have eaten and are satisfied, you shall bless the Lord your God for the good land which He has given you.
>
> Beware lest you forget the Lord your God by not keeping His commandments and His ordinances and His statutes which I am commanding you today; lest, when you

have eaten and are satisfied, and have built good houses and lived in them, and when your herds and your flocks multiply, and your silver and gold multiply, and all that you have multiplies, then your heart becomes proud, and *you forget the Lord your God* who brought you out from the land of Egypt, out of the house of slavery....Otherwise, you may say in your heart, "My power and the strength of my hand made me this wealth." But you shall remember the Lord your God, for it is He who is giving you power to make wealth, that He may confirm His covenant which He swore to your fathers, as it is this day" (Deut. 8:6-18, emphasis added).

According to Moses, the indication that one has forgotten God is that he no longer keeps God's commandments, many of which, even in the Mosaic Law, stipulated self-denying stewardship. Moses also believed that one could be distracted from devotion to God by the abundance of his material possessions. *Things tempt us to love them.* And according to Moses, this is not the only temptation faced by those who possess wealth. They might also be lifted up in pride, deceiving themselves into thinking that their prosperity is due to their own strength.

The result of yielding to either of these temptations is that one "forgets God," an expression that indicates one knew God in the past.

Moses' old covenant message makes clear that wealth can be a blessing or a curse. If wealth keeps us ever mindful of God's faithfulness and goodness, and if we use it to glorify the Lord as His faithful steward, it is a blessing. If wealth usurps God's rightful place in our lives, however, it is a horrible curse. Money can be a wonderful servant, but is always a poor master.

The psalmist warned, "If riches increase, do not set your heart upon them" (Ps. 62:10). When riches increase, there exists the temptation to set our hearts upon them. If we do, our hearts are no longer God's. That is precisely why Jesus told us not to lay up treasures on earth, but to lay them up in heaven: "For where your treasure is, *there will your heart be* also" (Luke 12:34, emphasis added). He wants our hearts in heaven, where God is. When we lay up earthly treasures, it proves that God does not have our hearts.

Did not John warn of the same danger? He wrote:

Do not love the world, nor the things in the world. If anyone loves the world, the love of the Father is not in him. For all that is in the world, the lust of the flesh and the lust of the eyes and the boastful pride of life, is not from the Father, but is from the world (1 John 2:15-16).

John was not only warning against loving the "world's system." He also warned against loving "the *things* in the world" (1 John 2:15, emphasis added), specifically those things that the flesh and the eyes desire and that tempt people to be boastful. As John declared, if we love the world and its things, it proves that we don't really love the Father. *If you were asked to testify in your church next Sunday as to how your lifestyle demonstrates that you don't love the world and its things, what would you say?*

Agur, the human author of a chapter of the book of Proverbs, penned a wise prayer that also echoes Moses' counsel:

> Two things I asked of Thee, do not refuse me before I die:
> Keep deception and lies far from me, give me neither poverty nor riches; feed me with the food that is my portion, lest I be full and deny Thee and say, "Who is the Lord?" Or lest I be in want and steal, and profane the name of my God (Prov. 30:7-9).

This was an Old Testament version of "Lead us not into temptation" (Luke 11:4). Agur was fearful that even a full stomach might tempt him to forget the Lord. How much more temptation lurks behind our more abundant earthly treasures?

The Many Temptations of Wealth

There is no doubt that the rich are exposed to numerous unique temptations that imperil them spiritually, temptations that the poor never encounter. For example, statistics indicate that wealthy people generally give a smaller percentage of their incomes to charity than do poorer people.[11] Does this not indicate that the wealthy face greater temptation to be greedy, and that they are more likely to yield?

The wealthy face greater temptation to be prideful and conceited (see 1 Tim. 6:17). How difficult it is for rich people not to think of themselves as being superior to others! Pride stalks them continually. Even as the rich man donates large sums (but small portions) of his wealth to charitable causes, his pride swells within him as he imagines what a good person he is. Most of his charitable giving benefits him in subtle ways.

And what a fertile seedbed is pride for numerous other vices. How well impatience, anger, jealousy, unforgiveness, and self-indulgence grow in the garden of pride. The rich person is swimming in such temptations.

How difficult it is for the possessor of wealth not to trust in his riches. They speak to his inner thoughts all the time, reassuring him that his future is secure: "A rich man's wealth is his strong city, and like a high wall

---

[11] One study in 2001 showed that U.S. residents whose annual incomes were over $100,000 gave an average of 2.2% to charity, while those who make less than $10,000 per year gave an average of 5.3%. Other studies have shown similar statistics.

in his own imagination" (Prov. 18:11).[12]

Not only is the wealthy person tempted to use his wealth for self-indulgence, but he is also tempted to multiply for himself what he doesn't spend, investing in what God hates and helping to build Satan's kingdom. He thus profits by the promotion of sin and by what causes others to stumble. Hidden within the mutual funds he holds are lives wrecked by alcohol, tobacco and pornography, babies aborted with products manufactured by companies in which he owns shares, and foreign slaves scraping out an existence on behalf of shareholders. He reaps earthly returns that others envy but eternal fire in hell.

Riches deceive and tempt in so many other ways. Wealth promises happiness and fulfillment, but never delivers on its promise. In fact the more one possesses, the more it seems one desires to possess. Like saltwater to a thirsty man, gaining wealth only creates more craving. Discontentment surfaces on every side of the one grasping at the illusive happiness of wealth.

Greed also drives people deep into debt—they are thoughtlessly lulled into mortgaging their future in a vain attempt to satisfy their current unquenchable lust for more things.

According to Scripture, entire churches can be ensnared. Read what Jesus Himself once said to the Church in Laodicea:

> I know your deeds, that you are neither cold nor hot;
> I would that you were cold or hot. So because you are
> lukewarm, and neither hot nor cold, I will spit you out
> of My mouth. Because you say, "*I am rich, and have become
> wealthy, and have need of nothing,*" and you do not know
> that you are *wretched and miserable and poor and blind and
> naked* (Rev. 3:15-17, emphasis added).

The Laodiceans had become rich, and their devotion to Jesus had cooled. In a lukewarm condition, their hearts were no longer fully His. Mammon may well have become their god. Worse yet, they were completely deceived about their spiritual state. *Riches had deceived them.* Blinded by darkness, they thought nothing could be better. Possessing a comfortable religion, they considered themselves to be in need of nothing. It was well with their souls. But Jesus saw them as they really were—wretched, miserable, poor, blind and naked. They were rich, but not rich toward God. Their only hope was repentance before it was too late:

> I advise you to buy from Me gold refined by fire, that

---

[12] A common smokescreen of the rich is their claim that they don't "trust in their wealth," but keep their trust in God. How can that be true as long as they keep large sums stashed away to protect them from the future?

you may become rich, and white garments, that you may clothe yourself, and that the shame of your nakedness may not be revealed; and eye salve to anoint your eyes, that you may see. Those whom I love, I reprove and discipline; be zealous therefore, and repent. Behold, I stand at the door and knock; if anyone hears My voice and opens the door, I will come in to him, and will dine with him, and he with Me (Rev. 3:18-20).

Jesus advised them to exchange their earthly wealth for what was much more valuable—richness toward God, righteousness (white garments) and spiritual insight (eye salve). Note that Jesus depicted Himself as standing on the outside, patiently knocking and calling to those behind the door, hoping to gain entrance so that they might enjoy a meal with Him. This picture does not portray Jesus desiring a more intimate relationship with regenerate people (as is often said in sermons about this text). Rather, it portrays Jesus desiring to get in to those He does not indwell (see Rev. 3:20). Had the Laodiceans become so deceived by riches that Jesus was no longer on the inside? It seems so. He had warned that it is impossible to serve God and mammon.

Lover of God! Beware of the deceitfulness of riches!

SEVEN

A Worthless Slave
Matthew 24:36-25:46

I could hardly believe the letter I was reading. The author of the letter was accusing me of "blatantly dismissing Jesus' very clear demands for investment productivity"! My accuser went on to explain how those who stand before Jesus without a track record of prudent and successful investments will be cast into hell, just like the unfaithful servant in the Parable of the Talents. Even when I questioned how an impoverished subsistence farmer in the developing world could ever hope to be saved under such requirements, my accuser retorted, "Indeed, Jesus does expect returns from Third-World people. Such is part of being converted and a follower of Him. We are no longer helpless parasites without light from Heaven and dependents of government handouts and redistribution of other people's work." He then went on to question my salvation, and ended his letter with the gracious compliment, "Your darkness is great, your ignorance greater!"

Who was my accuser? His letterhead read, "Bible Missions to America," and his vocation, according to his letterhead, was that of a teacher and consultant of "Christian Stewardship." I had been receiving his unsolicited, multi-paged, quarterly newsletters for some time, in which he offered his advice for financial planning. His magazine not only contained sales pitches for his services, but was also full of his opinions of what was wrong with the church and the world. He made it very clear that he was an enemy of all sin and unrighteousness. Jesus was his absolute Lord. He decried the spiritual state of our greedy country and the lukewarm church.

Within his newsletters that were sent to 20,000 people, he always recommended seven top-performing mutual funds as being excellent investments for Christians who wanted to be good stewards and adequately funded for retirement. I took a few minutes to check out the composite companies of his recommended mutual funds and discovered that almost all of them invested in companies that profit by grievous sin. Thinking that he, a devout follower of Christ, would surely want to know what I had discovered, I wrote him a letter, the majority of which follows:

> Dear Mr. Wolfer (not his real name),
>
> I have received several issues of your ---------- ------- ------ ----- *Journal* via mail over the past year. I took some time to investigate your recommended mutual funds on page 5 of the Winter issue and I am consequently alarmed by your recommendations. Almost all of the funds you recommend invest in companies that profit by doing things that Christ said would send people to hell, such as murder/abortion, homosexuality, and immorality/pornography. Moreover, there are companies within the mutual funds you recommend that are involved in the gambling industry, or the manufacture of alcohol and tobacco. Surely you don't want to recommend that Christians profit by the murder of unborn babies, by the manufacturing and distribution of pornography, or by the production of an addictive product that results in innumerable tragedies and costs our society billions of dollars each year!
>
> No true follower of Christ would want to support Planned Parenthood, but if they invest in any of the majority of mutual funds you recommend, they would. No true believer in Jesus would want to profit from dividends from Johnson and Johnson, which manufactures abortion products. Neither would they want to be unequally yoked with Philip Morris, Time-Warner, Anheuser Busch, Columbia Health Care, United Health Care, Starwood Hotels and Resorts, or Hilton Hotels [two purveyors of porn]. Yet these are the companies that are recommended within your recommended mutual funds.
>
> Because you use terms such as *righteousness, stewardship, spirituality, Christian disciple, morality, God's rule, Christian focus, obedience, rebuking evil doers, hypocrisy, repentance* and so on, throughout your publication, I must assume that you simply didn't realize what you were doing in making such immoral recommendations. If that is the case, I'm sure you will immediately right your wrong and inform your readership of your error, asking their forgiveness.

The Astounding Reply

Mr. Wolfer's reply surprised me. It became very clear that he knew what he was doing, but he was rationalizing it all. His reply and a subsequent letter he sent me could be used in psychology courses as model examples of how self-deceived greedy people can become.

Mr. Wolfer's first defense was that he wasn't responsible for the decisions of the managers of his recommended mutual funds (which is certainly true). Then attempting to prove that his moral standards were higher than theirs, he declared that if he were to invest in individual companies, he would not invest in some of the companies that the managers of his recommended mutual funds chose. Mr. Wolfer's justification was a classic case of self-deception. He had fooled himself into thinking that he would never do the very thing that he was doing. In my reply I subsequently attempted (in vain) to open his eyes to this:

> Mr. Wolfer, are your actions not then hypocritical? Because you knowingly invest in mutual funds that invest in companies that you know are immoral, it is just as if you chose to invest individually in those companies. What you are doing is just as wrong as investing in the individual companies.

> If I lent my money at interest in order to profit from someone whom I knew was using my money to purchase and sell illegal drugs on the street, I would be guilty of sin, promoting and profiting by what harms others. I would not be loving my neighbor as myself. If that drug pusher told me that only 10% of my money would be used to buy and sell drugs on the street, and that the rest would be used to buy clothes for his children, would that make any difference? Would that be a legitimate investment for a child of God? Would Jesus invest His money that way? How is my example any different from what you are recommending to your readers? You know that the mutual funds you recommend help ruin lives, kill babies, promote gross sin and anger God. Dear Mr. Wolfer, you know this and so you are accountable to God! I beg you in sincere love, think about what you are doing!

> Have we no obligation to consider the morality of how our money (which is actually God's money) is invested? If the only consideration of good stewardship is the amount of return I receive, then why not invest in abortion clinics,

strip bars, and drug cartels? I hear the returns are out-standing. What would you think if I sent you a newsletter recommending that we Christians pool our money and start a prostitution ring because the returns are good and God expects us to get a good return on our investments? Surely you would vehemently object! Can you see that is exactly what you are doing, only to a lesser degree?

….Mr. Wolfer, please consider what I have written. Every time someone checks into a Hilton Hotel and watches porn on TV, you helped make it happen. You are partly responsible for every little child who sees that porn, and for every marriage that is ruined as a result of that porn because of your part-ownership in Hilton Hotels. You are partly responsible for every innocent person killed by a driver who was drunk from drinking products manufac-tured by a company you partially own. Every deformed child born with fetal alcohol syndrome is pointing his or her little finger at you and saying, "You profess to be a fol-lower of Christ, yet look what I have suffered, in part, be-cause of you!" Every baby aborted by means of a product produced by Johnson and Johnson, you helped abort. For every weeping child whose father died of lung cancer us-ing a product manufactured by a tobacco company which you partially own, and who decides that God must not exist since his father was taken from him, you share the blame. Your investments are partly responsible for people stumbling into sin. How can you deny this? And accord-ing to Jesus, it would be better for you if a millstone were hung around your neck and you were cast into the sea.

Our money and all our possessions belong to God, as "the earth is the Lord's and the fullness thereof." We are only stewards of that which is His, and He has commanded us to use every means at our disposal to "love our neighbor as ourselves" and "do unto others as we would have them do unto us." Are you obeying those foremost command-ments in how you invest your money and advise others to invest their money? What if one of your grandchildren is killed by a drunken driver, or falls into a lifestyle of bond-age to immorality because of yielding to the temptation of pornography? What if your daughter is raped by a sex-addict whose apartment is filled with porn? Who should share in the blame? Who will God blame?

Mr. Wolfer, please read your latest issue of the ------------ -
---- ------- *Journal*. Read all that you have written against
hypocrisy, moral bankruptcy, and disobedience to God's
laws, and all you have written in favor of Christ's lordship, repentance, stewardship, and doing what is right.
Everything you have written is true. Yet in the same newsletter, you recommend that Christians profit by investing
in what angers God, builds Satan's kingdom, and sends
people to hell. How can you repeatedly decry the sinful
state of our nation yet invest and profit by its sin?

The Second Defense

Mr. Wolfer's second defense was a pathetic attempt to expose the supposed hypocrisy of conscientious investors. It seemed as if I was not the
first person to question his mutual fund recommendations. He wrote:

> I realize some claimed Christians [note the word *claimed*]
> seek to operate professional investment companies that
> do not buy or use companies producing tobacco or alco-
> holic beverages. Perhaps some of them have further re-
> strictions. I do note they refuse to address the issue of the
> daily moral standards of the operators and employees re-
> lating to adultery, fornication, etc. Is this honest?

This was a classic case of twisted logic. I responded (again, in vain):

> And…to respond to your questioning the consistency of
> not investing in immoral companies while at the same
> time investing in companies whose operators and em-
> ployees are immoral: First, even if your logic was sound,
> i.e., if it was somehow hypocritical to shun investing in
> immoral companies while investing in companies run by
> immoral people, that would not annul the truthfulness of
> anything I've written so far. If it is wrong to invest in com-
> panies that are run by people who *view* pornography, that
> doesn't make it right to invest in companies that *produce
> and distribute* porn.
>
> Yet beyond this, your logic is not sound, because there is
> a vast difference between investing in immoral compa-
> nies and investing in companies where the "daily moral
> standards of the operators and employees" are immoral.
> Let us consider an example. If I invest in a company that
> produces and distributes pornography, I am promoting
> and profiting by the production and distribution of por-

nography. Every time someone views the porn I helped finance, I share responsibility of his sin. I helped him to stumble into sin, something against which Jesus solemnly warned.

However, if I invest in a company that manufactures and distributes paper towels, what I have a part in harms no one. The product that I have helped manufacture causes no one to sin. I have done nothing to promote sin or cause anyone to stumble. If the owner of the company chooses to sin, I share no responsibility for it. I didn't entice him or cause him to stumble.

The Third Defense

As his third defense, Mr. Wolfer brought out his big guns. He had a scripture to support his position. According to Mr. Wolfer, Jesus had made "clear demands for investment productivity" of His followers. I again quote Mr. Wolfer:

> But, there is a clear principle and Scripture that you seem to ignore, are ignorant of or dismiss. Let me explain.

> In the illustration of the different sums of money given to the servants (Matthew 25:14-30), Jesus was severe with the steward that had not produced an increase! Sincerely, you should carefully and prayerfully re-read the passage. That servant was condemned. The money originally given to him was given to the servant that had done the best! The unfaithful, unproductive servant was cast into hell. He hadn't been saved! (underline his).

Amazingly, Mr. Wolfer actually had convinced himself that the Parable of the Talents was a mandate for savvy financial investment by Christ's followers. Those who failed to produce required returns proved themselves as being unsaved, just like the unfaithful servant in the parable! Mr. Wolfer continued:

> Now note, Jesus told, admonished him, you ought to have put my money to the exchangers and then at my coming I should have received my own with usury!

> The question and issue you must answer is, do you believe and teach the money changers were honest, moral, holy people who only "invested" or used those funds in clearly right and moral things?

Thus I was to believe that Jesus' "demands for investment productivity" superseded everything else He had ever said about money or morality. Because the one-talent slave in Jesus' parable was condemned for not investing his one talent with a money-changer who may have used his money immorally, then there is supposedly nothing wrong with Christians investing God's money in such a way that Satan's kingdom is helped. I responded:

> The very Parable of the Talents that you cite to defend yourself actually indicts you. Surely you don't think that the point of the parable, in light of everything else Jesus taught and lived (not to mention every other commandment found in Scripture) was to warn us that we must make sure that we invest our money so that we get a decent return or we will go to hell! Are we to think that Jesus wanted His audience of poor subsistence farmers to know that they had better get a good return on their investments lest they go to hell? And even if that was the point of the parable, surely Jesus was not saying that getting a return on our money supersedes all His other commandments, or that it is OK to help murder babies and destroy people's lives as long as we get a good return on our money! Must we break many of His commandments in order to obey one of His (supposed) commandments?

I then briefly attempted to help Mr. Wolfer see the fallacy of his interpretation of the Parable of the Talents:

> Obviously, the talents in this parable represent the gifts (including wealth), abilities, opportunities, and responsibilities that God gives to His servants. Those who utilize those gifts, abilities, opportunities and responsibilities for His glory, bearing fruit for His kingdom, bringing Him a return as it were, on His "investment," will be rewarded proportionately one day. But those who "bury" what God has given them, bearing no fruit for His glory, will be considered "wicked and lazy," and will be cast into hell. The "return" God is looking for is obedience to His commands, the fruit of a living faith.
>
> ....Like all parables, the parable of the talents is a metaphor—a comparison of two things that are basically dissimilar, but which share some similarities (see Webster's definition). Every parable is imperfect in that sense, in that

a point is reached where similarities turn to dissimilarities. For example, is the "master" in the Parable of the Talents a perfect representation of Jesus? Obviously not, for he is described by the unfaithful servant and by himself as "a hard man....I reap where I did not sow, and gather where I scattered no seed." That is not at all what Jesus is like. [Would anyone consider a person who describes himself that way to be Christ-like?] The only similarities between Him and the master in the parable is that they would both be absent for a while, both would return, and both would reward or punish their servants depending upon their faithfulness to bear fruit.

Jesus was no more teaching in the Parable of the Talents the necessity of savvy investment for salvation than He was teaching the necessity of sufficient oil in antique lamps for salvation in the preceding parable. This is a *parable*. Nor was Jesus encouraging or commanding us to invest our money with the moneychangers, the very people He chased out of the temple, calling them robbers and thieves (who incidentally will all be in hell, see 1 Cor. 6:9-10). Nor was He endorsing the idea of gaining financial increase through usury, something also clearly condemned by Scripture (you see, God does have something to say about moral investing).

Isn't it pitiful that a person could become so enslaved to mammon that he would claim, based on Christ's teaching in the Parable of the Talents, that salvation is revealed by one's successful investments? Isn't it tragic that one could be so blinded by greed that he believes Jesus doesn't care if our investments are moral or immoral? We are amazed that a person could become so self-deceived. Yet millions more are just as blinded as Mr. Wolfer, only believing more subtle lies and less obvious perversions of Scripture.

Poor Mr. Wolfer may have concocted the most inane interpretation of the Parable of the Talents than any other person in history. Still, many others have construed interpretations that, although less absurd, are no less wrong. Let us take a closer look at the Parable of the Talents to search for the true meaning of Christ's words there.

The All-Important Context

First, it is important to note that the parable is found within a larger context of what is commonly called "The Olivet Discourse." Jesus had been teaching in the temple, and as He walked out His disciples pointed out the temple buildings to Him. He then made the astounding statement that "not one stone here shall be left upon another, which will not be torn down" (Matt. 24:2). Such a thing could only occur by means of a great catastrophe, and naturally Jesus' disciples wanted to know more. A short time later when they were together on the Mount of Olives, they privately inquired of Him, "Tell us, when will these things be, and what will be the sign of Your coming, and of the end of the age?" (Matt. 24:3). Jesus subsequently foretold numerous signs that would precede the destruction of the temple (see Luke 21:12-24), His return, and the end of the age (see Matt. 24:4-42).

Jesus' obvious reason for foretelling the signs of His eminent return was so that His followers would be anticipating it and ready when it occurred (see Matt. 24:32-34, 42-44). As He continued, Jesus repeatedly warned them about not being ready at His return, making it plain that such a danger was a real possibility. Note that Jesus was speaking privately to His own disciples, not to unsaved people (see Matt. 24:3). Clearly, He did not want them to assume that they were guaranteed to be ready when He returned just because they were ready at that moment. This is so obvious from a cursory reading of the entire Olivet Discourse that it is amazing that anyone would attempt to refute it. Let us take a moment to read carefully Jesus' warning to His disciples, a warning that directly follows His foretelling the signs of His return and that directly precedes the Parable of the Ten Virgins and Parable of the Talents:

> Therefore be on the alert, for you [My disciples to whom I am privately speaking] do not know which day your Lord [clearly, Jesus is not speaking to the unsaved, as He is not the Lord of the unsaved] is coming. But be sure of this, that if the head of the house had known at what time of the night the thief was coming, he would have been on the alert and would not have allowed his house to be broken into. For this reason you [My disciples] *be ready too* [which indicates the possibility of their not being ready]; for the Son of Man is coming at an hour when you [My closest disciples] do not think He will.
>
> Who then is the faithful and sensible slave whom his master put in charge of his household to give them their food at the proper time? Blessed is that slave whom his master finds so doing when he comes. Truly I say to you, that he will put him in charge of all his possessions. But if that evil slave says in his heart, "My master is not coming for a long time," and shall begin to beat his fellow slaves and eat and drink with drunkards; *the master of that slave will come on a day when he does not expect him and at an hour*

> *which he does not know, and shall cut him in pieces and assign*
> *him a place with the hypocrites; weeping shall be there and the*
> *gnashing of teeth* (Matt. 24:42-51, emphasis added).

How can anyone intelligently claim that Jesus was only warning those who were presently unsaved to get ready for His coming? Obviously, Jesus was warning those who were presently ready to remain ready. Jesus used an example of a master and his slave to illustrate His relationship with His disciples. The slave in His example could not represent an unsaved person, because unsaved people are in no way slaves of Jesus. They are rebels to the core.

Notice also that the slave in the example was obedient for a time, but he had a change of heart because he believed his master would be absent for a long time. *That is, at one time he was ready, but he became unready.* Those who have never been saved have never been ready for Christ's return.

How did the slave in Christ's story become unready? He began to act like an unsaved person, no longer loving his fellow slaves and also associating with drunkards (people whom Scripture states are unsaved; see 1 Cor. 6:9-10). When his master returned unexpectedly, he was assigned "a place with the hypocrites," that is, among those who profess to be true but are actually false. In that place among the hypocrites, Jesus said there will be "weeping and gnashing of teeth," obviously referring to hell.[1]

Jesus made it very clear that one who is saved could ultimately forfeit his salvation. And how is such a thing possible? It is possible when belief changes to unbelief, resulting in a change of lifestyle. The fundamental problem of the slave in Jesus' example was that of faith. He did not believe that his master would return soon, and so he began to act like it, unconcerned if his life was pleasing to his master. Again, keep in mind that Jesus was speaking to His own disciples. He was warning Peter, James, John and the rest. His words apply to every one of His disciples, past, present and future.

The Next Parable

To underscore this solemn warning, Jesus then immediately told the Parable of Ten Virgins (see Matt. 25:1-13). Again, it was directed to the ears of His closest disciples, the only ones present when He shared it, and not to the unsaved. It is the story of ten women who were waiting for the arrival of a bridegroom, a common custom in Christ's day. All ten took their oil lamps, but only five carried extra flasks of oil—just in case their lamps ran out of oil while they waited.

---

[1] Incredibly, some who subscribe to the doctrine of unconditional eternal security claim that the place of weeping and gnashing of teeth is representative of a temporary state in heaven where unfaithful believers will mourn their loss of rewards! This is a perfect example of the truth, "It takes a scholar to misunderstand what is clear to a child." Anyone who takes a few minutes to research and study how Jesus used the phrases "weeping and gnashing of teeth" and "outer darkness" must conclude that such expressions are always a reference to hell.

When the bridegroom, who was delayed in coming finally arrived, all ten trimmed their lamps, but the five who didn't bring extra oil realized their lamps were going out. They had to run to an oil dealer to purchase what they lacked, and by the time they returned, the wedding feast was in progress and the door was shut. The five foolish virgins cried out, "Lord, lord, open up for us," but he answered, "Truly I say to you, I do not know you" (Matt. 25:12).

What was the lesson Jesus was trying to communicate in this parable? That is obvious. He ended the parable by saying to His disciples, "Be on the alert then, for *you* [My disciples] do not know the day nor the hour" (Matt. 25:13, emphasis added). Jesus wanted them to be ready for His return, which proves that there existed the possibility that they might not be ready, otherwise He would have had no reason to warn them.

Notice that all ten virgins were ready initially. Had the bridegroom arrived earlier, they would have made it into the wedding feast. All ten were anticipating the appearance of the bridegroom and specifically waiting for Him.

Could the five foolish virgins perhaps represent those who have never believed? That seems improbable to say the least. Are unbelievers waiting with believers for the return of the bridegroom? If the five foolish virgins represent those who were never saved, what was Jesus' purpose in telling His own disciples this parable and ending it with a warning to them to be on the alert since they didn't know when He would return? His point to His disciples was obvious: *You don't want to be like the five foolish virgins!* For these reasons, the five foolish virgins *must* represent believers who were initially ready for Christ's return, but who become unready, the same point Jesus had just made in his example of the unfaithful slave. Contextually and exegetically, that is the only reasonable interpretation.

Those who theorize that the unfaithful slave and five foolish virgins represent those who were never truly saved must satisfactorily explain why Jesus used both illustrations to warn His own disciples to be ready at all times for His return. That is impossible to do.

The Parable of the Talents

Finally, we come to the Parable of the Talents, which immediately follows and mirrors the same theme as the Parable of Ten Virgins and the example of the unfaithful slave, as well as underscores Jesus' repeated message to be ready for His return. It begins with the conjunction *for*, linking it to what Christ has just said. The Parable of the Talents however, like Jesus' foretelling of the judgment of the sheep and goats which follows it, emphasizes to an even greater degree what one must do to be ready for His return—in light of everyone's future personal judgment. Let us read what Christ said:

For it is just like a man about to go on a journey, who called his own slaves, and entrusted his possessions to them. And to one he gave five talents, to another, two, and to another, one, each according to his own ability; and he went on his journey. Immediately the one who had received the five talents went and traded with them, and gained five more talents. In the same manner the one who had received the two talents gained two more. But he who received the one talent went away and dug in the ground, and hid his master's money. Now after a long time the master of those slaves came and settled accounts with them. And the one who had received the five talents came up and brought five more talents, saying, "Master, you entrusted five talents to me; see, I have gained five more talents." His master said to him, "Well done, good and faithful slave; you were faithful with a few things, I will put you in charge of many things, enter into the joy of your master." The one also who had received the two talents came up and said, "Master, you entrusted to me two talents; see, I have gained two more talents." His master said to him, "Well done, good and faithful slave; you were faithful with a few things, I will put you in charge of many things; enter into the joy of your master." And the one also who had received the one talent came up and said, "Master, I knew you to be a hard man, reaping where you did not sow, and gathering where you scattered no seed. I was afraid, and went away and hid your talent in the ground; see, you have what is yours." But his master answered and said to him, "You wicked, lazy slave, you knew that I reap where I did not sow, and gather where I scattered no seed. Then you ought to have put my money in the bank, and on my arrival I would have received my money back with interest. Therefore take away the talent from him, and give it to the one who has the ten talents." For to everyone who has shall more be given, and he shall have an abundance; but from the one who does not have, even what he does have shall be taken away. "And cast out the worthless slave into the outer darkness; in that place there shall be weeping and gnashing of teeth" (Matt. 25:14-30).

The first item of importance is the identity of the slave who was given the one talent. Does he represent a saved or unsaved person? He obviously represents an unsaved person at the *end* of the parable, because his master called him a "wicked, lazy" and "worthless slave," and then cast him into outer darkness to weep and gnash his teeth. Does he, however, at the beginning of the parable, represent a person who is *saved*?

I am persuaded that he represents a saved person at the beginning of the parable for several reasons.

First, because he was indeed a slave of the master, just as much as the other two slaves were (see Matt. 25:14). Their master was also his master (see Matt. 25:18-19, 26). The same master that had entrusted them with talents entrusted him with a talent. The only difference between the three slaves was the number of talents entrusted to each one. In every other respect they had the same relationship with the master. Jesus, of course, does not have a Lord/slave relationship with unsaved people because they are rebels against Him.

Second, there is nothing within the parable that would indicate that the man was unsaved at the beginning of the parable. In fact, if the final verse of the parable, which tells about the man being cast into hell, had not been included, many would conclude that the one-talent slave represents a disobedient Christian, just as saved as the other two slaves. Read the entire parable except for the last verse to see what I mean. The primary reason commentators jump to the conclusion that the one-talent slave was unsaved at the beginning is because their theology doesn't allow for any other possibility. If the man was unsaved at the end, then he must never have been saved, they say.

Third, Jesus was still speaking to His closest disciples as He related the Parable of the Talents. He began the parable by saying to them, "Be on the alert then, for *you* do not know the day nor the hour. For it is just like a man about to go on a journey, who called his own slaves..." (Matt. 25:13-14, emphasis mine). The parable following that introduction was an obvious warning to them: You don't want to be like the one-talent slave who buried his talent in the ground. Again, if such a thing were impossible, Jesus would not have warned them of the possibility.

Fourth, the context before this parable supports such an interpretation. The preceding Parable of Ten Virgins was a warning to Jesus' disciples to stay ready. They should not copy the five foolish virgins, who were initially ready, but who became unready. The example of the unfaithful slave directly before that was also a clear warning to Jesus' disciples to stay ready. They should not imitate the unfaithful slave, who was initially ready, but who also became unready. Moreover, just seconds before He related the Parable of the Talents, Jesus emphatically warned His own disciples three separate times to be ready for His return:

> Therefore *be on the alert*, for you do not know which day your Lord is coming....For this reason *you be ready* too; for the Son of Man is coming at an hour when you do not think He will.... *Be on the alert* then, for you do not know

the day nor the hour" (Matt. 24:42, 44; 25:13, emphasis added).

All this being so, it seems only reasonable to conclude that the one-talent slave represents a person who was saved initially, but who forfeited his salvation by his unfaithfulness. He abandoned the faith he once possessed, and his lack of any fruitfulness proved it. Jesus' message to His disciples was and still is obvious: *I am about to depart from this world. I'm entrusting you with opportunities, abilities and gifts. I will eventually return, so always be ready. The way to be ready is to be fruitful. You don't want to be like the one-talent slave. That would have dire consequences.*

An Objection Answered

But doesn't the one-talent slave's attitude about his master indicate that he was unsaved? Do not his words, "I knew you to be a hard man, reaping where you did not sow, and gathering where you scattered no seed" (Matt. 25:24), reveal that he really didn't know the Lord?

Please note that the one-talent slave made that statement when his master returned, and he apparently possessed that same attitude when he originally buried his talent. But that does not prove that he was never a slave. Nor does it prove that he always possessed such an attitude or that he represents a person who was never saved. If it proves anything at all about his spiritual state, it only proves that he was on dangerous ground from the time he buried his talent. Even after burying it, however, he could have unburied it at any time before his master's return to begin using it wisely.

Of greater significance, however, is the fact that the master agreed with the one-talent slave's description of himself, affirming that he was indeed a "hard man, reaping where [he] did not sow, and gathering where [he] scattered no seed" (see Matt. 25:24). But such a description is certainly not appropriate for Jesus! Jesus does not reap where He does not sow, nor does He gather where He scatters no seed, both of which would be equivalent to stealing. For this reason, we can safely assume that this particular detail of the parable is of no spiritual significance. As I pointed out to Mr. Wolfer, every parable reaches a point where the similarities between details in the parable and spiritual truths end. Surely we have come to that point. The only similarities between Jesus and the parable's master are that both would be absent for a while, both entrusted their servants with special gifts, and both, when they returned, would reward or punish their servants depending upon their faithfulness in bearing fruit. But that is where the similarities end. Jesus is not just a man; He has more than three slaves; He has not entrusted us with bars of silver (the "talents" of Jesus' day); He did not just "go on a journey." Moreover, He does not reap where he hasn't sowed, as that would be sinful. Thus, trying to determine the one-talent slave's spiritual status by means of his description of his master is unjustified.

The Application to Us

Keeping all of this in mind, we recognize that the Parable of the Talents is just as applicable to us as it was to Peter, James and John. There exists the possibility that we, like they, could imitate the one-talent slave and not be ready when Jesus returns. The way to avoid being like the unfaithful slave is to make certain that we are using our "talents" for the Lord's purposes, bringing a return on His "investment."

To many people, this may sound like salvation by works. However, as I've said before, their error is in separating what cannot be divided—faith and works. Many suppose that faith and works oppose each other, like repelling magnets. The truth is that true faith and true works of righteousness cannot be torn apart. Each is embodied within the other, and if either is removed, the other ceases to exist. Those who continue to believe in Jesus continue to obey Jesus. Those who don't continue to obey Jesus prove they no longer believe in Jesus. Faith works. Believers obey.

In this parable, what do the talents represent, and what are the returns that Jesus expects from us? Do the talents represent our investment capital? Do the returns represent the increasing value of our shares of Mr. Wolfer's recommended mutual funds?

No, the talents of which Jesus spoke must represent more than wealth alone, because Jesus entrusts us with much more than that. They must represent anything and everything that God entrusts to us, including opportunities for service, spiritual gifts and abilities, natural talents, and of course, wealth. All of these things are gifts from God for which we must one day give an account. Scripture declares,

> We have as our ambition, whether at home or absent, to be pleasing to Him. For we must all appear before the judgment seat of Christ, that each one may be recompensed for his deeds in the body, according to what he has done, whether good or bad (2 Cor. 5:9-10; see also Rom. 12:1-8; 14:10-12; 1 Pet. 4:10).

Our time, talents and treasures are a stewardship from God, and if we selfishly bury those gifts in the ground, not using them as God intended, we stand in grave spiritual danger, just like the one-talent slave.

God expects that we will use His gifts to love Him and our neighbor. If we believe in Jesus, that is exactly what we will do. If we don't, we expose our unbelief and reveal our hypocrisy. Jesus couldn't have emphasized this solemn fact any more graphically than He did by what He said directly after the Parable of the Talents. There He tells of the future judgment that will occur when He returns. The theme is still the same—Be ready for

His coming. Although I quoted these words in the previous chapters, let us consider His words within their context:

> But when the Son of Man comes in His glory, and all the angels with Him, then He will sit on His glorious throne. And all the nations will be gathered before Him; and He will separate them from one another, as the shepherd separates the sheep from the goats; and He will put the sheep on His right, and the goats on the left. Then the King will say to those on His right, "Come, you who are blessed of My Father, inherit the kingdom prepared for you from the foundation of the world. I was hungry, and you gave Me something to eat; I was thirsty, and you gave Me drink; I was a stranger, and you invited Me in; naked, and you clothed Me; I was sick, and you visited Me; I was in prison, and you came to Me." Then the righteous will answer Him, saying, "Lord, when did we see You hungry, and feed You, or thirsty, and give You drink? And when did we see You a stranger, and invite You in, or naked, and clothe You? And when did we see You sick, or in prison, and come to You?" And the King will answer and say to them, "Truly I say to you, to the extent that you did it to one of these brothers of Mine, even the least of them, you did it to Me." Then He will also say to those on His left, "Depart from Me, accursed ones, into the eternal fire which has been prepared for the devil and his angels; for I was hungry, and you gave Me nothing to eat; I was thirsty, and you gave Me nothing to drink; I was a stranger, and you did not invite Me in; naked, and you did not clothe Me; sick, and in prison, and you did not visit Me." Then they themselves also will answer, saying, "Lord, when did we see You hungry, or thirsty, or a stranger, or naked, or sick, or in prison, and did not take care of You?" Then He will answer them, saying, "Truly I say to you, to the extent that you did not do it to one of the least of these, you did not do it to Me." And these will go away into eternal punishment, but the righteous into eternal life (Matt. 25:31-46).

Remember that Jesus was still speaking to His closest disciples. His theme had not changed. He wants His followers to be fruitful, thus always ready for His return. The goats in this passage clearly correspond to the one-talent servant, the five foolish virgins and the unfaithful slave in the three preceding passages. Like all of them, the goats weren't ready to give an account before the Master at His coming. In this foretelling of future judgment, Jesus underscores everything He has just been saying. The message couldn't be clearer: *You don't want to be among the goats at this future judgment. Therefore, use your time and treasures to show your love for Me by loving My brethren. If you do, you validate your profession of faith. If you don't, you reveal that you are not really Mine.*

Notice that every good work Jesus mentioned requires the sacrifice of one's time or money. None of them require any supernatural gifts. Practically anyone can do them. Every one of them is a simple act of loving one's neighbor as himself. All of them are indicative of a love for the Master, so that by doing them, one fulfills the two greatest commandments and exhibits his living faith.

The question is, how many of today's professing Christians, if they would stand at this judgment right now, would be counted among the goats? How many would be exposed as complete hypocrites, because they never, or only on rare occasions, have done what Jesus unmistakably said marks all true Christians? Although they had time to acquire money and spend it selfishly, they had no time or money to assist those with desperate needs who were members of their own (supposed) spiritual family.

The Hardness of Some Professing Christians' Hearts

Incredibly, I've found that when I preach about this very judgment, there are always some (often many) professing Christians who dismiss me as a legalist. Yet all I'm doing is telling them what Jesus plainly taught. If I'm a legalist, then so is He. The truth is, Jesus has told us about a future test that is impossible for us to avoid. He's also told us what we must do to pass that test, and we're still unprepared. We think Jesus is mistaken, even though He will be the Judge at the judgment. We imagine that we can be saved by a faith that has no works—a faith that exists nowhere in the universe—a faith that is an utter impossibility.

As you would suspect, strange, elaborate, and perverse interpretations have been suggested to soften or explain away the obvious message that is found in Christ's foretelling of the sheep and goats judgment. For example, some claim that we will somehow be exempt from this judgment. They say that it applies only to those people who are alive when Christ returns at the end of the seven-year tribulation.

Even if such an interpretation is true, what makes us think we will be judged by different criteria than the sheep and goats? Can it only be said of those Christians who are alive when Christ returns that they know they have passed from death to life because they love the brethren (see 1 John 3:14)? Is it only that final group of Christians who can be identified as Christ's disciples by their love (see John 13:35)? No, love is what identifies all Christians of all time. Additionally, all of us shall be judged by our works (see Matt. 12:36-37; John 5:28-29; Rev. 20:12-13), because our works are what validate our faith. To write off the sheep and goats judgment as being irrelevant to us is a foolish error. If you would have asked Peter, James or John if they thought what Jesus said about the sheep and goats applied to them, they would have answered in the affirmative. Jesus was speaking to *them*, warning *them* to be ready for His return.

Some claim that the sheep and goats judgment is a judgment just of nations, not people, depending on how they treated Israel during the future seven-year tribulation. This interpretation is so far-fetched that it is a wonder anyone has the nerve to present it seriously. According to Jesus, this judgment determines one's eternal destiny, whether it be heaven or hell (see Matt. 25:46). In light of all that Scripture teaches, are we actually to believe that at some time in the future, some people will be cast into hell forever because they lived in a nation whose government was opposed to Israel for seven years? And are we to believe that others will receive eternal life because they lived in a nation that was kind to Israel for seven years?

The True Test of Faith

May I also point out that Jesus did not ask these sheep and goats what church they attended. He didn't ask them about their theology concerning the Trinity. He didn't question if they were Republican or Democrat. He didn't quiz them about their eschatology. He didn't ask if they ever prayed the sinner's prayer or possessed assurance of their salvation. He didn't ask for their baptismal certificate. He didn't ask which TV preacher or Christian music group was their favorite. He didn't ask if they believed in Him. He only cared if they loved His brethren and expressed that love by meeting pressing needs. Their eternal salvation depended on what they did and didn't do, because that is what clearly revealed their faith or unbelief.

Question: How much do you love Jesus? Answer: How much do you sacrifice for the sake of His poor brethren? When you do it for them, you do it for Jesus. It is just that simple.

Ask yourself: If I were to stand at this judgment at this moment and be judged by the same criteria, would I be among the sheep or goats? If your answer is "goats," then you are a goat. You are unprepared to stand before Jesus. If He came back at this moment, you would spend eternity in hell. All that Jesus said in the Parable of the Talents, the Parable of the Five Foolish Virgins, and the example of the unfaithful slave, He was saying to warn you. Don't wait another second. Fall on your face before God and cry out for His forgiveness and transforming grace. Repent of a lifestyle of breaking the greatest commandments. Believe in Jesus. Begin following Him, even if other people think you are crazy.

Following Jesus clearly includes feeding the hungry, clothing the naked, helping those in distress, and visiting the sick and imprisoned, among other things. So give as generously as you can of your time and money to meet pressing, essential needs of brothers and sisters in Christ. The majority of them live in developing nations. Don't lay up treasures on earth; lay them up in heaven. Those are the returns that Jesus expects from His investment in you, not the ever-increasing value of your share of Mr. Wolfer's recommended mutual funds.

Perhaps the best maxim on stewardship was one coined by John Wesley, Anglican evangelist and unintentional founder of the Methodist Church. Wesley taught the early Methodists regarding money: "Earn all you can; save all you can; give all you can."

Good stewards are not lazy, but work hard to earn what they can reasonably, so they have more to give. They, of course, must earn their money lawfully, keeping a good conscience and not being so devoted to their vocation that their devotion to the Lord or His commandments is neglected in any way. They should not earn their money by exploiting other people.

Good stewards also save all they can. That is, they are frugal and use wisdom in their financial affairs. They don't spend needlessly, and they deny themselves the nonessentials in order to have more to give.

Finally, having earned all they can and saved all they can, good stewards give all they can. They don't limit themselves to giving just ten percent, but give 99% if God enables them.

Wesley lived what he preached, subsisting on a small portion of the large income he received from the sale of his books. His devotion to the greatest commandments even affected his diet. He ate only what was necessary to sustain his strength and health, in order not to rob someone who needed a touch of Christ's love that he could not have otherwise supplied. He died owning very little.

The Conclusion

What does the Parable of the Talents have to do with what Jesus taught about money, possessions and stewardship? We must all give an account one day for what we've done with the money that God has entrusted to us. If we've been unfaithful, proving ourselves to be poor stewards, using for ourselves what God intended that we use for His glory, we're unprepared to stand before Him. We're professing Christians but practicing atheists.

EIGHT

The Rest of What Jesus Taught

We've now completed our study of Jesus' major statements regarding stewardship. If you're still reading, you've probably made some very significant stewardship decisions. Yet the flow of the world and most of the church may well be tempting you to wonder if you are out of your mind. Let me assure you that you are not, and this chapter will assure you all the more.

In order to arrive at a balanced understanding of any biblical subject, the devoted student knows he must consider every relevant scripture. In regard to our topic, there are over one hundred scripture passages in the four Gospels that have some relevancy to the subject of money, possessions and stewardship. Thus the reason for this chapter: we want to consider everything Jesus taught on the subject, and I've commented on every relevant passage in the Gospels. You will first need to read the scripture passages that are referenced in order to best understand my commentary.[1]

In many cases, the scriptures we are about to examine will serve to support what we've already learned. In other cases, they will enlighten us to truths that we've not yet considered. In still others, they will bring some gentle balance to our understanding, lest we lean more to one side. It is, of course, possible to make the Bible say anything one wants it to say by isolating scriptures from their context. It never ceases to amaze me how people will justify their greed with one obscure scripture, ignoring everything else God has to say about money.

It is also important to keep in mind that the Bible is a progressive revelation. God did not reveal everything to Adam that He revealed to Paul. Moses did not have the understanding that Jesus did. Even Jesus Himself once told His own disciples that He had more revelation to share with

---

[1] This chapter is written so as to serve as a reference for everything Jesus said on stewardship.

them but would have to share it later because that they were unable to receive it at the time (see John 16:12-13).

If we ignore this fact, we may end up emphasizing early revelation at the expense of ignoring later revelation, and consequently become very unbalanced. In a nutshell, this is the error of the majority of the so-called prosperity preachers. They essentially ignore or twist every scripture relating to money, except those that promise prosperity, the majority of which are found in the Old Testament. Such scriptures, ripped from their biblical context, become a very convenient way for any greedy person to justify his sin.

This is certainly not to say that the Old Testament is somehow unbalanced regarding money, void of any direction regarding godly stewardship. It is in the Old Testament that we first find the commandment to love one's neighbor as oneself (see Lev. 19:18), as well as numerous other scriptures that specifically spell out how that is done, in part, by the means of one's money.

In later chapters, we'll consider what the Old Testament and the epistles teach about money, possessions and stewardship. For now, let us examine everything else that Jesus said on the subject, as well as any scripture that is relevant to our topic that is found in the four Gospels.

Matthew

2:11 The magi demonstrated their authentic belief that baby Jesus was divine by their long journey to see Him, their falling before Him, their worshiping Him, and their opening their treasures to present Him with gifts of gold, frankincense and myrrh. *Their faith affected what they did with their possessions.*

It is a matter of speculation as to what became of their gifts. Perhaps the selling of those items is what sustained Mary, Joseph and Jesus during their ensuing flight to, sojourn in, and return from Egypt (see 2:13-21). It is absurd to claim, however, in light of everything else we know about Jesus' adult lifestyle and living standard, that those three gifts made Him rich all His life (see Matt. 8:20; Luke 8:1-3), as some claim.

3:4-12 John the Baptist evidently lived very simply, sustained by a diet of locusts and wild honey, and wearing a garment of camel's hair with a leather belt. It seems quite unlikely that he would have owned much more clothing than that. He told his penitent audience that if they owned two tunics, they should give one to a person who had none in order to validate their professed repentance (see Luke 3:10-11). His instruction to them was nothing more than an application of the second greatest commandment.

If modern professing Christians had been in John's audience, would they have followed his instruction? Or would they have said, as did many then, that John had a demon (see Matt. 11:18)? Jesus, of course, did not need to repent at the preaching of John because He never sinned. He always loved His neighbor as Himself throughout His entire life. Jesus owned only one tunic.

4:17 Jesus began His ministry by preaching the identical message as John the Baptist (compare with 3:2). Are we to think that what Jesus meant by repentance was different than what John meant? If penitent people had asked Jesus what they must do, would Jesus have answered differently than John, as recorded in Luke 3:10-14? Would He have disagreed with John, one whom He considered to be the greatest man "born of women"? (see Matt. 11:11).

4:18-22 Peter, Andrew, James and John left everything behind when Jesus called them to follow Him. They would later remind Him of their sacrifice when He told them that it was easier for a camel to go through the eye of a needle than for a rich man to enter the kingdom of God. He then assured them of future kingdom blessings as well as eternal life (see Matt. 19:23-30).

5:40 Does this mean that we are not to contest unfair lawsuits that could potentially result in our having to borrow a large sum of money in order to make a payment to our opponent? Beyond that, are we to borrow additional money to give our opponent more than what he wants? No, Jesus was talking in this passage about showing extra mercy when we suffer minor offences (see 5:38-41).

The Pharisees considered it their holy obligation to take revenge for petty offences. Their justification was based on a twisted interpretation of a commandment that was meant to insure justice in court for major offences (such as poking out another person's eye). In petty offences, Christ's followers are to be more tolerant and loving than people expect, showing them God's love and shaming them in the process. If someone wants to knock out our teeth, Jesus does not want us to also offer our arm for breaking. He was simply correcting the practice of the Pharisees, who had a zero-tolerance policy regarding any small offence.

5:42 Followers of Christ should be characterized by their willingness to give and lend. Keep in mind, however, that Jesus was not talking about giving or lending money to people who don't have enough cash this month to make payments on their luxuries purchased with borrowed money. Helping people with pressing, essential needs was more of what He must have had in mind (see 6:1-4).

If Christ's followers are to lend, they must first have some surplus. What a blessing it is to have God supply more than we need, that we might have some to give or lend.

6:1-4 Note that Jesus didn't say, "If you give alms," but "When you give alms." He expected His followers to give to the poor and here stressed the importance of doing it with the right motives. The Pharisees sounded trumpets at their public distributions, ostensibly to attract the poor. But God knew their true motives. Followers of Christ should give as secretly as possible.

What exactly is the reward that is promised by Christ to those who secretly give alms? Is it a larger sum of money received while we are still on earth? Perhaps, but Jesus later said that we lay up treasure in heaven by giving to charity, indicating a heavenly reward (see also Luke 14:13-14). If our reward is indeed a larger sum of money received in this life, we then must decide if we want to use that blessing to lay up treasures on earth or heaven, disobeying or obeying Jesus. Our desire to gain more ought to be so we can give more.

6:11 In this prayer we are taught to pray for our basic need of food. This should fill us with faith that it is always God's will that we have enough food to sustain us. David testified, "I have been young, and now I am old; yet I have not seen the righteous forsaken, or his descendants begging bread" (Ps. 37:25). According to what Christ taught in this prayer, however, we should be content with only one day's supply, our "daily bread." If we possess more, we should consider ourselves as possessing abundance. There is certainly no hint of greed found in this prayer. Christ's followers are to be content with what they have, even if it is only food and covering (see Phil. 4:11-14; 1 Tim. 6:6-10; Heb. 13:5).

Notice also that we are not to pray, "give *me* this day *my* daily bread," but "give *us* this day *our* daily bread." Our prayer reflects our concern for everyone who is related to our Father. We sincerely desire that all of God's children have their daily bread. How can we pray this prayer without hypocrisy if God has given us more than we need and we don't share it with our brothers who lack daily bread?

6:19-24 Jesus' commandment not to lay up treasures on earth is just as valid as His commandments forbidding adultery, lust, murder and hatred (see 5:21-30). It can only be ignored if it is twisted and stripped of its obvious meaning, which it has been by many professing Christians. I have fully commented on this passage in Chapter Five.

6:25-34 This passage again underscores that our real needs consist of nothing more than food and covering, and promises us that God will supply those needs. We should therefore not be concerned about lacking them and devote ourselves foremost to seeking God's kingdom and righteousness. So many fall far short from obeying this commandment. Not only are they not seeking first God's kingdom and righteousness, but they are seeking to possess much more than what they need. I've also commented on this passage in Chapter Five.

7:7-11 Practically any time North American preachers mention this passage, they are forced to explain "what Jesus really meant" in light of the fact that we don't receive so much of what we ask for. Yet the fact remains that Jesus declared, "Ask, and it shall be given to you…For every one who asks receives." Could part of the problem be that what we are asking for is not God's will? Unlike the son in Christ's example who asked only for food, our requests are often a reflection of our greed. We want more material riches so we can indulge ourselves.

Did not James warn of this very thing in his epistle that so often parallels the Sermon on the Mount?: "You ask and do not receive, because you ask with wrong motives, *so that you may spend it on your pleasures*" (Jas. 4:3, emphasis added; see also 1 John 5:14-15). Jesus promised that the Father would give "what is good to those who ask Him." Would God consider something to be good if it would tether our hearts to this earth, distract us from devotion to Him, fill us with pride, make us more selfish, and ultimately drag us into hell?

8:20 If Jesus had owned a home, as some prosperity preachers claim, could He have made this statement without lying?

10:9-10 Jesus did not want His twelve disciples to take any future provision with them when He sent them out to preach and heal. Their needs would be supplied as they arose. Thus, there was no reason for any of the twelve to purchase an extra tunic or pair of sandals before their departure. They needed only one tunic and one pair of sandals. When what they had wore out, God would provide a replacement. They wore the same clothing every day, as do so many hundreds of millions of people today in the developing world. What a different perspective we have concerning our needs in contrast to Jesus, His apostles, and multitudes of people living on the earth today!

12:1 Elaborately-prepared meals were not always the means God used to meet the nutritional needs of Jesus' disciples. Sometime they enjoyed fresh fruit, or in this case, raw heads of grain. Could you be content with such a meal and eat with thanksgiving?

13:22 I have fully commented on "the deceitfulness of riches" against which Christ warned in Chapter Six.

13:44-46 How would Jesus' disciples, who heard Him say that it would be easier for a camel to go through the eye of a needle than for a rich man to enter into heaven, and who witnessed His lifestyle of self-denial, have interpreted these two parables? At bare minimum, both parables teach that gaining heaven is worth giving up everything one possesses, because heaven is of infinite value. This being so, are we then to conclude that we must not give up *anything* to gain heaven? Why would Jesus even communicate that gaining heaven was worth sacrificing *everything* if one could gain heaven without giving up anything? Was He only trying to teach those who possessed eternal life that they should value it more than anything else they possess? Or was He again trying to enlighten hell-bound people who, like the rich young ruler and rich fool (see Matt. 19:16-30; Luke 12:16-21), selfishly cling to earthly things, refuse to repent of greed, and esteem earthly riches above true heavenly wealth?

14:15-21 Is there any example in the Gospels of Jesus providing people with any other material things besides the necessities of food, drink, and money to pay taxes? No, there is not one. God has promised to supply our needs, and Jesus, the "exact representation of [His Father's] nature" (Heb. 1:3) clearly revealed what our needs actually are. In this case, Jesus actually provided more food than the crowds needed. He gathered the excess, however, and I think it is safe to assume that it was all eventually eaten.

15:3-9 Here we learn that obeying the fifth commandment, when it is rightly interpreted, could mean giving money to support one's elderly parents. Thus, five of the Ten Commandments can be said to have something to do with money and possessions.

The first commandment, having no other gods before God, is certainly applicable to money and possessions when we consider what Jesus said about the impossibility of serving God and mammon. Money can be one's god.

The fourth commandment, keeping the Sabbath, obviously regulates one's profiting through labor on one day of the week.

And the eighth and tenth commandments that forbid stealing and coveting one's neighbor's property teaches us our proper relationship to material things that belong to others.

All this being so, how foolish we must be to think that the topic of money, possessions and stewardship is of little importance to God. May we not ignore God's clear commandments regarding these things, lest He also say of us: "This people honors Me with their lips, but their heart is far from Me. But in vain do they worship Me, teaching as doctrines the precepts of men" (15:8-9).

15:32-39 Again Jesus supplied people's basic needs. If every man present was married and had just two children with him, Jesus fed at least 16,000 people. No need to worry if He can take care of you!

16:5-12 Jesus here reminds His disciples, men of little faith, that they don't have to fear going without bread. He can and will supply their need for food, as proven by two recent miracles.

16:24-27 Obviously, Jesus was talking about salvation and damnation here. Why else would He use such expressions as, "save his life," "loses his life for My sake," "find his life," "gains the whole world, and forfeits his soul"? Why else would He warn that everyone will be recompensed according to his deeds when He returns? This being so, does "denying ourselves" and "losing our lives for Jesus' sake" affect what we do with our money and possessions? Does "gaining the whole world," which guarantees that one forfeits his soul, have anything to do with money and possessions? If Jesus is going to repay us according to our deeds, do those deeds include what we've done with the money He has entrusted to us? Obviously, the answer to all these questions is *yes*.

17:24-27 Here is another miracle of provision for someone's basic needs, a tax from which Peter was not exempt.

18:1-4 If the greatest in the kingdom of heaven is the one who humbles himself the most, we ought to be striving to become as humble as possible. What is humility? It is, in part, thinking of others as being more important than ourselves (see Phil. 2:3). Humble people serve others, putting their needs first. Proud people consider themselves to be more important than others. Their own needs selfishly come first. Jesus set the greatest example of humility. Although He was God, He humbled himself to die on the cross, considering that our salvation was more important than His comfort (see Phil. 2:5-8). If we view others as being more important than ourselves, will that affect what we do with our money and time? Certainly.

19:16-30 I have fully commented on the rich young ruler in Chapters Two and Three.

21:12-13 To say that Jesus was upset would be an understatement. What provoked Him to such a degree? God intended that the temple would be a place where His people would pray, prayer being an expression of their devotion to Him. However, the main activity around the temple was an expression of devotion to money. It was the perfect business location for the moneychangers and dove sellers, who apparently were not all honest in their dealings. Profits, not prayers, were on their minds.

Does one have to be selling something at Jerusalem's temple before considering if this passage has any personal application? No. When making money supersedes our devotion to God, even if our earnings are honest, we are guilty of serving mammon.

21:22 If we are to pray believing, we must have some promise from God so that we know His will, otherwise it is impossible to pray with assurance of one's prayer being answered. For example, it would be impossible to pray with faith that Jesus will return tomorrow or that adultery won't be a sin during the first weekend in November. Yet many make this error when they attempt to "believe God" for more personal luxuries. How can one have faith to possess more earthly treasures when Jesus commanded us not to lay up treasures for ourselves on earth? *It is absolutely impossible to have faith for earthly treasures.* A greedy person may pray with hope for such things, but he cannot pray with faith for them. As I mentioned when commenting on Matthew 7:7-11, James plainly told us why God doesn't answer such prayers: "You ask and do not receive, because you ask with wrong motives, *so that you may spend it on your pleasures*" (Jas. 4:3, emphasis added). On the other hand, we know it is God's will for us to spread the gospel to the whole world, as well as feed the hungry and clothe the naked. Thus we can ask in faith that He will provide for us so we can do those things.

In light of this, it is interesting that prosperity preachers are always trying to convince everyone of how much faith they have by the abundance of their possessions. In reality, they show what little faith they have. If their faith were really so great, they would give everything away and trust God to supply their daily needs.

22:15-22 We learn here it is God's will that we pay our rightful share of taxes, so we can trust that He will help us to do it. Jesus also affirmed that just as we have financial obligations to our governments, so we also have financial obligations to God.

22:35-40 It is amazing that this profound statement by Jesus is so rarely esteemed and emphasized. Jesus told us that God's total will for us is embodied in just two commandments. Jesus came and died for all the times we disobeyed these commandments, and He lives in us now to enable us to obey these commandments. If a person loves God will all his heart and his neighbor as himself, will it have any affect on what he does with his money and possessions? It most assuredly will!

23:10-11 To be a servant of all should obviously be the aspiration of every follower of Christ. If one is a servant, will it have any affect on what he does with his money and possessions? Of course.

23:14 To "devour widow's houses" must be some reference to the scribes and Pharisees' practice of taking financial advantage of poor widows, who are often trusting and gullible, thus easy prey. Under the "pretense of making long prayers," that is, under a guise of love and spirituality, these wolves in sheep's clothing were somehow able to coerce donations from those who could least afford to part with them. Their houses were "devoured," leaving them with nothing. Jesus severely condemned them for their greed. They blatantly disregarded the second greatest commandment.

23:16-17 Why are we not surprised that the scribes and Pharisees, lovers of money (see Luke 16:14), valued the gold in the temple above the temple itself? This is just one more indication that they were servants of mammon.

23:23-26 When we combine Matthew and Luke's versions (see Luke 11:42) in order to know every word Christ said here, we come up with, "And yet [you] disregard the weightier provisions of the law: justice, mercy, faithfulness and the love of God." Justice, mercy and faithfulness are simply facets of loving one's neighbor. "The love of God" speaks for itself. Thus, once again, Jesus is emphasizing what is truly important. The weightier provisions of the law are loving God and one's neighbor. Isn't it obvious that one may scrupulously tithe, but still be guilty of laying up treasures on earth? Likewise, an ardent tither may love money, not love his neighbor as himself, live in self-indulgence (see 23:25) and not love God as He should be loved. What message is found here for those whose Christianity consists of little more than going to church on Sunday and faithfully tithing out of their abundance? Why is tithing emphasized so much of the time in so many churches at the neglect of what is most important?

25:14-46 I have fully commented on this passage in Chapter Seven. The question every person who reads this passage should ask him/herself is this: If I was to die at this moment and find myself at the sheep and goats' judgment, would I be counted among the sheep or the goats? Perhaps more sobering is the fact that our love for Jesus is revealed by our love for His family, expressed by meeting their pressing needs. It is amazing that millions of people claim to love Jesus, but sacrifice nothing to feed and clothe His impoverished believers. They are completely deceived.

26:6-13 Mark tells us that the value of this woman's ointment was equivalent to about three hundred days' wages for a common laborer (see Mark 14:3-4). To bring it into some perspective, imagine a perfume worth fourteen months of your labor, working five days a week for fifty weeks each year. It was "very costly" (26:7) indeed.

The woman who poured it on Christ may have been wealthy herself to be able to afford such ointment, or she may have received it as a gift, perhaps by inheritance. Regardless, it was without any doubt, an earthly treasure, and as one who obviously loved Christ, she wanted to lay up treasure in heaven and show her love for Him.

Had she poured her perfume upon anyone other than Jesus, the disciples would have had a valid complaint. But she realized, as they should have, that Jesus was of greater importance and value than all the people of the world combined, as He was God in the flesh. Beyond that, there would always be opportunities to help the poor, but only a short time to express her great love for Him. We must, however, give the disciples credit for at least attempting to follow Jesus' commandments regarding good stewardship. Their criticisms of this woman indicate that they cared for the poor, just as He had taught them. Their fault was that they didn't rightly value Jesus.

26:14-16 There is no need to speculate about Judas' reason for betraying Jesus. He had no higher motive than the love of money. Amazingly, Judas had heard Jesus say everything we have considered in this book so far, but perhaps he was tired of a life of self-denial. Mammon, the god who competes for the hearts of people more than any other false god, enticed and deceived him.

Was Judas' character tainted even from the beginning of his relationship with Jesus? Perhaps it was. We know that Judas periodically stole from the corporate moneybox, at least near the close of Jesus' ministry (see John 12:6). Jesus once announced that one among the twelve was a devil (see John 6:70). Yet Judas had preached the gospel, healed the sick, cast out demons and fed the five thousand, just as much as the other eleven. When Jesus announced at the Last Supper that He would be betrayed by one of the twelve, no one suspected Judas (see Matt. 26:22; Luke 22:23; John 13:22). Thus it seems possible that mammon gradually enticed him. If so, what a sobering warning to us of the powerful seduction of riches! Even one who literally lives with Jesus is not beyond its temptation. If he yields and does not repent, it can also be rightfully said of him, "It would have been good for that man if he had not been born" (26:24).

Judas' fundamental fatal flaw was yielding to the temptation to gain wealth at the expense of obedience to Christ. One is guilty of that same sin, to a lesser degree, whenever he gains or uses money in a way that is contrary to God's will. When he does, he is serving mammon, allowing it to direct his life rather than God.

27:57-60 Joseph of Arimathea is another example of a wealthy man who became "a disciple of Jesus" (27:57). Keep in mind that biblical disciples are those who met Jesus' requirements for discipleship, one of which is giving up all of one's possessions (see Luke 14:33). We don't know what Joseph did with the rest of his possessions, but his sincere devotion to Jesus is revealed in this passage as he gave his own tomb for the burial of Jesus' body.

28:11-15 Here is one more obvious example of people who served mammon rather than God. The chief priests did not use money according to God's will, and the Roman soldiers took money against God's will. Anyone who knowingly gains or uses money in a way that is contrary to God's will is serving mammon, because money, not God, is directing his life.

28:18-20 Jesus wanted His disciples to make disciples of their own, teaching them to obey everything He had commanded them, including everything he commanded concerning money, possessions and stewardship. This they did, as is so clearly revealed in the epistles and the book of Acts. Why aren't spiritual leaders doing this today? In fact, why are so many spiritual leaders teaching what contradicts what Jesus taught regarding wealth? Why are so many living in luxury? Why are so many teaching wealthy, self-indulgent people that God loves them and thus wants them to be even more wealthy and self-indulgent? We have just surveyed Matthew's entire Gospel for relevant scriptures about money, possessions and stewardship. Where is the modern prosperity doctrine found in Christ's teachings? We have read scores of scriptures that contradict not only the prosperity gospel, but that also condemn standard American evangelical doctrine as well as the normal American lifestyle. Who will dare say in North America that it is easier for a camel to go through the eye of a needle than for a rich man to enter the kingdom of heaven?

Mark

There is essentially nothing regarding stewardship in Mark's Gospel that isn't also included in Matthew's Gospel. I have, therefore, only given the corresponding references.

2:23 See my comments on Matt. 12:1.

4:19 I have fully commented on "the deceitfulness of riches" against which Christ warned in Chapter Six.

6:7-9 See my comments on Matt. 10:9-10.

6:33-44 See my comments on Matt. 14:15-21.

7:9-13 See my comments on Matt. 15:3-9.

8:1-9 See my comments on Matt. 15:32-39.

8:13-21 See my comments on Matt. 16:5-12.

8:34-38 See my comments on Matt. 16:24-27.

9:33-35 See my comments on Matt. 18:1-4.

10:17-31 I have fully commented on the rich, young ruler in Chapters Two and Three.

10:42-45 See my comments on Matt. 23:10-11.

11:15-17 See my comments on Matt. 21:12-13.

11:24 See my comments on Matt. 21:22.

12:17 See my comments on Matt. 22:15-22.

12:28-34 See my comments on Matt. 22:35-40.

12:41-44 I have made mention of this story in Chapter Four. Jesus' reaction to those who give out of their surplus is no different today.

14:3-9 See my comments on Matt. 26:6-13.

14:10-11 See my comments on Matt. 26:14-16.

Luke

1:53 This Spirit-inspired utterance from a humble bond slave is a revelation of God's justice. God delights in righting wrongs, and the hungry are so often the victims of the wrongs of others, particularly the rich. But at times in the past, God has judged the unrepentant rich by forcing them to beg just like the hungry poor they previously ignored.

This verse is not only historically true (at least to some degree), but is prophetically true as well. Although not everyone has reaped what he's sown in this life, without exception, every person will be repaid according to his or her deeds in the next life, believers and unbelievers (see Matt. 16:27; Rom. 2:6-10). The greedy rich who never repent of ignoring the starving poor can never enter heaven, or else God would be unjust. The only thing that could make a greedy person imagine that he will enter heaven is a false gospel. The truth is, Jesus died, not just to forgive us of our selfishness, but to deliver us from it for the rest of our lives and throughout eternity.

2:22-24 From these verses, we certainly don't get the impression that Jesus' parents were wealthy at this point in their lives. Mary and Joseph gave the offering that was required of poor parents, being unable to afford a lamb (see Lev. 12:6-8).

3:7-18 As I mentioned in an earlier chapter, practically every specific thing that John told his convicted audience to do in order to validate their repentance involved money. Clearly, John wanted his hearers to realize that, unless they repented of greed and produced the fruit to prove it, hell was their eternal home. I'm afraid that many modern professing Christians, if they heard John preaching "the gospel," as Luke calls it (3:18), would call him legalistic, unbalanced, harsh, or extreme (see also my comments on Matt. 3:4-12).

4:18 When the Holy Spirit descended upon Jesus, He was anointed to preach the gospel specifically to the poor, as Isaiah had foretold. The reason Jesus didn't target the wealthy is not because God didn't love them. In fact, some wealthy people repented and were saved under Jesus' ministry. Jesus primarily targeted the poor for a number of possible reasons.

Perhaps first because it is so difficult for the rich to be saved—as difficult as it is for a camel to go through the eye of a needle (to quote an authority on the subject). The rich rarely repent of their greed. Why target the least receptive group?

Perhaps second, because of God's justice. The poor so often get the short end of the stick, and the God of love hates injustice.

And perhaps third, because of God's great compassion toward the marginalized citizens of the world, as Jesus' constant ministry to the sick, to the demonized, to the hungry, to women and children, and to the poor so abundantly demonstrated. James wrote that "God choose the poor of this world to be rich in faith and heirs of the kingdom" (Jas. 2:5; see also 1 Cor. 1:26-29).

Some prosperity preachers have a standard rhetoric that revolves around this verse. It goes as follows: "Jesus said He was anointed to preach the gospel to the poor! So what is good news to the poor man? That's simple: 'Poor man, you don't have to be poor any more!'" At which point the wealthy and greedy crowd wildly applauds.

Of course, we never find Jesus preaching such a gospel. Jesus also preached good news to the Pharisees, tax collectors and prostitutes. Shall we determine what Christ's message was to them based on what they would have liked to hear? "Hey prostitutes, you can keep your profession and still go to heaven!" I'm sure prostitutes would have given Him a standing ovation.

It is indeed true, however, that those who repent of their sin (including the sin of greed) and become His followers need not worry about food or clothing. Now that's good news to believers who are truly poor.

5:4-11 It is often pointed out by prosperity preachers how Jesus blessed Peter's business with abundance. These same people, however, rarely point out that Peter left all those fish on the beach (along with everything else) to start following Jesus, which of course was Jesus' original intention.

May I also ask: As Peter and his companions frantically worked to get every fish they could into their boats to the point of sinking them, all under the calm and holy gaze of Jesus, what was going through their minds? Could Peter suddenly have realized that his actions revealed his heart? Could he have realized that his frantic attempt to fill the boats to the point of sinking was a revelation of his greed? That he was only thinking of profits while he was standing in the midst of a miracle, and that his excitement was wrongly directed at the fish instead of the Miracle Worker? Could that have been why he then fell at Jesus' feet saying, "Depart from me, for I am a sinful man, O Lord!"?

Even if not, the fact remains that as soon as Peter decided to become a disciple of Jesus, he "left everything and followed Him" (5:11). His priorities all changed with his repentance. His focus was no longer fish, but fishing for men. How do you suppose Jesus would have reacted if Peter had announced that he was seeking speaking engagements for his new message, "Secrets for Divine Prosperity"?

5:27-32 Like Peter, Andrew, James and John, Matthew also left everything behind at his workplace when Jesus called him. There was nothing more important than following Jesus. Matthew immediately began using what he possessed to serve the Lord, hosting a large banquet in Jesus' honor as a means of introducing his corrupt associates to Him. Jesus considered Matthew's invitation to be an opportunity to call more sinners to repentance, and Matthew hoped his friends would yield.

6:1 See my comments on Matt. 12:1.

6:20-26 This passage either begins Luke's summary of the Sermon on the Mount, recorded more fully in Matthew 5-7, or more likely is an account of another of Jesus' sermons in which the content was very similar to His Sermon on the Mount. Regardless, Jesus here clearly contrasts heaven's view of people with the world's view. Which people are to be pitied, and which ones are to be envied? God's view is the exact opposite of the world's. The world envies those who are rich, comfortable, well fed, laughing, and popular. But Jesus warned that their happiness is only temporary. They will ultimately be very uncomfortable, hungry and hated, as they weep and gnash their teeth in hell.

Contrasted with them are those who had decided to follow Jesus, His disciples, to whom He was speaking (see 6:20). Although they are hated and ostracized now, one day they will be living forever in a perfect society of perfect love. Although they are poor in material things, they are spiritually rich and will one day be walking on streets of gold (see Rev. 21:21). Although they are not well fed, they will one day dine at the marriage feast of the Lamb (see Rev. 19:9). Although they sometimes weep, one day their God will wipe away every tear (see Rev. 21:4), and they will enter into the eternal joy of their Master (see Matt. 25:21).

And why might Christ's disciples weep? Because following Christ means loving God and neighbor, which means inevitable sorrow. Friends are lost, relationships broken, families are divided and persecution is endured. Beyond this, Christians weep because they care, weeping with those who weep (see Rom. 12:15). And like Paul, they carry "great sorrow and unceasing grief" (Rom. 9:2) in their hearts for those who are still in darkness.

6:29 See my comments on Matt. 5:40.

6:30 See my comments on Matt. 5:42.

6:31-35 Jesus wants to put an end to selfish lending, which always expects something in return. Unselfish lending would include lending without charging interest, as well as loaning money or goods without making a mental debit against the borrower's account for future reference.

The Old Testament condemned *usury*, which was not the sin of charging exorbitant interest as it is thought today, but the sin of charging *any* interest to a countryman facing pressing needs (see Ex. 22:25; Lev. 25:35-37; Deut. 15:7-11; 23:19-20). Here Jesus extends the Old Testament prohibition against usury to include loans made even to one's enemies, at the same time commanding such unheard of acts of kindness.[2]

In order to lend, one must first have something to lend. Thus, this commandment indicates that Jesus was not advocating destitution for His followers. Of the first believers it is recorded that "not one of them claimed that anything belonging to him was his own; but all things were common property to them" (Acts 4:32). This is another way of saying that they very generously lent to each other. Some must have owned contemporary conveniences, such as plows, oil presses, work animals and so on.

Good stewardship is characterized by owning only what one needs, giving away what one doesn't need, and lending what one doesn't always need. For example, one who owns a larger home than he needs is able to lend a room to someone who has no home of his own.

6:38 This is not a "formula for obtaining divine wealth," as some want us to believe, because that would stand in contradiction to everything else Jesus said in this sermon about unselfish love (not to mention the entire tenure of Scripture). Giving to get is pure hypocrisy, nothing more than selfishness under the guise of love. Rather, this promise is an assurance that we need never fear impoverishing ourselves by our giving to others, because God will abundantly return our kindness. As Paul would later echo to the Corinthian Christians when he admonished them to give generously to the poor, promising them a bountiful return: "And God is able to make all grace abound to you, that always having all sufficiency in everything, you may have an abundance *for every good deed*" (2 Cor. 9:8, emphasis added). Notice Paul assumed that the generous Corinthians, once blessed with their return, would want to use their God-given abundance for more good deeds. Those who are motivated to give because of love for God and neighbor will naturally want to continue to lay up treasures in heaven with what God abundantly repays them.

7:2-10 Because salvation has always been offered by grace and received

---

[2] Jesus, would not, of course, be commanding His followers to lend their money to enemies whose purpose in borrowing was some evil design. Loans made to enemies who were facing pressing needs was more of what He must have had in mind.

by a living faith (see Rom 4:1-17), it only seems reasonable to conclude that this Gentile Centurion was a saved man. Jesus declared that He had not found such great faith in Israel. His faith was evidenced by his humility (considering himself unworthy for Jesus to visit his house), his great respect for Jesus, his testimony concerning Jesus' authority, and the Jews' testimony about him. "He loves our nation" (7:5), they said, indicating a very unusual relationship between these Jews and a soldier who worked for the hated occupying power. Obedience to the second greatest commandment is a primary identifying mark of God's true people (see Luke 6:35; John 13:35; 1 John 3:14).

This centurion's living faith in God was also evidenced by the use of his money. He must have been quite generous, as the Jews gave him the credit for building their synagogue (see 7:5). This man lived his faith and others could see it. He loved God and neighbor.

7:24-25 Sadly, what Jesus said here is not true in our day. "Those who are splendidly clothed and live in luxury" are no longer found only in royal palaces—they are often found in church pulpits. Clearly, Jesus was contrasting a true man of God with those who lived in luxury. *Splendidly clothed men who live in luxury can't preach the true gospel, because their selfish lives testify that they don't believe it themselves.* Jesus considered that John was the greatest man who had ever lived (see 7:28).

8:1-3 Here we gain a glimpse of how God provided for the needs of Jesus and His band of twelve. Those who had been touched by His grace were interested in seeing Him succeed at His mission. Their faith was manifested by their self-denial.

9:1-3 See my comments on Matt. 10:9-10.

9:12-17 See my comments on Matt. 14:15-21.

9:23-26 See my comments on Matt. 16:24-27.

9:46-48 See my comments on Matt. 18:1-4.

9:58 See my comments on Matt. 8:20.

10:1-8 As when He sent out the twelve, Jesus allowed the seventy to take no future provision with them when He sent them to evangelize. As Christ's ambassadors, they were required to demonstrate faith, contentment with little, and humility to receive food and lodging from those who received their message.

10:30-37 The scribes and Pharisees apparently defined the word *neighbor* as being anyone who loved them (see Matt. 5:43-47). Thus, one fulfilled the second greatest commandment by loving one's friends, which meant one could and should hate his enemies. In this parable, however, Jesus revealed from God's perspective who one's neighbors are. They include members of other ethnic groups, strangers, and even our enemies. Scripture tells us that Samaritans and Jews in Jesus' day hated each other (see Luke 9:51-55; John 4:9).

Jesus also defined the word *love* in this parable. It involves meeting the pressing needs of other people in trouble, and our responsibility is based upon our knowledge of their needs and the resources we have to meet those needs. Love may require the sacrifice of time and money. How are we any different from the priest and Levite in this story if we close our hearts to starving, dying people? If there are so many hundreds of millions of Christians in the world today, why is anybody on earth starving? Are we loving our neighbors as ourselves? Finally, is it not safe to assume that two zealous tithers walked by before the Samaritan arrived on the scene of the crime?

11:3 See my comments on Matt. 6:11.

11:9-13 See my comments on Matt. 7:7-11.

11:42 See my comments on Matt. 23:23-26.

12:13-34 All of Chapter One of this book was devoted to this portion of Luke's Gospel. While some modern preachers are telling us to believe God for more possessions, Jesus told His followers to sell what they didn't need and give the proceeds to charity! Can you see that many modern preachers are telling people the exact opposite of what Christ said? They are telling their followers not to follow Christ.

14:12-14 Too much of our kindness extends no further than our own family or circle of friends, something that Jesus said amounts to nothing. Even the Gentiles do that much (see Matt. 5:46-47). Beyond that, our acts of kindness are often nothing more than subtle acts of selfishness, done in order to make the beneficiary feel obligated to reciprocate. We wine and dine potential clients in hopes of future profits.

God, however, expects us to use our resources to serve those who cannot repay us, the marginalized people of the world. By so doing, we are laying up treasures in heaven, something that is not accomplished when we serve those who reciprocate. Are you using a portion of your resources to serve the poor, crippled, lame and blind (particularly, but not exclusively, those who are believers), people who, in the developing world, are often forced to depend on the generosity of others for their survival?

14:16-24 A preoccupation with their newly-acquired possessions kept the first two people from accepting the gracious dinner invitation. What fools! Their earthly focus blinded them to potential heavenly joy. The poor, crippled, blind and lame face no such temptation, and in that sense are blessed.

14:25-35 The notion that one can be a believer in Christ, securely saved, but not be a disciple of Christ, is a modern theory that cannot be supported by Scripture. Those who claim that Jesus' requirements for discipleship here stand in contradiction to "salvation by grace through faith" do not understand the nature of true grace or true faith. God's grace instructs us to "deny ungodliness and worldly desires and to live sensibly, righteously and godly in the present age" (Tit. 2:12). The grace He offers says, "I don't condemn you, so go and sin no more." It does not say, "I don't condemn you, so you may continue to live in sin." Likewise, true faith obeys (see Gal. 5:6; Jas. 2:14-26; 1 John 2:3). Those who don't meet the requirements listed here to be Christ's disciples are not true believers in Him. They are not saved.

Not only must we love Jesus more than any other person (see 14:26), obediently following Him as we deny ourselves (see 14:27), but we must also "give up all [our] own possessions" (14:33). How we fool ourselves when we imagine that we fulfill this requirement by a supposed *mental* relinquishment that results in no *actual* relinquishment. If there is no actual relinquishment, neither has there been any mental relinquishment. How would the government react if you told them that you had *mentally* paid your taxes? How would the tax auditor respond if you said, "I'm holding my tax money loosely, and I don't consider that money to be mine any longer, even though it is still in my bank account"?

16:1-31 I have fully discussed this portion of Scripture in Chapter Four.

18:18-30 I have fully discussed the story of the rich ruler in Chapters Two and Three. What American pastor would remain employed if he told a rich man seeking salvation what Jesus told this man? Very few. Thus, Jesus Christ, whom Scripture calls the *Good Shepherd* (John 10:14), the *Great Shepherd* (Heb. 13:20) and the *Chief Shepherd* (1 Pet. 5:4), would not be employed as a shepherd in most churches because He apparently doesn't understand the truth about salvation. He believes that greedy people must repent in order to be saved.

19:1-10 I've already discussed the repentance and salvation of Zaccheus in Chapter Three. When Zaccheus repented of greed, salvation came. Why is it that so many today suppose that it is not necessary to repent of greed in order to be saved? The New Testament declares that no greedy person will inherit eternal life (see 1 Cor. 6:10; Eph. 5:3-6).

Note that Zaccheus repented of both forms of his greed. No longer would he make money by taking advantage of others, and no longer would he neglect the poor.

Here is a thought-provoking question: What if Zaccheus had continued to defraud people but gave all his profits to the poor? Would God have approved? An amazing phenomenon is the philanthropist who gains his money by disobeying the golden rule. Yet people applaud him for his great generosity, ignoring the fact that all he gives he has gained by selfishly exploiting other people to enrich himself! Moreover, what he donates to charity actually requires no self-denial on his part, because he continues to live in luxury. Although the world may applaud such people, in God's eyes they are hypocrites of the worst sort, greedy people who pretend to be caring.

Finally, if you are a pastor, how would you respond if a wealthy person told you what Zaccheus told Jesus? Would you caution that wealthy person against becoming too extreme in his zeal? Would you tell him that fourfold restitution to those he defrauded was going a bit too far, because God has forgiven him? Would you suggest the money could be better used for the building fund?

19:45-46 See my comments on Matt. 21:12-13.

20:20-26 See my comments on Matt. 22:15-22.

20:46-47 See my comments on Matt. 23:14.

21:1-4 See my comments on Mark 12:41-44.

22:3-6 See my comments on Matt. 26:14-16.

22:24-27 See my comments on Matt. 18:1-4.

John

2:1-11 Jesus again provided basic needs, in this case drink for thirsty people. There is no record of Him providing anything other than food, drink and taxes.

2:14-17 See my comments on Matt. 21:12-13.

4:5-8 Have you ever considered the fact that Jesus lived His entire earthly life in what we would consider an undeveloped nation? His disciples had gone to buy food, not in a supermarket, but in a marketplace like you would find today in any village in the developing world. Moreover, Jesus drank water from wells. He never once turned on a faucet or stood under a shower in a bathroom. He never washed His clothing in a washing machine. He never opened the door of a refrigerator. He never drove a car or even a bicycle for that matter. Not once did He listen to a radio, speak to someone over a phone, cook a meal on a stove, or preach through a public address system. He never watched a television show, turned on an electric lamp, or cooled off in front of an air conditioner or electric fan. He never owned a lawnmower, a lawn chair, a wristwatch, or even a pair of sunglasses. He didn't have a closet full of clothing. How could He have been happy?

6:5-14 See my comments on Matt. 14:15-21.

12:3-8 When we compare the specific details of Mary's anointing of Jesus with the anointing by an unnamed woman mentioned in all three Synoptic Gospels, it seems they are not the same incident (see Matt. 26:6-13; Mark 14:3-9; Luke 7:37-39). In this case, John highlights the hypocrisy, deception, thievery and greed of Judas, who under the pretense of concern for the poor, complained about the waste. Yet Judas actually stole from the treasury that which was meant for the poor, and we are just like him when we selfishly use for ourselves what God intends that we use for the poor. Is the money that God has entrusted to us any different than the money in Jesus' treasury?

13:27-29 Here we gain insight concerning the treasury of Jesus and His disciples. It was most commonly used for their essential needs, such as food, and to supply the essential needs of the poor. Jesus always loved His neighbor as Himself. Thus, meeting their needs was a priority. Is it not our goal to become like Him? Is that not God's goal for us? (see Rom. 8:29; Phil. 3:12).

13:34-35 This was, indeed, a new commandment, heretofore unheard. Christ's disciples are to love each other by a new standard. They are not just to love each other as themselves (as the second greatest commandment enjoins), but as He has loved them. They are not to view one another as being equal to themselves, but as being more important than themselves (see Phil. 2:3), just as Jesus did. Jesus elaborated on this theme a short time later in 15:12-14: "This is My commandment, that you love one another, just as I have loved you. Greater love has no one than this, that one lay down his life for his friends. You are My friends, if you do what I command you."

Jesus loved His friends, whom He defined as those who do what He commands, by laying down His life for them. So His disciples are to love one another by laying down their lives for one another. John reiterated this thought in his first epistle: "We know love by this, that He laid down His life for us; and we ought to lay down our lives for the brethren" (1 John 3:16).

Does such a laying down of one's life have anything to do with what one does with his money and possessions? John thought so, and continued in the very next verse, "But whoever has the world's goods, and beholds his brother in need and closes his heart against him, how does the love of God abide in him?" (1 John 3:17). Clearly then, one who has the ability to meet the pressing needs of one of Christ's disciples but "closes his heart against him," does not obey Jesus' new commandment and does not distinguish himself with the identifying mark of Christ's true disciples, as Jesus said in 13:35.

14:15 In this statement, Jesus was not excluding His commandments regarding money, possessions and stewardship. Our stewardship is a measure of our love for Him.

14:21-24 What Jesus said here is not a promise of special bonuses for Christians who love Jesus, bonuses that will not be enjoyed by those heaven-bound Christians who don't love Jesus. Rather, Jesus was talking about the benefits of being saved. All true believers love and obey Jesus (see John 3:36; 1 Cor. 16:22). Both Father and Son make their abode in every true Christian by the indwelling Spirit (see Rom. 8:9). Thus we once again see the correlation between faith and works, belief and behavior. Those who are truly born again love Jesus and are characterized by obedience to His commandments, including His commandments regarding money, possessions and stewardship.

15:12-14 See my comments on John 13:34-35.

19:23-24 From the information found here, some prosperity preachers have attempted to prove that Jesus was wealthy, because only wealthy people supposedly could afford a seamless inner garment! It is utterly amazing what significance can be found in the biblical text if one wants to prove what contradicts numerous other scriptures. Can you imagine presenting such evidence in court to prove that someone was wealthy?

With the completion of this eighth chapter, we have now studied everything that Jesus taught and lived concerning money, possessions and stewardship. Have we found evidence in any of the four Gospels that Jesus wants us to trust Him to prosper us even more so we can live in greater self-indulgence and ignore the poor multitudes and those who have never heard the gospel? No, we have found that Christ taught and lived the exact opposite. The essence of following Him is self-denial, yet millions of professing Christians have embraced a theology of selfishness that is nothing more than greed sanctified by a few out-of-context scriptures.

NINE

The Early Church Follows Jesus

Have I perhaps misinterpreted what Christ taught about money, possessions and stewardship? If I have, a study of what was taught and practiced by the apostles and early church would reveal my error. Did the apostles encourage their disciples to "believe God" for more material things so they could possess their "covenant rights" and enjoy life as "king's kids"? Did the apostles live in luxury, as do so many modern "ministers," touting their ministerial success by their wardrobes, new cars and jewelry? Were the early Christians unconcerned about the poor, believing that people's poverty is always a result of their sinful choices or lack of faith? Were they focused primarily on their careers and accumulating more material wealth so as to guarantee comfortable retirements? I suspect you already know the obvious answers to those questions.

The apostles, of course, obeyed Jesus' final commandment to "make disciples of all the nations...teaching them to observe all that [He] commanded [them]" (Matt. 28:19-20). They faithfully taught their disciples what He had taught them, including all He had commanded them regarding money, possessions and stewardship. Those disciples, being true believers in Christ, obeyed Christ's commandments, relayed through the apostles. This will have to be admitted by anyone who is honest in reading the book of Acts and the New Testament epistles, because the evidence is overwhelming.

From the very beginning, the early Christians were *devoted* to the apostles' teaching (they didn't just *listen* to it). Thus they laid down their lives for one another, sold their possessions, and laid up treasures in heaven, just as Jesus had commanded. Read the earliest description of common Christian life:

And they were continually devoting themselves to the

177

apostles' teaching and to fellowship, to the breaking of bread and to prayer...And all those who had believed were together, and had all things in common; and *they began selling their property and possessions, and were sharing them with all, as anyone might have need* (Acts 2:42-45, emphasis added).

Note that Luke, unlike many modern commentators, added no disparaging commentary to his report. We are told by some today that these early Christians were overly zealous, or were mistakenly treating capital as if it were income, thus insuring their own future poverty. Others claim, with no biblical support, that there were unusual circumstances that dictated unusual actions by the early Christians. For example, it has been claimed that there were multitudes of Jewish pilgrims in Jerusalem during the Passover who became Christians. Supposedly, they would have wanted to stay in Jerusalem to learn more about Christ, or would have found it impossible to return to their homes elsewhere, having become (to quote one theorist) "the victims of social and economic ostracism, ecclesiastical excommunication, and national disinheritance.[1] Their business enterprises must in most cases have collapsed in ruins and family bonds been heart-breakingly severed." Thus, the early Jerusalem church supposedly found itself with multitudes of unemployed, homeless persons from far-away places within its ranks.

This is, however, a matter of *great* speculation, and we must wonder why Scripture is silent about those multitudes of believing, unemployed, homeless Passover pilgrims who remained in Jerusalem after Christ's crucifixion. I find no record of multitudes believing in Jesus from the time of His crucifixion until almost two months later on the day of Pentecost, when about three-thousand people repented at Peter's preaching (see Acts 2:41). There is nothing said about any Pentecost pilgrims (much less Passover pilgrims) being unable to return to their homes in far-away places. What would have prevented them from doing so? How would they even have known the reaction of their families to their conversions had they not journeyed back home to tell them? (Incidentally, at this point in church history, it was said that the Christians enjoyed great favor with all the people; see Acts 2:47). Would not those newly-converted Pentecost pilgrims have had a strong desire to return home and tell their loved ones the good news about Jesus?[2]

All of this being so, why should we accept a theory for which there is

---

[1] Why are we more easily persuaded that someone knows what he is talking about if he uses impressive words? Rather, we should be suspicious that he is trying to replace with language what he lacks in logic and facts.

[2] I must add that the multitudes of Jews from foreign countries who gathered to witness the Pentecost miracle were not said to be *visiting* Jerusalem. Rather, it is twice stated that they *lived* in Jerusalem (see Acts 2:5, 14). If Luke meant that they permanently resided in Jerusalem, then they would not have become a burden to the church.

no scriptural basis and that contradicts simple logic? Even if this particular theory is true, how is the early church's supposed situation unique in Christian history, in light of the multitudes of very poor Christians living today in the developing world whom we can assist?

The truth is that the early Christians were simply obeying Jesus' commands to sell their possessions, lay up treasure in heaven, and love each other as He loved them. They demonstrated a "faith working through love" (Gal. 5:6). Because "God's love abided in them," they were not "closing their hearts against brethren in need," as the apostle John no doubt taught them (see 1 John 3:17). They were fulfilling Jesus' prayer that they might be one (see John 17:20-23), caring for each other. The world knew they were Christ's disciples by the love they had for one another (see John 13:35). It is just that simple.

This was not a short-lived phenomenon in the early church. It continued to be a regular feature of New Testament life. For example, two chapters later, Luke tells us,

> And the congregation of those who believed were of one heart and soul; and not one of them claimed that anything belonging to him was his own; but all things were common property to them.... and abundant grace was upon them all. For there was not a needy person among them, for all who were owners of land or houses would sell them and bring the proceeds of the sales, and lay them at the apostles' feet; and they would be distributed to each, as any had need (Acts 4:32-35).

I cannot help but wonder how many professing North American Christians, if they read in a newspaper the above description of a modern religious group, would immediately conclude that sect was a dangerous cult?

The unity of the early church included an economic unity, so that there was no needy person among them. The reason was because believers who owned land that they didn't need, or more than one house, sold it in order to supply the pressing, essential needs of other believers. This attitude of love and generosity was manifested not only among the wealthy of the church, but among all the members: "Not one of them claimed that anything belonging to him was his own; but all things were common property to them" (Acts 4:32). They were true believers and thus obedient followers of Christ, striving to keep His commandments and enter by the narrow gate (see Matt. 7:13-14). Keep in mind that none of them owned cars, electric appliances, lawn mowers, and so on. For the most part, they owned only what people in modern developing nations own.

Note also that the proceeds of what the early disciples sold was laid at the apostles' feet. Those giving knew that these men who unfailingly modeled Christian contentment, stewardship and generosity could be trusted to administer the distribution.

Let us continue to explore what the remainder of the New Testament teaches regarding money, possessions and stewardship. This chapter, like the previous one, is so written so that it can be used as a reference to everything relevant to stewardship found in Acts and the epistles. You will need to have your Bible open so you can reference the relevant passages before reading my commentary.

Acts

2:38 When Peter called for repentance here and in 3:19, are we to think that the repentance of which he spoke was any different from the repentance of which John the Baptist and Jesus spoke? When John's convicted audience asked what they should do to demonstrate their repentance, practically every specific thing he told them to do involved money (see Luke 3:10-14). Are we to think that the repentance of which Peter had in mind was unrelated to the sins of greed and covetousness?

2:45-46 We shouldn't conclude that every Christian who owned only one house sold his home to give the proceeds to charity. Only those who owned houses (plural) sold their extra homes (see 4:34; see also Acts 2:46; 5:42; 12:12; 20:20; 21:8 for proof that Christians continued to own houses). A home provides the necessity of shelter, a place to share meals, have church gatherings and house strangers (see Matt. 25:43).

4:36-5:11 The sins of Ananias and Sapphira were lying and hypocrisy. They publicly claimed that they were giving all the proceeds from the sale of their property. It is likely, however, that some degree of greed was what motivated them to lie. If they had kept back a portion of the proceeds for themselves in order to meet some personal pressing need, why would they have lied about the selling price? They would simply have told the apostles that they were giving only a portion of the selling price, as they themselves were suffering need just as were the beneficiaries of their kindness. Wanting, however, to appear that they were just as generous as all the other Christians, they conspired to cover their selfishness. Their hypocrisy cost them their lives, and God's judgment upon them had its intended effect: "Great fear came upon the whole church, and upon all who heard of these things" (Acts 5:11). They received a new revelation regarding God's holiness. You have "heard these things" as well. Has "great fear" come upon you? If not, why not?

How are we to interpret Peter's questions to Ananias regarding his land and the proceeds of its sale, ""While it remained unsold, did it not remain your own? And after it was sold, was it not under your control?" (Acts 5:4)? Does this prove, as some say, that Ananias had no obligation as a follower of Christ to sell his land, and once sold, had no obligation to give any of the proceeds away?

In light of Christ's commandments regarding self-denial, loving fellow believers, selling possessions and laying up treasures in heaven rather than on earth, it seems unlikely that Peter was telling Ananias that he could do whatever he wanted with his land or the money gained from its sale, regardless of Christ's commandments. Perhaps Peter simply pointing out that Ananias was responsible for his actions. It was Ananias' land and the proceeds of its sale were completely under his control, thus he stood condemned, and had no legitimate excuse for his actions. Or perhaps Peter was exposing Ananias' deception, namely in how the value of his land changed between the time he owned it, sold it, and brought the proceeds to the apostles. Or perhaps he was pointing out Ananias' contradiction in his selling his land *supposedly* in obedience to God but then attempting to deceive the entire church regarding his generosity. Since he had supposedly decided to sell it out of conviction to obey Christ's commandments (as were all the rest who sold their land), he was also just as obligated not to lie to the Holy Spirit and the entire church regarding the price of the land.

Even if none of those interpretations of Peter's words to Ananias are correct, does any other interpretation annul everything that Christ taught regarding stewardship? Are we to believe that Peter was attempting to convey to the church, "None of you has any obligation to sell land that you don't really need, even though Christ commanded us not to lay up earthly treasures"?

6:1-6 From the beginning, the church was involved in meeting the pressing needs of the poor, in this case, feeding impoverished widows. Although the apostles knew they had a higher calling, they did not neglect to see that the daily serving of food was properly administrated.

8:3 Paul ravaged the church by "entering house after house." Again we see that those Christians who owned one house didn't sell their houses to give the proceeds to charity. They needed places to live. We also note that the early Christians didn't live together in a commune. The "salt of the earth" was sprinkled throughout society for maximum seasoning. (For other references to houses owned by Christians, see Acts 2:46; 5:42; 12:12; 20:20; 21:8).

8:9-24 We are tempted to think that Peter overreacted to Simon's request to purchase the authority to impart the Holy Spirit. Peter sternly rebuked him, warning Simon that he was in danger of perishing with his silver, and creating doubts in his mind that the Lord would forgive him. Did Peter really believe what he said to Simon? Apparently, yes.

9:36-39 Tabitha was an exemplary disciple, "abounding in deeds of kindness and charity, which she continually did" (Acts 10:36). She was no "Sunday Christian," and her faith in Jesus was expressed by her practical deeds of love, which required not an occasional, but a regular expenditure of her time and money. One facet of her ministry was the making of clothing for poor widows. Jesus eventually said to her, "I was…naked, and you clothed Me" (Matt. 25:35-36).

10:1-4 Luke specifically sites Cornelius' continual prayers and his generous giving to the poor as the evidence that he was devout and feared God. The angel who appeared to him declared that God had taken note of both. How is it that Cornelius, as a Gentile without the indwelling Holy Spirit, was more devout than many professing Christians, who pray only on Sundays and give nothing to the poor?

11:27-30 Note that it was not just a few of the disciples who contributed to the relief of the brethren living in Judea, but all of the disciples who had means to help. Every believer in Antioch gave in proportion to his resources. Keep in mind that the early church did not subscribe to the modern theory that one can be a believer in Christ without being a disciple of Christ. In fact, it was in Antioch where "the disciples were first called Christians" (Acts 11:26). Thus, when Luke tells us that every disciple made a contribution according to his means, he was not referring to a special group of very committed believers, distinct from the "regular" Christians. He was referring to all the Christians. Because the Christians in Antioch were true believers in Jesus, they loved other believers and demonstrated their love. Jesus would one day say to them, "I was hungry, and you gave Me something to eat" (Matt. 25:35).

12:12 Here is another example of a believer who didn't sell her home to give away the proceeds. She put it to good use for God's kingdom as a gathering place for the church to pray. It was also probably used for regular church gatherings as well.

17:30 Paul, like Peter, Jesus, and John the Baptist, preached the necessity of repentance for salvation (see also 20:21). Paul also believed that repentance involved much more than just a change of mind about who Jesus is. He later testified that he "kept declaring both to those of Damascus first, and also at Jerusalem and then throughout all the region of Judea, and even to the Gentiles, that they should repent and turn to God, *performing deeds appropriate to repentance*" (Acts 26:20, emphasis added). Would such appropriate deeds include anything to do with what one did with his money? Paul clearly believed that one had to repent of greed and covetousness to be saved, as he wrote to the Corinthians that covetous people would be excluded from God's kingdom, just as would be idolaters, homosexuals, drunkards, and thieves (see also Eph. 5:3-6).

182

19:18-19 Some treasures should not be sold and the proceeds given to the poor. Don't sell your music and movie collection if the contents might cause others to stumble. Dispose of them.

20:33-35 Speaking to the spiritual leaders of Ephesus, Paul reminded them of the example he had set before them, an example worthy of their imitation. He had shown that his motives were pure. He did not desire to possess what belonged to others. Rather, he desired to give to others what belonged to him, proven by the fact that his own labor helped provide for the needs of his traveling band. The Ephesian elders should likewise live to serve rather than to be served, remembering what Christ said, recorded only here in Scripture: "It is more blessed to give than to receive" (Acts 20:35).

24:17 Even as Paul journeyed to Jerusalem, knowing that "bonds and afflictions" (Acts 20:23) awaited him there, he remembered the poor, bringing alms with him.

24:26 Felix, a lover of money, hoped for a bribe from Paul in exchange for his release. This does not prove that Paul was wealthy, as some want us to believe, especially in the light of so many other scriptures that indicate otherwise (see, for example, 1 Cor. 4:11). Felix must have noted that Paul had many friends and supporters who ministered to him (see 24:23). This was a prisoner whose loyal friends would surely pool their money in order to gain his release.

28:30 Just because Paul lived in his own rented quarters in Rome does not prove he was wealthy, as some would like us to think. Because someone has the ability to rent a house, does that make him rich? Paul was obviously assisted by the brethren in Rome, to whom he had previously written a letter which revealed that he knew quite a few of them even before he arrived (see Rom. 16:1-15). This scripture simply reveals that God supplied Paul's needs.

Romans

1:28-32 Paul listed the sin of greed, along with many other sins, as plain evidence that God has given people over to depraved minds because they did not see fit to acknowledge Him any longer. Clearly, Paul did not believe that greedy people are saved people.

12:13 Here Paul lists "contributing to the needs of the saints" and "practicing hospitality" as being an expected practice of all Christians. He must have known what Jesus said in Matthew 25:31-46.

12:19-21 Not only are we not to take revenge upon our enemies, but as followers of Christ, we are to do good to them, loving them as ourselves, which includes meeting their pressing, essential needs. Yet professing Christians today ignore the essential needs of their own spiritual family around the world!

15:25-32 The early Christians did not excuse themselves from helping fellow believers who lived far away from them, as do so many modern professing Christians. The saints in Macedonia and Achaia entrusted Paul with an offering for the poor believers in Jerusalem, a thousand miles away.

So much of benevolence money that American churches distribute helps local people who are wealthy by the world's standards, and who are facing financial difficulties only because they are unwilling to lower their standard of living. In some cases, it is because they will not forsake their sins. As a pastor in past years, I've often been tempted to ask those who request benevolence help, "Has it gotten so bad yet that you've had to cancel your cable-TV subscription, quit smoking, drive a used car and no longer have pets?"

1 Corinthians

4:8 If Paul's words here are proof that the Corinthians had "applied God's prosperity principles and reaped an abundant financial harvest" (as some claim), we would have to wonder why he didn't apply those supposed principles and deliver himself from his own present poverty. Just three verses later he wrote, "To this present hour we are both hungry and thirsty, and are poorly clothed, and are roughly treated, and are homeless" (1 Cor. 4:11). So what did Paul mean in this verse?

Clearly, pride had crept in among the Corinthian believers. Having received an abundance of God's gracious gifts (see 1:7), they boasted about them, revealing their arrogance. They regarded themselves as "superior" (4:7). By their own estimation they were like kings who were "already filled," as well as "rich...prudent...strong...[and] distinguished" (4:8-10). All of this revealed their pride.

Paul, however, did not consider them to be "superior" (4:7), and he reminded them that they didn't have any reason to boast, because their blessings were "received," not earned (see 4:6-7). Neither did he consider them to be kings, although it would be great if they were, he mused, so that in light of his current situation he could reign with them (see 4:8-13)!

Clearly, Paul's purpose in this portion of his letter was to admonish the Corinthian Christians to repent of their arrogance and imitate him (see 4:16).

5:9-13 Paul could not have made it more clear that covetous people, just like idolaters, swindlers, drunkards, revilers, and those who are immoral, are not true Christians regardless of their professing to be. They are only "so-called" (5:11) Christians. Such hypocrites should be excommunicated from the church, and true Christians should not associate with them.

The question is, *How can we know if a person is covetous or not?* If covetousness is only an attitude of the heart, as so many think, then there would be no way of identifying those who are guilty of this sin and thus worthy of excommunication. Paul, however, obviously believed that covetousness was manifested by a person's actions, and that it could be identified just as could drunkenness, idolatry and immorality. Keep in mind that the word translated *covetous* here is translated elsewhere as *greedy*. A person can be identified as greedy or covetous by his actions. What actions characterize greedy and covetous people?

Certainly, one who "has the world's goods, and beholds his brother in need and closes his heart against him" (1 John 3:17) reveals his greed by his actions. John declared that God's love does not dwell in such a person. Certainly, he does not love his brother as Christ commanded, nor does he possess the mark of the true disciple of Christ (see John 13:34-25). Did not the actions of the "goats" of which Jesus spoke in Matthew 25, who ignored the pressing, essential needs of His brethren, reveal their selfish, greedy hearts?

In the early church, those who had the resources, but who did not relieve the sufferings of impoverished brethren, were marked as covetous or greedy, and deserving of excommunication. They were obviously not true believers, showing no love for the brethren. If such discipline were practiced in the modern church, it would significantly thin the ranks.

6:9-11 Repeating the message of 5:9-13, Paul emphatically states that no unrighteous person shall inherit the kingdom of God. Clearly, Paul was speaking of those who lacked *practical* righteousness, not imputed, legal righteousness, because he immediately listed certain examples of unrighteous people, including the covetous. They, just like fornicators, idolaters, adulterers, effeminate, homosexuals, thieves, drunkards, revilers and swindlers, will not enter heaven.

Some have theorized that Paul's phrase, "inherit the kingdom of God," is not a reference to entering heaven, but to experiencing God's best on the earth (or something similar). Supposedly then, some people who don't inherit God's kingdom on *earth* will inherit God's kingdom in *heaven*.

This theory is easily disproved, however, by considering Paul's use of the same phrase later in the same epistle. In 15:50, Paul writes, "Now I say this, brethren, that flesh and blood cannot *inherit the kingdom of God*; nor does the perishable inherit the imperishable" (emphasis added). Paul is clearly speaking of entering heaven in the future, as he goes on to reveal how true believers will receive new, glorified bodies "at the last trumpet" (see 15:51-53).

Paul probably borrowed the expression, *inherit the kingdom*, from Jesus, who used it in reference to entering heaven. He told of the future judgment of the sheep and goats, when He will say to those who loved His brethren, "*Inherit the kingdom* prepared for you from the foundation of the world" (Matt. 25:34, emphasis added).

9:7-14 The overriding message of these verses is summed up in verse 14: "So also the Lord directed those who proclaim the gospel to get their living from the gospel." True ministers of the true gospel should be supported financially by those who have received the good news through them. Those who claim to believe the gospel but have no interest in supporting those who brought them the gospel or those who are spreading the gospel are fooling themselves. They don't really believe the gospel.

Although Paul had the divine right to make his living from the Corinthians' support while he preached the gospel to them, he waived his right so that he would "cause no hindrance to the gospel" (9:12). That is, because he received no money from the Corinthian Christians, no one could rightfully accuse him of preaching just for personal financial gain, using that judgment as an excuse to dismiss his message. Paul did, however, receive money from Christians in other cities while he was in Corinth according to his own testimony (see 2 Cor. 11:7-9).

Every minister should have the same concern as Paul, lest the gospel be hindered by his financial dealings. He should live humbly enough so that no one can justifiably accuse him of being a minister for the sake of gaining money. Even if he is well paid, he should live humbly and use the excess to be a blessing.

10:6-8 These verses are a further warning against greed, idolatry and sexual immorality, the practice of which Paul had previously declared will exclude one from inheriting God's kingdom (see 1 Cor. 6:9-10).

Paul's admonition against "craving evil things" is probably a reference to the story found in the eleventh chapter of the book of Numbers, when the Israelites, not satisfied with the manna God provided each day, wept for meat. Angered by their complaining, God promised to send meat the next day that would last for a month, "until it comes out of your nostrils and becomes loathsome to you; because you have rejected the Lord" (Num. 11:20). The next day, God sent quail that fell in piles all around the Israelites' camp about three feet deep, so that the Israelites spent the next two days gathering them. Scripture tells us that the person who gathered the least gathered 110 bushels of quail (see Num. 11:32). We then read, "While the meat was still between their teeth, before it was chewed, the anger of the Lord was kindled against the people, and the Lord struck the people with a very severe plague. So the name of that place was called Kibroth-hattaavah [meaning, 'the graves of greediness'], because there they buried the people who had been greedy" (Num. 11:33-34).

God killed people who were greedy, and their greed only related to food. Paul wrote, "These things happened as examples for us" (10:6).

13:3 Here we learn that it is possible to give all one's possessions to feed the poor but not have love. Such a person must be motivated by some form of selfishness, perhaps to receive the praises of people. Thus we see the importance of checking our motives when we assist those with pressing needs. Giving in secret is a good way to avoid selfish giving.

16:1-4 Paul instructed each of the Christians of Galatia and Corinth to "put aside and save, as he may prosper" on behalf of a collection for the poor believers in Jerusalem. This indicates that he was not writing to wealthy people who could liquidate some of their assets in order to give, but to those who lived week by week from their earnings. Their "prospering" consisted of what they earned above what they needed each week when the collection was made. To "prosper" in this context certainly didn't mean that one had an abundance of wealth, but simply that one had more than he needed, thus enabling him to share with others.

I mention this because a favorite proof text for some prosperity preachers is 3 John 2. There the apostle John wrote to Gaius, "I pray that in all respects you may *prosper* and be in good health, just as your soul prospers" (emphasis added). John was not praying that Gaius would become fabulously wealthy so that he could disobey Jesus and lay up earthly treasures for himself. Rather, he was praying that God would bless Gaius with more than he needed so that he could continue to experience the joy of giving and laying up heavenly treasures. What a blessing it is to have more than you need in order to be an agent of God's blessing. As Jesus said, "It is more blessed to give than to receive" (Acts 20:35).

Note that this was an offering for poor Christians, a common practice in the early church (see Acts 11:27-30; 24:17; Rom. 15:25-28; 1 Cor. 16:1-4; 2 Cor. 8-9), a true expression of Christian love. So often we find a portion of 1 Cor. 16:1-4 quoted on church offering envelopes, where the collections rarely benefit the poor in the least.

2 Corinthians

6:10 Here Paul describes himself and his associates as being "poor" and "having nothing," hardly the picture of material wealth. Yet, although he was poor, Paul had the satisfaction of "making many rich." He obviously did not mean that he made other people materially rich, but spiritually and eternally rich, a much more significant wealth. If Paul had somehow been able to make others materially rich, we would have to wonder why he didn't make himself materially rich as well, if by no other means, at least by the offerings he received from all the people he made materially rich.

Just two chapters later in this epistle, Paul used a similar expression that is often used as a proof text for modern prosperity preachers. In 8:9 we read, "For you know the grace of our Lord Jesus Christ, that though He was rich, yet for your sake He became poor, that you through His poverty might become rich."

Some prosperity preachers claim that it is material poverty and material wealth that Paul had in mind throughout this entire verse. That is, Jesus was *materially* rich in heaven, but He became *materially* poor in His incarnation, living with little all His earthly life. The result of His material poverty is that we can supposedly become materially rich. Bigger houses, more expensive clothing, and exotic vacations are now ours to be claimed by faith because Jesus became poor that we might become rich.

It is certainly true that Paul was speaking of material wealth when he wrote that Jesus was rich but became poor. We could think of Jesus as being very wealthy in heaven, walking on streets of gold, but becoming very poor by comparison during His incarnation.

There is certainly good reason to doubt, however, that earthly, material wealth was the benefit Paul had in mind when he wrote of our becoming rich because of Christ's poverty. Such an interpretation stands in contradiction to its immediate biblical context (not to mention the entire context of the New Testament). Paul was writing to the Corinthians in chapters 8 and 9 to admonish them to participate in an offering for poor Christians. If Jesus became poor so that Christians might become materially rich on earth, why were there any poor Christians who needed an offering? Let them claim their gospel right as "king's kids"! And why did Paul describe himself as being poor in 6:10? Why didn't he also claim his rightful, earthly, material wealth that Jesus made possible?

Also keep in mind that just because Paul was writing about material wealth or poverty in one part of a sentence, that doesn't prove that he was talking about material wealth in another part of the same sentence. For example, Jesus Himself said to the poor believers in Smyrna, "I know your tribulation and your *poverty* (but you are *rich*)" (Rev. 2:9, emphasis added). Who would debate that Jesus was saying that the Christians in Smyrna were material poor and also materially rich? No, Jesus was saying that they were materially poor but spiritually rich, and He said it all in one sentence.

When Paul wrote that Jesus became poor that we, through His poverty, might become rich, his meaning was similar to what he wrote just 33 verses earlier, when he said that he himself was poor, yet made others rich. Jesus, because of His incarnation and death on the cross (during which He lost even His clothing, the ultimate poverty), has provided spiritual and eternal riches for us beyond our dreams. So too, Paul, impoverished as he was at times, through His ministry was able to make many people spiritually wealthy through the gospel.

8:1—9:15 (I have fully commented on 8:9 in the previous comments regarding 6:10.) These two chapters beautifully reveal a full and balanced picture of Christian stewardship. An honest reading here exposes many modern myths.

The occasion was the receiving of an offering by Paul from the churches on behalf of poor believers. He began by informing the Corinthians of what had recently happened among the churches of Macedonia. Even though they were suffering "an ordeal of affliction" as well as "deep poverty" (8:2), they had given liberally. In fact, by God's grace, and without being pressured, they had given even "beyond their ability" (8:3), to the degree of "begging...with much entreaty for the favor of participation in the support of the saints" (8:4). The Macedonian Christians were the ultimate cheerful givers, and Paul expected that the Corinthian Christians would follow their example.

Paul stressed that one's giving is limited by his resources (see 8:12) but that one's responsibility is also determined by his resources (see 8:13), twice using a word that is almost anathema in capitalistic vocabulary, the word *equality* (see 8:13-15). If one Christian has abundance, he should use it to supply another Christian's need (see 8:14). And if that formerly-poor Christian prospers while the formerly-prosperous one becomes needy, their roles should then be reversed (see 8:14). It amounts to nothing more than "loving our neighbors as ourselves" and "doing unto others as we would have them do unto us" (see Mark 12:31; Luke 6:31). This is perhaps the most foundational principle of Christian stewardship, yet one that professing Christians in wealthy countries have ignored. God loves all His children; thus, those with more should share with those who have less, and it's just that simple.

Paul also understood the need for accountability in the administration of such benevolence projects, and he was careful to insure that the offering he received would be used for the purpose for which it was collected. A number of men who had proven their trustworthiness would be involved in the project (see 8:16-23). Financial accountability is of utmost importance in corporate offerings to the poor, otherwise people are given an excuse to cling to their treasures, claiming that their potential gifts might be mishandled.

The Corinthians had previously promised a "bountiful gift" (9:5), which would of course be made possible only by bountiful giving. Thus Paul cautioned against covetousness (or better translated greed)[3] that might affect the Corinthian's giving (see 9:5). Here again, we clearly see that covetousness/greed is not just an attitude; it is an attitude revealed by actions. If the Corinthians yielded to greed, they would give less. Their selfish *attitude* would affect their *actions*.

---

[3] The word translated *covetousness* here is translated *greed* in Luke 12:15; Rom. 1:29; Eph. 5:3; Col. 3:5; 1 Thes. 2:5; and 2 Pet. 2:3, 14.

Paul continued with a warning to those who might yield to greed and a promise to those who would be generous: "Now this I say, he who sows sparingly shall also reap sparingly; and he who sows bountifully shall also reap bountifully" (9:6).

Paul was not revealing "divine secrets for abundant prosperity," encouraging his readers to "sow a big financial seed and reap abundant riches" so that they could then own many possessions and enjoy a lavish lifestyle, as some prosperity preachers might want us to believe. If he was, then he was promoting the very thing he was warning against in 9:5, that is, greed. If people give just so they can grow rich and have many possessions, that is nothing more than giving from a motive of selfishness. Giving to get is hypocritical—it is selfishness under the guise of love.

Thus, the reason one should want to "sow bountifully" and thus "reap bountifully" is so one can "sow even more bountifully," blessing more people. This truth Paul plainly repeats three times in the next few verses:

> And God is able to make all grace abound to you, that always having all sufficiency in everything, you *may have an abundance for every good deed*; as it is written, "He scattered abroad, he gave to the poor, His righteousness abides forever." Now He who supplies seed to the sower and bread for food, *will supply and multiply your seed for sowing* and increase the harvest of your righteousness; you will be enriched in everything *for all liberality*, which through us is producing thanksgiving to God (9:8-11; emphasis added).

Once a sower reaps, he then must decide what to do with his harvest. If he still has more than he needs, and there are still others with pressing needs, then there is no doubt what he should do. His former self-denial certainly wouldn't give him the right to be greedy now. The whole reason to reap is not so one may lay up earthly treasures in disobedience to Christ, but so that one may sow some more.

What constitutes sowing that is "sparing" or "bountiful"? That, of course, is different for each person. The widow who put her two copper coins into the treasury gave more than all the rich people who put in large gifts, according to Jesus (see Mark 12:41-44). She "sowed bountifully" while they "sowed sparingly," even though their gifts were much larger. What impresses God is self-denial. Bountiful and sparing sowing are determined by what one keeps.

Another reason the Corinthians should give liberally was because it was an opportunity for them to show their faith by their works. Their giving was an indication of their "obedience to [their] confession of the gospel of Christ" (9:13). Those who believe the gospel of Christ act like it, obeying Christ and loving the brethren.

Finally, Paul also instructed each of the Corinthians to "do just as he has purposed in his heart; not grudgingly or under compulsion; for God loves a cheerful giver" (9:7). This verse has often been ripped from its context and twisted to relieve the consciences of selfish people. They are told, "God wants only what you can give cheerfully, so let that be your gauge. Only give what you can give without grudging." Consequently, greedy people give little or nothing, demonstrating no self-denial or love, and think God approves, since He doesn't want what they can't give cheerfully.

Paul, however, was not trying to make greedy people think that God is comfortable with their greed, as the context so clearly reveals (see 9:5). He was trying to help each person consider what is in his heart. If one is giving under compulsion or grudgingly, he is not giving because he loves needy brethren. By the same token, the reason God "loves a cheerful giver" is because a cheerful giver is motivated by love for God and neighbor. He finds joy in sacrificing on behalf of those with pressing needs because he loves them. The one who gives grudgingly or under compulsion, however, reveals a greedy heart, and thus gives hypocritically, because he is doing what his heart would prefer not to do. Thus, it would be better for him not to give at all, but let him not think that God approves of him in either case. God wants him to repent of his selfishness, be transformed by His grace, and become a cheerful giver who denies himself with joy. God, and only God, can turn greedy people into cheerful givers. They then become imitators of Him, who gave sacrificially from a heart of grace and love (see 9:15).

10:14-16 Paul expressed his hope to preach the gospel in the future, with the help of the Corinthian Christians, beyond the regions of Corinth. This is a perfect example of church/missionary partnership, working together to fulfill the Great Commission.

11:7-9 While Paul was preaching the gospel in Corinth, he received no money from them, as we previously learned reading 1 Cor. 8:6-15. This fact was apparently used against him by certain false apostles (see 11:1-4, 12-15, 20-33) to somehow undermine the legitimacy of his ministry (see also 12:11-18).

11:27 Reluctantly boasting of his devotion to Christ in order to authenticate his apostleship and win back the Corinthians' full affections, Paul mentioned some of the hardships he had endured. They included temporary hunger and thirst as well as exposure to the elements, all for the sake of the gospel. If Paul were alive today, he would be disdained in many "Christian" circles as lacking faith for prosperity.

12:11-18 Again, the issue of Paul's not receiving money from the Corinthians surfaced. From his repeated defense, it once more seems that this fact was somehow being used against him by certain false apostles. We don't know the particulars, however.

Paul promised that on his next visit he would again not be a burden to the Corinthian believers (see 12:14). The reason, he said, is because he wasn't seeking to gain their money, but was seeking them (see 12:14). He also added, "Children are not responsible to save up for their parents, but parents for their children" (12:14).

This principle and practice is certainly endorsed by Paul through his using it to explain and justify his own actions. Thus, Christian parents may rest assured that they have a legitimate reason to save some money on their children's behalf if possible, to help them get a start in life. This can be considered part of parents' God-given responsibility to provide for their own children. On the other hand, parents sometimes foster their children's irresponsibility by providing too much for them. A balance is needed.

Galatians

2:10 Considering the context of the first two chapters of Galatians (Paul's defense of his gospel of grace), this verse almost seems out of place. It is not, however, because Peter, James, John and Paul all believed that ministering to the poor was an essential part of what it meant to follow Christ.

3:10-14 These verses are often used as proof texts for prosperity preachers. Before we consider their reasoning, however, let us not forget everything we've learned from pertinent New Testament passages already, as well as what we just read in Galatians 2:10 about the importance of ministering to the poor. Also, let us keep in mind that the same man who wrote these verses also wrote that no greedy/covetous person will inherit the kingdom of God (see Eph. 5:3-6).

According to what is written in the Mosaic Law, anyone who didn't keep the Law was "under a curse" (3:10). Paul directly quoted the last verse in Deuteronomy 27 to prove this fact (see 3:10).

In the very next verses in Deuteronomy, in fact in all of chapter 28, Moses told the Israelites the specific blessings that would be enjoyed by those who kept the Law (see Deut. 28:1-14), as well as the specific curses that would be suffered by lawbreakers (see Deut. 28:15-68). The specific curses certainly included material poverty (see Deut. 28:17-18, 29-31, 33, 38-40, 42-44, 47-48, 51-63), as well as sickness, disease, war, famine, and deportation to a foreign land.

Paul wrote, "Christ redeemed us from the curse of the Law, having become a curse for us" (Gal. 3:13). Prosperity preachers argue that, since we've been redeemed from the Law's curse, we've been redeemed from the curse of poverty that is part of the Law's curse.

I have no objection to such teaching, as long as we are talking about being redeemed from what the *Bible* refers to as poverty as opposed to what North Americans refer to as poverty. If we will do that, then Jesus taught the very same thing, promising His followers that God will supply the needs of His children, supplying their food and covering (see Matt. 6:25-34). Let us not overlook, however, the fact that Jesus only promised to supply the needs of those who sought first His kingdom, which certainly includes obeying everything He commanded regarding stewardship. Thus, those who attempt to claim God's promise to supply their needs while neglecting what He said about stewardship are fooling themselves.

Now back to our text. If Paul was saying that we are redeemed from the curses promised to law-breakers in Deuteronomy 28, then we must first ask if we are suffering those curses. Specifically, are any of us suffering the kind of poverty described in Deuteronomy 28:17-18, 29-31, 33, 38-40, 42-44, 47-48, 51-63? Very few, if any of us, are suffering anything close to what is described there. Most people in North America, even those who are unsaved, would identify more with the blessings of prosperity described in Deuteronomy 28:4-5, 8, 11-13. Why then do we imagine that we need to claim our redemption from the Law's curse of poverty if we aren't experiencing that curse, but are already enjoying the blessings?

Prosperity preachers sometimes attempt to show a correlation between the Israelites when they were delivered from Egypt and New Testament Christians, pointing out how God prospered the Israelites by their plundering of the Egyptians. Thus, we too, should supposedly expect abundant wealth now that we've been delivered from the kingdom of darkness.

Are we, however, really economically comparable to slaves prior to our salvation? North American Christians, already extremely wealthy by the world's standards, are more comparable to the Egyptians, who became rich at the expense of the slavery of others. We, above all people on earth, should be content as well as generous, holding so much of the world's wealth in our hands. For us to "believe God" for more wealth so we can live in greater self-indulgence must be reprehensible in God's eyes.

Prosperity preachers also want to convince us that "the blessing of Abraham," of which Paul wrote in 3:14, is another promise that God will make us rich. Because God made Abraham rich, if we receive "the blessing of Abraham" that is promised to the Gentiles, we will also become rich. *Abraham's Blessings are Mine* is a favorite song and sermon topic.

I must wonder, however, why these preachers don't claim that they will live in a tent, like Abraham did all of his life (see Gen. 12:8; 13:3, 18; 18:1-2, 6, 9-10). Or why they don't claim that they will have a child in their old age, also like Abraham, since Abraham's blessings are theirs!

In reality, the "blessing of Abraham" of which Paul wrote, is a reference to God's promise to Abraham that in his seed "all the nations of the earth [would] be blessed" (Gen. 22:18), as the context reveals (see 3:8-9, 16). That singular seed, as Paul explained in 3:16, is Christ, and everyone who is in

Him is truly blessed in many ways. Thus, in 3:14, Paul was only describing how Christ, who became the curse that redeemed us from the Law's curse, fulfilled God's promise to Abraham that all the nations would be blessed in his seed.

Two things I have often observed about those who follow the teaching of the prosperity preachers.

One is that they usually aren't very prosperous at all, but maintain some appearance of prosperity through borrowing money. Yet, not having to borrow is one of the facets of the prosperity that God promised Israel (see Deut. 28:12). The primary reason such people borrow is because of their lack of contentment with what they possess, and because of the desire to appear prosperous, which is nothing more than pride. I found that when I became content with what God gave me, I was soon out of debt, and I was enabled to give more. If I own an eight-year-old car debt-free worth $3,000, and someone else drives a one-year-old car worth $20,000 on which they owe $23,000, who is more prosperous?

Second, a small percentage of the disciples of prosperity preachers are indeed wealthy by American standards, and they live luxuriously. This is often because greedy people are attracted to teaching that they think will help them become even wealthier. These people will agree to tithe (which requires little if any self-denial on their part), but they can only be motivated to do so by the promise of a big return on their giving. Every financial achievement they consider a direct blessing from God (in spite of the fact that nonbelievers receive the same "blessings' when they put forth the same effort), which in turn seals their deception to a greater degree. These kinds of people are in for a rude awakening when they stand before Christ's judgment seat.

The primary people who really get rich as a result of modern prosperity preaching are the prosperity preachers themselves, who are always encouraging people to sow financial seeds into their ministries, promising them riches in return.

5:14 God clearly stated the standard by which we are to love our neighbors: as ourselves. Some have twisted this commandment, teaching that it is, first of all, a commandment to love ourselves, because we must first love ourselves if we are to love our neighbor as ourselves. Therefore, we must work on loving ourselves more. This interpretation effectively nullifies the very purpose for the commandment.

Paul once said that husbands should "love their own wives as their own bodies" (Eph. 5:28). He certainly wasn't trying to convince husbands to work on first loving their own bodies so that they could then really love their wives. Rather, he was stating what is obvious, that all husbands naturally love their own bodies, which is why they take care of them. Likewise, they should love their wives just as they naturally love their own bodies. This becomes obvious in the very next verse, where Paul says, "For no one ever hated his own flesh, but nourishes and cherishes it" (Eph. 5:29).

So, too, God knows that people naturally love themselves. Self-interest is endemic. All people are very much wrapped up in their own comfort, fulfillment, happiness and so on. No one needs to work on loving himself more, regardless of what today's pop psychologists want us to believe. The whole problem with the world is that people *only* love themselves, and they don't love their neighbors. This is called *sin*.

Thus, God commands us to love others as we love ourselves, being interested in their fulfillment and happiness as we naturally are in our own. If we love our neighbor as ourselves, will that affect what we do with our money and possessions?

5:22-23 If one is manifesting the fruit of the Spirit, particularly love, kindness, goodness and self-control, will it have any affect on what he does with his money and possessions?

6:2 The phrase, *the law of Christ*, is found only twice in the New Testament, here and in 1 Corinthians 9:21. In both cases, it is clear that the law of Christ is something that Christians are supposed to obey. It seems reasonable to conclude that the law of Christ consists of everything Jesus commanded, just as the Law of Moses consists of everything Moses commanded. Jesus told His apostles to make disciples, teaching them to obey everything He had commanded them (see Matt. 28:19-20).

The Law of Moses can be summarized by the commandment to love one's neighbor as one's self, or to treat others as you want to be treated (see Matt. 7:12; Rom. 13:10; Gal. 5:14). Perhaps the law of Christ can also be summarized by His commandment to love each other as He has loved us (see John 13:34). Those who bear the burdens of fellow believers are certainly fulfilling this law, imitating Christ's love for all of us.

Since His love for His own is the standard by which we are to love each other, may I point out that there is no evidence that Jesus enjoyed a higher standard of living than His apostles. He shared with them what was His, and their needs were met from a common treasury (see John 12:6; 13:29). He loved them as Himself, of course, perfectly obedient to the second greatest commandment. If we obey the law of Christ, will we not share our material substance with our impoverished brothers and sisters in Christ, bearing their financial burdens?

6:6-10 What did Paul mean when he wrote, "For the one who sows to his own flesh shall from the flesh reap corruption, but the one who sows to the Spirit shall from the Spirit reap eternal life"? (6:8). What is the "seed" that we sow into these soils of flesh and Spirit? What is the "corruption" that is reaped from sowing to the flesh? And how is it that "eternal life" is reaped by sowing to the Spirit?

These questions can be answered by considering the immediate context. Paul wrote in the previous chapter of the battle between the flesh and Spirit that every Christian faces: "But I say, walk by the Spirit, and you will not carry out the desire of the flesh. For the flesh sets its desire against the Spirit, and the Spirit against the flesh; for these are in opposition to one another, so that you may not do the things that you please" (Gal. 5:16-17).

Paul continued by describing the "deeds of the flesh," which included "immorality...idolatry...strife...drunkenness" and so on, warning that "those who practice such things shall not inherit the kingdom of God" (Gal. 5:21). Obviously, if Christians face a battle between the flesh and Spirit, then it is possible for them to yield to the flesh, practicing the very sins against which Paul warned. The result could ultimately be that they would not inherit the kingdom of God. That is precisely why Paul was warning the Galatian Christians (see Gal. 5:21).

Of course, those who believe, contrary to Scripture,[4] that a truly saved person could never forfeit his salvation have difficulty accepting this interpretation. And since they can't argue against the fact that all Christians face the battle of the Spirit and flesh, nor can they debate that those who practice the deeds of the flesh will not inherit God's kingdom, they are left to redefine what it means to inherit God's kingdom. They usually claim that it doesn't mean that one won't get into heaven, but that one will forfeit inheriting all of God's blessings on the earth.

I have, however, already proved that the phrase, "inherit the kingdom of God," as Paul uses it, is clearly a reference to entering into heaven. In 1 Corinthians 15:50, Paul wrote, "Flesh and blood cannot *inherit the kingdom of God*; nor does the perishable inherit the imperishable" (emphasis added). Paul then continued by revealing how God will change our bodies from being mortal to immortal when we inherit the kingdom of God.[5] Obviously, he was referring to the future time when we enter heaven.

All this being so, it is quite possible for authentic Christians to forfeit their salvation by returning to the practice of sin.[6] That is what is meant by the phrase, "sowing to the flesh." Those who practice the deeds of the flesh reap the harvest of "corruption," or as the NIV translates it, "destruc-

[4] See, for example, Matt. 18:21-35; 24:4-5, 11-13, 23-26, 42-51; 25:1-30; Luke 8:11-15; 11:24-28; 12:42-46; John 6:66-71; 8:31-32, 51; 15:1-6; Acts 11:21-23; 14:21-22; Rom. 6:11-23; 8:12-14, 17; 11:20-22; 1 Cor. 9:23-27; 10:1-21; 11:29-32; 15:1-2; 2 Cor. 1:24; 11:2-4; 12:21-13:5; Gal. 5:1-4; 6:7-9; Phil. 2:12-16; 3:17-4:1; Col. 1:21-23; 2:4-8, 18-19; 1 Thes. 3:1-8; 1 Tim. 1:3-7, 18-21; 4:1-16; 5:5-6, 11-15; 6:9-12, 17-19, 20-21; 2 Tim. 2:11-18; 3:13-15; Heb. 2:1-3; 3:6-19; 4:1-16; 5:8-9; 6:4-9, 10-20; 10:19-39; 12:1-17, 25-29; Jas. 1:12-16; 4:4-10; 5:19-20; 2 Pet. 1:5-11; 2:1-22; 3:16-17; 1 John 2:15-2:28; 5:16; 2 John 6-9; Jude 20-21; Rev. 2:7, 10-11, 17-26; 3:4-5, 8-12, 14-22; 21:7-8; 22:18-19.

[5] In Matthew 25:34, Jesus also used the expression, "inherit the kingdom," in reference to entering into heaven.

[6] For further information about the believer's conditional security as well as God's discipline of wayward believers, see pp. 184-208 in my book, *The Great Gospel Deception*.

tion." Note that in the passage under consideration, Paul contrasts the reaping of corruption/destruction with the reaping of eternal life, leading us to believe that corruption/destruction is a reference to eternal death and damnation.

On the other hand, "sowing to the Spirit" is a reference to following and being obedient to the indwelling Holy Spirit. One who does so will be characterized by the "fruit of the Spirit," which Paul listed in 5:22: "love, joy, peace, patience, kindness, goodness, faithfulness, gentleness [and] self-control."

This interpretation of what it means to "sow to the Spirit" is buttressed by the two verses that follow the verse containing the phrase. Paul wrote, "And let us not lose heart in doing good, for in due time we shall reap if we do not grow weary. So then, while we have opportunity, let us do good to all men, and especially to those who are of the household of the faith" (Gal. 6:9-10). If we continue "doing good…especially to those who are of the household of the faith," not losing heart, "we shall reap" eternal life.[7] Thus we see that "sowing to the Spirit" and "doing good" are used synonymously.

Clearly, "doing good" and "sowing to the Spirit" include the sharing of our material resources with other Christians. This, in fact, is the initial reason Paul wrote what he did in this passage, as he began it by saying to his readers, "And let the one who is taught the word share all good things with him who teaches" (6:6). True believers in Jesus want to learn and grow spiritually. Thus they will avail themselves to the ministry of God-called teachers, to whom they have a responsibility to support materially. Supporting such teachers is one aspect, among many, of "sowing to the Spirit."

Ephesians

4:17-19 Here again, Paul declares that greediness, like sensuality and impurity, is a sin that characterizes one as being unsaved.

4:28 Paul expects the former thief to do just the opposite of what he used to do. Not only should he cease taking from others what does not belong to him, he should also work to gain more than he needs so that he can give of his surplus to others. This should be the motivation for any Christian who labors, not just former thieves.

5:3-6 The Greek word translated *greed* in verse 3 (pleonexia) comes from the root word that is translated *covetous* in verse 5 (pleonektes). It is obvious that Paul saw little difference between these two Greek words, as we compare his triplet in verse 3, *immorality, impurity and greed*, with his parallel triplet in verse 5: *immorality, impurity and covetousness.*

---

[7] Because salvation is only secure for those who continue to believe in and follow Jesus, Scripture speaks of salvation as something that believers experience in the present tense and as something they can experience in the future.

Greed should be not "even be named" (5:3) among Christians, as Paul says, because it so improper among saints, a word that means "holy ones."

Paul also equates greed/covetousness with idolatry, because it amounts to serving another god (see 5:5). He is only echoing Jesus' teaching about the impossibility of serving two masters. For this very reason, no covetous person has "an inheritance in the kingdom of Christ and God" (5:5). Greedy/covetous people will go to hell. Paul solemnly warns against being deceived in this matter, because God hates greed. His wrath will one day fall in fury, in part, because of that very sin. How foolish it is to think that one can be a Christian and greedy.

6:5-9 Clearly, there were Christians in Paul's day who had slaves (see also Col. 4:1; 1 Tim. 6:2). Is not the holding of slaves an indication of opulent wealth and selfishness? Not necessarily.

According to Wayne A. Grudem, a professor at Trinity Evangelical Divinity School, first-century slaves "were generally well treated and were not only unskilled laborers but often managers, overseers, and trained members of various professions (doctors, nurses, teachers, musicians, skilled artisans). There was extensive Roman legislation regulating the treatment of slaves. They were normally paid for their services and could expect eventually to purchase their freedom." Thus, Grudem informs us that, "the word 'employee', though not conveying the idea of absence of freedom, does reflect the economic status and skill level of these ancient 'slaves' better than either of the words 'servant' or 'slave' today."[8]

For this reason, the Christian masters to whom Paul writes, who lived within the framework of the Roman economic system, were very much like modern employers, and their slaves were very much like modern employees who sign legal contracts to work for a specified time period. And certainly it is not wrong to own one's company or farm and employ others, as long as one treats his employees as he would want to be treated as an employee, and as long as one uses his personal profits from his business according to God's will.

Philippians

2:3-7 If we "do nothing from selfishness" and "regard one another as more important than" ourselves, looking out "for the interests of others," that will be the end of selfish spending and the beginning of real Christ-like generosity. For many Christians, obedience to these commands would mean dramatically scaling down their standard of living so that they could be enabled to share more. If they did, they would certainly be imitating Jesus, who dramatically "scaled down" in His incarnation in order to save us.

---

[8] Wayne Gruden: *1 Peter* of the *Tyndale New Testament Commentaries* (Inter-Varsity Press: Leicester, England; 1988) p. 124.

2:25-30 As we will discover in the fourth chapter, the Philippians had recently sent an offering to Paul, delivered by a man named Epaphroditus who apparently became deathly ill on his journey.

3:17-20 Here Paul contrasts Christians with non-Christians, writing that the latter are those who "set their minds on earthly things" (3:19). The former, whose citizenship is in heaven, have their minds focused on the return of their heavenly Savior. Thus, they are always thinking about how they can be more prepared to see Him, and every earthly thing, including every possession, is considered in the light of eternity.

4:10-19 As Paul closes his letter, he expresses his gratitude for the offering he has received from the Philippians via their messenger, Epaphroditus. As those who believed the gospel, the Philippian Christians naturally wanted to help one whom God was using to take the gospel to others. What a privilege it is to "participate in the gospel" (see 1:5) by supporting God's messengers!

Paul made it clear that, although he "rejoiced in the Lord greatly" when he received their gift, it wasn't because he was in "want" (4:11) that is, suffering destitution, although he admitted to being in an "affliction" (4:14). His joy had more to do with the fact that the Philippians were laying up heavenly treasures, or as Paul beautifully said it, "Not that I seek the gift itself, but I seek for the profit which increases to your account" (4:17).

Even prior to the arrival of Epaphroditus, Paul was content in his circumstance by the power of Christ (see 4:11, 13). He had learned to "get along with humble means" as well as "live in prosperity" (4:12).

Of course, when Paul referred to being periodically prosperous, he did not mean that there were times when he lived in lavish luxury and self-indulgence. That would make him a hypocrite, since he instructed the Philippians to "do nothing from selfishness" (2:3) and so on. Paul more clearly defined the periodic prosperity he enjoyed in verse 12. When he was prosperous, he was "filled" rather than "hungry." When he was prosperous, he had "abundance," that is, more than he needed, contrasted with when he found himself "suffering need." As a result of the Philippians' offering, he was now again enjoying "abundance" and was "amply supplied" (4:18). Obviously, he did not mean that he could now live in luxury like a modern prosperity preacher, as he was in jail when he wrote those words. Yet Paul considered himself prosperous even while incarcerated.

The gift sent by the Philippians was sacrificially given (see 4:18), and "well-pleasing to God" (4:18). Paul was confident that because the Philippians had "sought first God's kingdom" (see Matt. 6:33), God would keep His promise to supply all their needs "according to His riches in glory" (Phil. 4:19). The only Christians who can rightfully claim the promise of 4:19 are those who meet the conditions of the promise thereby imitating the Philippians.

Colossians

3:1-7 Christians are obviously subject to the temptations of immorality, impurity and greed, otherwise Paul would not have admonished the Colossian Christians to "consider the members of [their] earthly body as dead" (3:5) to those sins. We may have formerly "walked" (3:7), or lived, in them, but now we must avoid them at all costs. Those who want to please God will not want to be guilty of these sins because "the wrath of God will come" (3:6). As those who are spiritually alive, we should now set our minds "on the things above, not on the things that are on earth" (3:2).

Notice that Paul, once again, equated greed with idolatry, the worship of a false god (see 3:5). His teaching about money was, of course, perfectly consistent with Christ's.

1 Thessalonians

2:3-9 It is quite possible to do the right thing for the wrong reasons. Our motives may be hidden from people, but they are known to God, "who examines our hearts" (2:4). No one should preach the gospel in order to enrich himself. We have to wonder, however, how many modern "ministers" preach the gospel "with a pretext for greed" (2:5) when the majority of their sermons are designed to motivate people to give to their "ministries" and they live in lavish luxury. In many congregations, the pastor is the wealthiest member. How do these pastors compare to Paul, who labored "night and day, so as not to be a burden" (2:9) to the Thessalonians?

On the other hand, pity the poor pastor whose congregation is too stingy to support him! That is a form of greed on the part of the congregation. Paul wrote, "the Lord directed those who proclaim the gospel to get their living from the gospel" (1 Cor. 9:14). He also wrote, "Let the elders who rule well be considered worthy of double honor, especially those who work hard at preaching and teaching" (1 Tim. 5:17).

4:9-12 The "love of the brethren" does not consist solely of warm sentiments within the heart, but includes (among other things) working hard so as not to be a burden upon others. Laziness is a sin because it violates the second greatest commandment. One who loves his neighbor as himself would not expect to be supported by his neighbor's labor when he is capable of supporting himself.

This is not to say that we have no obligation to assist those with pressing needs. If, however, the needy one is capable of work but lazy, no one is obligated to assist him (see 2 Thes. 3:10). He should be left in his laziness until Proverbs 16:26 becomes a reality to him: "A worker's appetite works for him, for his hunger urges him on." When charity removes the incentive to work from those who are capable of work, such charity is void of authentic love, hurting those it is supposed to help.

2 Thessalonians

3:6-12 Paul addressed more pointedly a problem that he alluded to in his first letter to the Thessalonians (see 2 Thes. 4:11-12). Some of the Thessalonian Christians were "leading an undisciplined life, doing no work at all, but acting like busybodies" (3:11). Such behavior is a violation of the second greatest commandment, because we won't want to be a burden on someone if we love that person. Lazy people should not expect or receive charitable assistance. If those who are capable of work are unwilling to work, they should be allowed to go hungry.

I read some years ago about a pastor who was periodically visited by unemployed men requesting financial help. He would ask them, "Have you searched for a job?" They would always reply in the affirmative but explain that no work was available. "Would you be willing to work if I could find a job for you?" would be the pastor's second question. Again, the answer would always be in the affirmative. Finally, the pastor would say, "Out behind the church is a cord of wood that needs splitting, and there's an ax in a shed beside it. Go out and split as much wood as you can, and then come see me, and I'll pay you fairly." In almost every case, the men would thank the pastor for the job, walk out the door, and never return.

1 Timothy

2:9 To spend excessive time and money on one's outward appearance is nothing more than vanity, a form of selfishness. Better to spend your money on providing clothing for the naked than in elaborately decorating your body to gain the stares of others. Immodest dress is also displeasing to God, as it can cause the opposite sex to stumble into impure thoughts and actions. God is looking for "the beauty of holiness" (Psalm 96:9, KJV).

3:3 A candidate for overseer, which is the same office as biblical pastor (shepherd) and biblical elder (compare Acts 20:17, 28; 1 Pet. 5:1-2; Tit. 1:5-7), must be "free from the love of money." How does one know if he is free from the love of money? The author of the book of Hebrews (perhaps Paul, who authored 1 Timothy as well), wrote, "Let your character be free from the love of money, being content with what you have" (Heb. 13:5). Thus, biblical pastors display contentment with what they have, and those who don't should be avoided.

Later in this same epistle, Paul definitely links discontentment with the love of money. There he wrote, "If we have food and covering, *with these we shall be content*. But those who want to get rich fall into temptation and a snare and many foolish and harmful desires which plunge men into ruin and destruction. For the love of money is a root of all sorts of evil, and some by longing for it have wandered away from the faith, and pierced themselves with many a pang" (1 Tim. 6:8-10, emphasis added).

3:8 A fondness for illegitimate gain disqualifies candidates for the office of deacon, as well as the office of elder (see Tit. 1:5-7).

5:3-16 The primary theme of this passage is the church's responsibility to support worthy widows who would otherwise be destitute. Because a major part of church-life was taking care of the poor, naturally it was something of which people might take advantage. Good stewardship made it necessary to lay down strict ground rules. The church should provide only for those who are "widows indeed" (5:3, 5, 16). What characterizes a "widow indeed"?

Paul first stated that the church should not support those widows who have children or grandchildren who can support them. In fact, in terms that couldn't be stronger, Paul declares that the church shouldn't support anyone who has family members who can provide assistance. Any professing Christian who "does not provide for his own [his household and extended family], and especially for those of his own household...has denied the faith, and is worse than an unbeliever" (5:8).

Second, the church should only provide for widows who were and are wholly devoted to Christ, as evidenced by their prayer lives, their good reputations, and their deeds of mercy and kindness (see 5:5, 10). A widow who "gives herself to wanton pleasure is dead even while she lives" (5:6). She has no warrant to claim to be Christ's follower; nor is the church obligated to subsidize her carnal life.

Third, the church should only support older widows, at least sixty years of age, who are unlikely to be remarried. Younger widows should seek to be remarried and supported by their husbands (see 5:9-14).

It seems as if qualifying widows practically became employees of the church, as they apparently took a pledge to Christ, a pledge of singleness and devotion (see 5:11-12). No doubt their ministry provided rich blessings to the body. What a contrast are they with so many modern widows who profess to be Christians but who live the final years of their lives in a continual testimony of their devotion to self.

Finally, if a female believer, out of devotion to Christ, provided food and covering for widows, that is a worthy ministry that relieves the church of some responsibility (see 5:16).

5:17-18 Biblical elders, who are the equivalent of biblical pastors and overseers (see Acts 20:17, 28; 1 Pet. 5:1-2; Tit. 1:5-7), are paid church employees. This is made clear, first by the language Paul uses in 5:17, which is similar to his language in 5:3, regarding "honoring" widows, and second by his expressions in 5:18.

Surely "double honor" at least indicates that elders should not be paid less than what they need, and probably indicates they should be paid more, giving them the blessed opportunity to have something to share.

6:3-10 To "suppose that godliness is a means of gain" (6:5) is obviously a wrong supposition, and one that is held by "men of depraved mind and deprived of the truth" (6:5). Because their lives consist of their possessions, because money is their god, because they find their joy in material things, because they have no higher goal than accumulating more, they foolishly think that the only reason someone might live in a godly fashion is to gain earthly wealth.

Lest Timothy think that he was saying that nothing was to be gained by godliness, Paul quickly states that godliness, when accompanied by contentment, is indeed a means of great gain (see 6:6). He was speaking, of course, of *eternal* heavenly gain, not temporal earthly gain, as he makes so clear in the very next verse. There he says that we can take nothing more with us at death than we brought with us at birth. Thus the godly person sees the utter foolishness of devoting his life to gaining what he must one day forfeit. Likewise, he is wisely content with what he has for the present, even if it is only food and covering (see 6:8). He knows that his contentment, an indication of his freedom from greed, will ultimately be a means of "great gain" (6:6), for he will one day live forever in heaven, since God, not mammon, is his Master. Beyond that, any sacrificial giving, made possible by his contentment with little, will reap for him abundant heavenly rewards.

Those who are not content with having only their needs met, that is, those who "want to get rich" (6:9), face inevitable temptations that plunge them, according to Paul, into "ruin and destruction" (6:9). Paul certainly had more than financial ruin and destruction in mind here. He was referring to temporal *and* eternal consequences. He, as well as other New Testament authors, frequently used the word *destruction* (Greek, *apoleia*) to signify eternal damnation (see Matt. 7:13; Rom. 9:22; Phil. 1:28; 3:19; 2 Thes. 2:3; Heb. 10:39; 2 Pet. 2:1, 3; 3:7, 16; Rev. 17:8, 11). The *King James Version* translates the last of part of this verse, "destruction and *perdition*" (emphasis added).

In the very next verse, 6:10, Paul makes it even more obvious that he was thinking not just of the temporal consequences of desiring to be rich, as he states that some believers began to love money and consequently "wandered away from the faith, and pierced themselves with many a pang." To "wander away from the faith" is to no longer meet the qualification for salvation, that is, faith; thus one has forfeited his salvation. At death, unless he repents beforehand, he will be eternally condemned.

If desiring to be rich can result in eternal damnation, it would be helpful to know what it means to be "rich." When we consider Paul's contrast in

6:8-9, it seems he believed that anyone who had more than what he needed is rich: "And if we have food and covering, *with these we shall be content. But those who want to get rich* fall into temptation and a snare and many foolish and harmful desires which plunge men into ruin and destruction" (emphasis added). If Paul had said, "If we have a three-bedroom house, two cars, and plenty of clothing, with these we shall be content. But those who want to get rich fall into temptation," would we not assume he meant that anyone who isn't content with a three-bedroom house, two cars, and plenty of clothing, is among those who "want to get rich"? Certainly.

Webster's New World Dictionary defines the word *rich* no differently than Paul. It helps us to understand the modern definition of the word *rich* by comparing it with other synonyms:

> *Rich* is the general word for one who has more money or income-producing property than is necessary to satisfy normal needs; *wealthy* adds to this connotations of grand living, influence in the community, a tradition of richness, etc. [a wealthy banker]; *affluent* suggests a continuing increase of riches and a concomitant lavish spending [to live in affluent circumstances]; *opulent* suggests the possession of great wealth as displayed in luxurious or ostentatious living [an opulent mansion]; *well-to-do* implies sufficient prosperity for easy living.[9]

Thus we see that our own modern definition of the word *rich* reveals that if ones desires more than what "is necessary to satisfy normal needs," then one desires to be rich. Let us not fool ourselves then, to think that Paul's warning to "those who want to get rich" (6:9) applies only to those who long to be wealthy, affluent or live opulently. Most Americans don't see themselves as being rich, yet billions of people in the world consider all of us to be very rich, and rightfully so. Simply earning minimum wage in the United States puts one in the top 13% of the world in terms of income. And still we strive to gain more. Discontentment is the driving force in our materialistic culture, and the American church appears to be keeping right in step. Consequently, we continually "fall into temptation and a snare and many foolish and harmful desires which plunge men into ruin and destruction" (6:9).

The love of money is taking North Americans to hell by the millions,

---

[9] *Webster's Dictionary* likewise helps us understand the word *poor* by comparing it with common synonyms: "*Poor* is the simple, direct term for one who lacks the resources for reasonably comfortable living; *impoverish* is applied to one who having once had plenty is now reduced to poverty [an impoverished aristocrat]; *destitute* implies such great poverty that the means for mere subsistence, such as food and shelter, are lacking [left destitute by the war]; *impecunious* applies to one in a habitual state of poverty and suggests that this results from personal practices [an impecunious gambler]; *indigent* implies such relative poverty as results in a lack of luxuries and the endurance of hardships [books for indigent children]." By these definitions, God certainly does not want His children to be destitute, lacking food and shelter. And it could be said that He doesn't want them to be poor, if "reasonably comfortable living" means having food and covering.

many of whom think they are Christians. Yet what North American would admit that he is guilty of either "the love of money," or "longing for it"? I suspect very few. Even though our lives revolve around the acquiring and selfish spending of money, surely we don't love it. Yet Paul made his point very clear. If one's needs are met and he is not content, longing for more, he loves money. Is this not also made clear in Hebrews 13:5: "Let your character be free from the love of money, being content with what you have." If one is not content with having his needs met, he loves money.

Into what kind of temptations, snares and "foolish and harmful desires" (6:9) do lovers of money inevitably fall? One temptation is to gain wealth by unrighteous means. If one has no desire to get rich, one is not tempted to do something unrighteous to enrich himself. Yet how many of us are doing something or investing in what we know to be sinful? And why? Because getting rich is more important to us than obeying God. We love money more than Him, and it is just that simple.

The greatest temptation that lovers of money fall into is the temptation not to love God as He should be loved, making money one's master. The one who is discontent with having his needs met, who longs for more, will be devoting his life to money, making it impossible for him to devote his life to God. "No servant can serve two masters; for either he will hate the one, and love the other, or else he will hold to one, and despise the other" (Luke 16:13). It is impossible to serve God and mammon.

The lover of money also faces great temptation to act selfishly, not loving one's neighbor as he should (see 6:18), keeping what he ought to share, ignoring the second greatest commandment.

Does all this mean that every Christian should scale down to the point of having only food and covering? No, because as I've stated in an earlier chapter, our needs often exceed those bare necessities. However, Paul's words, which harmonize perfectly with what Jesus taught, indicate that every Christian should scale down to owning only what he needs (and there could be some variance from what one Christian needs compared to another depending on their circumstances). Those who have more or gain more than they need should generously share their excess, as Paul points out in 6:17-19 (the next passage we will consider).

6:17-19 In light of what we've just read eight verses prior to this passage, we don't have to wonder whom Paul means when he refers to "those who are rich" (6:17). They include everyone who has more than he needs, probably most people reading this book. What should they do?

First, because they will be tempted to think themselves as better than those who have less, Paul admonishes them not to be conceited, guarding themselves against pride (see 6:17).

Second, because they will be tempted to "fix their hope on the uncertainty of riches" (6:17), Paul reminds them to keep their hope fixed on God.

To "fix one's hope on the uncertainty of riches" is to hope one's future is secure because of his wealth. This is a very "uncertain" hope indeed, because it may well be a hope that never materializes. Moreover, one who is hoping in riches is thinking selfishly and probably hoarding his excess.

In contrast, the one who is "hoping in God" is looking forward to the brighter eternal future that He promises, and thus doesn't have his hope set on the "uncertainty of riches." Neither is he yielding to the temptation to think only of himself, hoarding for his future, while others suffer lack. His hope is in God, who holds the future in His hands, who has promised to supply all our needs, and who often gives us more than we need, or as Paul says, "who *richly* supplies us with all things to enjoy" (6:17, emphasis added).[10]

For this reason, Paul's final instruction for those who have more than they need is "to do good, to be rich in good works, to be generous and ready to share" (6:18). Those who are "rich" should be equally rich in good works.

Moreover, because their hope is fixed on God and not on the uncertainty of riches, they should be living their lives with their eternal future, not just their temporal, earthly future in focus. By being generous and sharing, they will be "storing up for themselves the treasure of a good foundation for the future" (6:19), an echo of Jesus' promise to those who lay up heavenly, rather than earthly, treasures.

If they will do this, they will then "take hold of that which is life indeed" (6:19). To me, this sounds like salvation, the promise of true life, eternal life, which begins when one believes in Jesus with a living faith. The *King James Version* translates the last part of 6:19: "that they may lay hold on *eternal life*" (emphasis added). As I have stated previously, if Paul had written, "Instruct them to believe in Jesus so that they may take hold of that which is life indeed," we would have interpreted him to mean that one must believe in Jesus to be truly saved. Then why not interpret what he did write to be consistent with what the rest of the New Testament teaches, namely, that rich people must repent of greed if they hope to be saved?

2 Timothy

3:1-2 In Paul's list of what will make the "last days difficult times" (3:1), he first lists that "men will be lovers of self, lovers of money" (3:2). Many of us think that we are living in the last days, and it is quite possible that "the love of money" is the most prevalent sin in the world today, yet the

---

[10] Paul does not necessarily have yachts and mansions in mind here. Grateful people can enjoy what greedy people cannot—God's provision of food and covering, as well as what He gives us beyond those things, because the excess allows us the blessed opportunity to be a blessing to others, as well as lay up heavenly treasures. True enjoyment comes from knowing, loving and serving God.

one that is least recognized because of its pervasiveness. The church hardly recognizes it and sometimes even promotes it. This should not surprise us, as Paul later wrote in this same letter that "the time will come when they will not endure sound doctrine; but wanting to have their ears tickled, they will accumulate for themselves teachers in accordance to their own desires; and will turn away their ears from the truth, and will turn aside to myths" (2 Tim. 4:3-4).

All of the various characteristics Paul lists of the ungodly during the end times (see 3:1-7) could be summarized by the first one Paul lists—"lovers of self." Certainly the love of money is a specific way that people reveal their love of self.

4:13 If Paul was so rich, as some want us to believe, why did he request that Timothy bring a cloak to Rome that he had left in Troas, 750 miles away? Surely he could have easily bought a new one with all his money, thus ensuring his warmth during the coming winter (see 4:21).

Titus

1:7-11 A fondness of "sordid gain" disqualifies one from being an elder / overseer as well as a deacon (see 1 Tim. 3:8). We gain a little better idea of what Paul means by the phrase "sordid gain" from 7:11, as he states that certain false teachers are motivated by sordid gain. They are making their money illegitimately, being paid for doing something that is in opposition to God's will. If a spiritual leader is receiving money for teaching people what is not true, he is guilty of making his money by "sordid gain." How many pastors, those who tickle people's ears by telling them what they want to hear, fall into this category? All of them. They are making their living illegitimately.

1:16; 2:14; 3:1, 8, 14 Five times in this short epistle Paul emphasizes the importance of believers doing good deeds. One's deeds are what validate one's relationship with God. Those whose lives are void of any good deeds effectively prove that they don't know God, even if they profess otherwise (see 1:16). God's purpose in showing us His grace was, in part, that we might become "zealous for *good deeds*" (2:14; emphasis added). Thus, we should always "be ready for every *good deed*" (3:1; emphasis added) and be "careful to engage in *good deeds*" (3:8; emphasis added).

What kind of good deeds did Paul have in mind as he so frequently wrote of them in this epistle? 3:14 gives us a better idea: "And let our people also learn to engage in good deeds *to meet pressing needs*" (emphasis added). These kinds of good deeds, as do all good deeds, require one's time and / or money. Paul goes on to say that, if we don't engage in such good deeds, we are "unfruitful" (3:14).

Philemon

1:18-19 Having run away from Philemon, his Christian master, a slave named Onesimus found himself incarcerated in the same prison as the apostle Paul, who then led him to Christ. Providentially, Paul and Philemon were friends in Christ, and Paul wrote this letter to him, sending it with Onesimus on his return to his master. Paul thus informed Philemon of his runaway slave's authentic conversion.

Onesimus had either stolen some money from his master or had incurred a certain debt by the absence of his labor. Paul now graciously requested that Philemon charge Onesimus' debts to his own account (see 1:18). Ironically, however, Philemon was already indebted to Paul, although it is not clear whether his debt was spiritual or monetary. Regardless, it certainly seems foolish to use these two verses to prove that Paul was wealthy. I rather think they prove that money was not Paul's god, and that he was gracious in the use of what God entrusted to him.

In regard to the question of how a Christian could have a slave, see my comments on Ephesians 6:5-9.

Hebrews

7:4-10 This is the only place in the New Testament epistles where tithing is mentioned, a fact that is often used to prove that under the new covenant, Christians need not concern themselves with tithing. Certainly, one would think that tithing would be mentioned more often in the epistles if it were as important as many think. Even in this passage, tithing is not spoken of in order to promote the practice of it among Christians. Rather, it is mentioned to prove the superiority of Melchizedek's priesthood over the Levitical priesthood, thus revealing Christ's superior ministry, who became a high priest "according to the order of Melchizedek" (6:20).[11]

Some also argue that since there is no longer a valid Levitical priesthood, there is no valid reason to tithe, as tithes were given under the old covenant to support their ministry. In contrast, however, one could argue that Christ's priesthood is certainly valid now, and there is indeed scriptural precedent for paying tithes to Melchizedekian priests in the very story mentioned in this passage. Thus, is could be said that modern ministers, who are authorized by our High Priest and members of His body, should be supported by the tithes of God's people. And isn't it also true that tithing was practiced long before the Law of Moses, so that it would be wrong to consider ourselves excused from practicing it on the basis that we are no longer under the Mosaic Law?

In my mind, however, all of these arguments reveal an inherent flaw

---

[11] Some feel that 7:8 is an endorsement of New Testament tithing because it speaks of Christ receiving tithes. In disagreement, I would say that the author is contrasting the Levites receiving tithes and Melchizedek receiving tithes. This is revealed from the context, and especially 7:9-10, which makes clear that the author was referring to a time in history when Melchizedek received tithes, and not to Christ presently receiving tithes.

on both sides: they ignore Christ's most basic lessons about stewardship. People who know that they can't be disciples of Christ unless they give up all their possessions (see Luke 14:33), who know that their Lord forbids them to lay up earthly treasures (Matt. 6:19), and who know that He expects them to love one another as He has loved them (see John 13:34), don't see the point of arguing about tithing. They aren't trying to find out how little they can give without feeling guilty.

This is precisely why there is no endorsement of tithing in the New Testament epistles. It is a mute point. Christ's true disciple's are not like the Pharisees who scrupulously tithed their garden herbs while neglecting "the love of God" (Luke 11:42) and the love of neighbor (see Matt. 23:23). Christ's true disciples live to please the One who redeemed them from sin.

10:32-39 We gain some insight into the persecution endured by the recipients of this letter: Hebrew believers who were being tempted to renounce Jesus and return to the practice of Judaism. Incredibly, they had "accepted joyfully the seizure of [their] property," knowing that a "better possession" (10:34) waited them in heaven. Public Jewish sentiment was so aroused against these "traitorous" followers of Christ that forcefully confiscating their property became acceptable, perhaps even virtuous. Yet these devoted Hebrew believers reacted with joy, knowing their loss was really gain. Here was an opportunity to demonstrate their living faith in their Messiah with a heavenly attitude about their possessions.

What possessions they lost, specifically, would be a matter of speculation. It would also be speculative to say that these Jewish believers had previously maintained wealthy lifestyles before their property was seized, proven only by the fact that Scripture states they owned property that could be seized. (They may even have lost their homes, as perhaps intimated in 11:37-38.) One could just as well speculate that God allowed the seizure of their property as a means of disciplining them (see 12:4-11) because they were lax in sharing or in contentment (see 13:5).

11:8-10, 24-26, 37-38 This entire eleventh chapter is a masterful encouragement to first-century Hebrew believers who were being tempted to revert to Judaism because of the persecutions they were suffering. The author shows how their experience is not unusual for those whose faith is alive. In fact, many of the patriarchs and well-known characters of Scripture endured afflictions because they took God at His word. Yet they were all anticipating a future reward. Likewise the Hebrew Christians should not "throw away [their] confidence, which has a great reward" (10:35).

Note that, for some of the "faith heroes" listed in this chapter, their faith resulted, not in financial prosperity, but in their having less. For example, Moses chose to "endure ill-treatment with the people of God...considering the reproach of Christ greater riches than the treasures of Egypt" (11:25-26). Others, because of their faith, "went about in sheepskins, in goatskins, being destitute, afflicted, ill-treated...wandering in the deserts and mountains and caves and holes in the ground" (11:38). All of these examples would serve to comfort and encourage the Hebrew believers who were also less prosperous now that they had come into the faith (see 10:34).

13:5 Clearly, one whose character is free from the love of money is one who is content with what he has. Thus, one who is not content with what he has is not free from the love of money. Such a concept is completely foreign to our thinking because our culture is built on discontentment. The goal of life is to improve one's life by gaining more money and possessions. A professing Christian once even accused me, without apology, of "ruining people's incentive to better their lives" when I've taught what the Bible says about contentment!

13:16 Because the Spirit wars against the flesh, we are continually tempted to be selfish. Thus the reason for admonitions like the one found in this verse.

James

1:9-12 James apparently wrote this general epistle during a time when the church was suffering persecution, perhaps what is recorded in Acts 8:1-4. There we read, "On that day a great persecution arose against the church in Jerusalem; and they were all scattered throughout the regions of Judea and Samaria" (Acts 8:1). We note that James addressed his letter to Jewish believers who were "dispersed abroad"(1:1) and who were enduring trials of their faith (see 1:2-3, 12; 5:10-11).

If the recipients of James' letter had been scattered because of persecution, we can easily understand why James had good reason to encourage "the brother of humble circumstances" (1:9). Scattered Christians would likely be suffering materially. Moreover, they would be more susceptible than usual to the temptation of envying those who had more. Thus James contrasted God's view of the "brother of humble circumstances" and the "rich man" (1:9-10).

The brother of humble circumstances should "glory in his high position," while the rich man should "glory in his humiliation" (1:9-10). The reason is because of their ultimate ends. The rich man will "like flowering grass...pass away...in the midst of his pursuits" (1:10-11), just like the rich fool of Luke 12 and the rich man who ignored starving Lazarus. The brother of humble circumstances, however, who "perseveres under trial...will receive the crown of life" (1:12), which is eternal life, given to all who love the Lord (see 1:12). Thus it is far better to be a poor believer than a rich unbeliever.

1:27 How often do professing Christians think that what is most important is to believe the correct doctrine? We are quick to write off anyone who has a little different perspective on the Trinity or speaking in other tongues. Yet, as James points out in this verse and all through his epistle, what a person *does*, not what he *professes to believe*, is what is most important to God. Throughout Scripture, He has repeatedly declared His concern for the marginalized of society. Thus, His true people will share His compassion and demonstrate it, taking care of those can't take care of themselves and assisting those with pressing needs.

Looking after widows and orphans consists of more than just praying, "God bless all the widows and orphans." It requires time and money. If you are looking for a way to help an orphan in a developing nation, visit www.OrphansTear.org.

2:1-9 Once again we have the opportunity to compare the church in James' day with the modern American church. James relates how a poor man dressed in dirty clothes might come into a gathering. If anyone is that poor in America, he would probably not consider visiting a church service due to his embarrassment about his clothing. He would also know that he runs a very good chance of not being permitted to enter many churches.

James also describes a rich man who might come into an assembly. Interestingly, what marks him as being rich is that he has "a gold ring and [is] dressed in fine clothes"! (2:2). That description fits the large majority of Americans who attend churches. Even if they aren't wearing "fine clothes," it is only because they chose to leave their fine clothes at home. Once again we are faced with the fact that by biblical standards we are rich, even though we may not be by American standards.

The sin James addresses here is the sin of showing partiality. When a rich person receives favored treatment over a poor person, the second greatest commandment is broken (see 2:8). One is not loving his neighbor as himself. He is not treating the poor person as he wants to be treated.

James questions why such partiality would be shown. Why would we automatically honor a rich man and dishonor a poor man, both of whom we know nothing about, when we know what God esteems and despises? We know that God loves the poor, having special compassion for them, choosing them to be "rich in faith and heirs of the kingdom" (2:5). Indeed, God has chosen "the base things of the world and the despised…the things that are not, that He might nullify the things that are" (1 Cor. 1:28). In contrast, the rich are often guilty of sins that arouse God's anger, not the least of which is their exploiting the poor, whom He loves so much, in order to enrich themselves. They also often blaspheme God's name (see 2:6-8). Thus how foolish it is to honor automatically a rich man and dishonor a poor man based on no other criteria than their apparent wealth or poverty.

If we are to err in the matter, better to err by honoring the poor over the rich. In most instances, the rich man is likely to be far from God, while the poor man is more likely to respond to God's love. Not knowing what is in the heart of either, however, we should honor them both with good seats when they visit our gathering. And we shouldn't be surprised when the poor man responds to the gospel while the rich man remains devoted to mammon.

The only reason that someone would show partiality to the rich is because of an evil motive, probably the hope of personal gain (see 2:4). As Solomon astutely observed, "Wealth adds many friends....and every man is a friend to him who gives gifts" (Prov. 19:4, 6). This phenomenon can be easily observed in American churches, where pastors often yield to the temptation of showing favoritism to those with the most wealth. This sin can at least be partially mitigated if the pastor does not know what any individual contributes to his church.

2:14-17 It is interesting that the example James uses to illustrate dead, useless faith is one about meeting the pressing needs of a fellow believer. Verbalizing one's concern for a homeless and hungry fellow believer while doing nothing to assist him is of no use. So faith, without works, is also utterly useless and dead. One cannot be saved by such a faith. Yet this dead faith is the predominant kind of faith today in the North American church. Multitudes of greedy people are deceived into thinking that they are on the way to heaven when in reality they will be cast into hell. Having done nothing to meet the pressing needs of suffering believers, they will join the other "goats" of which Jesus spoke in Matthew 25:31-46.

4:1-4 James addresses the problem of quarrels and conflicts in the church, immediately attacking the root, which was selfishness in various forms. They were desiring (probably a better translation for the word *lust* in 4:2) what they did not possess, and consequently committed murder. (I certainly hope that James was speaking metaphorically of the sin of cursing a brother, which Jesus condemned as being equally deserving of hell as murder; see Matt. 5:21-22.) They were envious of what others possessed, and so they fought and quarreled. Even their prayers revealed their selfishness, as they asked only for what they planned to use for self-indulgence (see 4:3).

Note that all of this selfishness seems to be related to material things. Such a focus makes one guilty of serving mammon, which is perhaps the reason James calls them "adulteresses" in verse 4. This expression is borrowed from the Old Testament prophets who equated idolatry with spiritual adultery, or unfaithfulness to the Lord (see Is. 1:21; Jer. 2:20; Ezek. 16:15-17). Greed is idolatry (see Col. 3:5).

Because the unsaved world is focused on money and is serving mammon (see Matt. 6:32), James additionally warns his readers that, "whoever wishes to be a friend of the world makes himself an enemy of God" (4:4). While selfish, worldly people live each day in servitude to Mammon, the love-filled servants of Christ live to show their love for God and fellow man. They are envious of no one, knowing that happiness is not found in material things. They pray for God to bless them with more than they need, not so they can indulge themselves, but so they can be a blessing to others.

4:13-17 James is not saying that it is wrong to travel to a distant city for a year to engage in profitable business. He is only saying that to declare what one will be doing in the future, without acknowledging God's sovereignty, is arrogant. As James states, we really don't even know what will happen to us tomorrow, much less over the next year. Being just a "vapor that appears for a little while and then vanishes away" (4:14), we could vanish at any time! Thus to assume that we can make any plans that God might not change is arrogant. We ought to say, "If the Lord wills, we shall live and also do this or that" (4:15). You will be alive tomorrow only if God wills it (see Luke 12:20). You will accomplish your plans only if God wills that you do.

James' theology certainly stands in contrast to the modern idea of speaking prosperity or long life into existence by one's faith. He would call such "positive confessions" boastful, evil arrogance.

5:1-6 James returns to his earlier theme (see 1:10-11; 2:6-7) of condemning the rich. He begins by telling them to weep and howl for the miseries that are coming upon them, a clear warning of hell (see also 5:3).

As we read the first verse of this passage, two inevitable questions come to our minds: "Is James talking about all rich people, or just evil rich people?" And, "If James is referring to all rich people, how much does one have to possess in order to be characterized as rich?" James does not leave these questions unanswered.

In the next two verses, James enumerates specific indications of the wealth of those he is condemning. They own riches that have "rotted" (5:2). It would seem reasonable to conclude that James was speaking of their possessing so much food that much of it rotted before it could be consumed. They had more than they obviously needed, and it could have been shared with those who needed it. Perhaps James was alluding to Jesus' story of the rich fool, whose stored-up treasure consisted, at least in part, of abundant food (see Luke 12:16-21). Regardless, one who has more food than he needs or uses is rich.

The garments of the rich whom James condemns "have become moth-eaten" (5:2). This certainly echoes Jesus' command that forbade His followers to lay up for themselves earthly treasures, "where *moth* and rust destroy" (Matt. 6:19; emphasis added). Moths eat clothing that isn't frequently worn. Having clothing that one doesn't need or use characterizes one as being rich.

The rich whom James condemns own "gold and silver" that has "rusted," or perhaps better rendered, "tarnished." That is, they have so much that they have some that is never touched or used. They don't need it, and it could be used to help others.

We might, perhaps, convince ourselves that we are not condemned by James if none of our food is rotting, none of our clothing is being eaten by moths, and we don't have stacks of tarnished gold coins. But is it not true that what characterizes the rich whom James condemns is simply the selfish use of their wealth, that they keep more than they need while others go without? They "lived luxuriously on the earth and led a life of wanton pleasure" (5:5), what seems to be the primary pursuit of so many.

Not only have the rich whom James condemns used their wealth selfishly, they have gained it selfishly. We learn in 5:4 that they had hired laborers to mow their fields but never paid them. Thus, they prospered by exploiting others.

Certainly one is not automatically exempt from James' condemnation if he owns no fields or hires no laborers to mow them. The principle behind James' example is universal. Enriching oneself by exploiting others is selfish, a violation of the second greatest commandment. James could have condemned the doctor who performs unnecessary surgery, the lazy welfare recipient, the used-car salesman who turns back odometers, the employee who lies about how many hours he worked, or the citizen who cheats on his taxes.

As I have mentioned in Chapter Five, those of us who live in North American cannot escape from benefiting from laborers in other nations who are often exploited by large corporations. Although such laborers do agree to work for low wages by American standards, and although the companies who hire them do pay them their agreed-upon hourly rate, we cannot help but question if James would not condemn such a practice as a means of enriching oneself by exploiting others. It certainly seems to violate the golden rule and the second greatest commandment. What would Jesus do?

What if the rich to whom James wrote had come by their money completely honestly? Would he then have written, "Your riches have rotted and your garments have become moth-eaten. Your gold and your silver have rusted, and it is in the last days that you have stored up your treasure! You have lived luxuriously on the earth and led a life of wanton pleasure; but you have no need to be concerned, because you came by your money honestly"? Obviously not. Greed is expressed not just by how money is gained, but also by how money is used.

James' words apply to anyone who has more than he needs, even if he gained his wealth without sinning in the process. If he did gain his wealth in an unrighteous way, he is all the worse off in God's eyes.

1 Peter

3:3-4 Spending excessive time and money on outward beauty reveals selfishness; inward beauty is characterized by selflessness.

5:2 See my comments on Titus 1:7-11.

2 Peter

2:3, 14-15 False teachers are characterized by, among other things, their greed. Their primary goal is to gain the money of their followers, thus they "exploit [them] with false words" (2:3). Many modern "successful ministers" fall into this category. They preach just what the servants of mammon want to hear, fueling their greed with twisted logic and out-of-context scriptures, enriching themselves in the process. As Peter warns, "their judgment from long ago is not idle, and their destruction is not asleep" (2:3).

1 John

2:15-17 Loving the world and "the things in the world" proves that one does not love the Father. John specifically warned against those things that the flesh and eyes desire, and what tempts people to be prideful, all of which would certainly include material wealth. He was echoing Jesus' declaration that one cannot serve God and mammon, because he will hate one and love the other (see Matt. 6:24).

3:14-20 Without dispute, John declares that the authenticity of one's salvation can be determined by his generosity toward fellow believers in need. "We know that we have passed out of death into life, because we love the brethren" (3:14). The kind of love of which John wrote is sacrificial, which imitates Christ, and that goes beyond just caring "with word or with tongue" (3:18). One who does not relieve the pressing need of his brother by sharing his excess does not posses this love, and confirms by his actions the unbelief in his heart. He is deceived if he thinks he is a Christian.

On the other hand, the one who opens his heart to his brother in need knows he is "of the truth" and assures his heart before God (see 3:19). That is, if he doubts in his heart his standing before God, his love in action restores his heart's assurance, relieving him of any condemnation. God, knowing everything, is thus "greater than our heart" (3:20), because He knows about us what sometimes even our own hearts don't know. Our giving to a brother in need does not earn our right standing with Him, it only confirms to our hearts what He already knew.

3 John

1:2-8 Verse 2 of this book is often used by prosperity preachers to prove that God wants His people to prosper. Certainly if the apostle John, a very spiritual man, desired that Gaius would prosper, then there is nothing wrong with wanting to prosper.

I have no problem with that conclusion, but must take exception with how prosperity preachers define prosperity and with their understanding of what God expects of Christians who do prosper.

In light of what we just read from John's first epistle, it would be incredibly foolish for us to conclude that John hoped Gaius would become rich so he could live in luxury and self-indulgence. The only reason John would want Gaius to prosper would be so Gaius would have more to share. Is this not abundantly clear from the verses that follow? Gaius was a loving servant of the brethren, a financial supporter of traveling missionaries (see 1:5-8), and if he prospered (and enjoyed good health, John's other desire) he could serve and give all the more.

To prosper financially simply means to gain more than one presently has. Very poor people can prosper and still have very little.

All of this being so, certainly it should be our desire that everyone who is seeking first God's kingdom prosper, because more good would be done by their obedience to Christ and their love for the brethren. But to teach that 3 John 2 proves that God wants us all to enjoy luxury homes and autos, designer clothing and exotic vacations is poor exegesis at best and a sign that one is a false teacher at worst.

Jude

1:11 Like Peter in his second epistle (see 2 Pet. 2:15), Jude also cites the prophet Balaam as illustrative of contemporary false prophets and teachers who were motivated mostly by money in their "ministries." Holiness is foreign concept to such greedy teachers, "who turn the grace of our God into licentiousness" (1:4). The only ones who can't discern their deception are their greedy followers, attracted to their meetings like hopeful gamblers are drawn to Las Vegas.

Revelation

2:9 Here is another example of a group of believers who were facing financial hardship, perhaps because of the persecution they were currently enduring. Although they were suffering poverty, Jesus told them that they were rich, and He could only have meant that they were spiritually rich, being destined to share His eternal glory. He did not rebuke them for their lack of faith (as modern prosperity preachers often do to Christians who aren't prosperous). In fact, of the seven churches Jesus addresses in

Revelation 2-3, there were only two that Jesus doesn't find fault with, and Smyrna was one of them.

3:15-20 We shouldn't be surprised that, of the seven churches Jesus addresses in Revelation 2-3, the one He accuses of being lukewarm was wealthy. Jesus warned that God's word can be choked by the "worries and riches and pleasures of this life" (Luke 8:14), a concept we considered in much more detail in Chapter Six. Nothing pulls people's hearts away from devotion to the Lord like money, which is why Jesus warned that we can't serve God and mammon (see Luke 16:13).

Indeed, money was the draw in Laodicea. They had grown wealthy and proud, now thinking they needing nothing. Jesus, however, had a vastly different viewpoint. To Him, they were "wretched and miserable and poor and blind and naked" (3:17), materially rich but spiritually impoverished. It was a cutting, humbling appraisal.

Jesus then graciously offered a remedy for their ills. They, being so wealthy, should buy three things from Him: (1) "gold refined by fire," that they "may become rich," (2) "white garments" to cover their nakedness, and (3) "eye salve to anoint [their] eyes" that they might see (3:18).

How much we should read into these figures of speech is debatable. At minimum, Jesus was calling for a repentance that would result in their being truly rich, righteous, and spiritually perceptive. Taking a little more liberty, could we not interpret Jesus' advice to buy refined gold from Him, that they might "become rich" (3:18), to be a command to use their wealth to lay up heavenly treasures? What else could one whom Jesus considers spiritually poor do with his money that would result in Jesus appraising him as then being rich?

A more important question concerns the Laodiceans' eternal status. Materially rich, laying up earthly treasures, spiritually poor, without white garments[12] spiritually blind, needing to repent, and about to be spit out of Jesus' mouth—I wonder, were they saved, in danger of forfeiting their salvation, or unsaved? What was their eternal destiny if they didn't repent? Are people whom Christ considers wretched, miserable, poor, blind and naked on the narrow road that leads to life? That seems unlikely.

Jesus' final words to the Laodicean church raise even more doubts. He portrays Himself as standing on the outside, knocking at the door, waiting for the one inside to hear His voice and open the door that He might come in and dine with him (see 3:20). Jesus indwells all those who are born again (see Rom. 8:10; 2 Cor. 13:5).

6:15-16 As we are told in Proverbs 11:4, "Riches do not profit in the day of wrath, but righteousness delivers from death."

---

[12] In the book of Revelation, having white garments is indicative of salvation; see Rev. 3:4-5; 4:4; 6:11; 7:9, 13-14; 19:14.

17:4-5; 18:3, 7, 11-19 Whatever world-renowned city this great harlot, also called Babylon, turns out to be, it is evident that it will be full of wealth when God's judgment falls upon it. Although her luxurious wealth is not the only thing God will hold against her, it will at least be part of the reason for His wrath upon her, as we read in 18:7: "To the degree that she glorified herself and lived sensuously (or *luxuriously*, as the margin indicates in the NASB), to the same degree give her torment and mourning…." The basis of her allotted wrath will be the degree of her glorifying herself and her luxurious living.

Having now considered the large majority of relevant scriptures in the New Testament epistles regarding money, possessions and stewardship, we can safely conclude that there is nothing within them that contradicts what Jesus taught on the subject. Rather, what Paul, Peter, James, John and Jude teach only reinforces what Jesus plainly taught, as we would expect, since He commanded them to teach their disciples to obey all that He commanded them (see Matt. 28:19-20).

So let me conclude asking the same question I asked at the outset. *Have I misinterpreted what Jesus taught about money, possessions and stewardship?* No, my interpretation has proved to be consistent with the apostles' interpretation of what Christ taught. Greed is equivalent to idolatry. It is impossible to serve God and mammon. Greedy people won't go to heaven unless they repent of greed, which is an attitude that is expressed by actions. Those who profess to be Christ's disciples should, by their good stewardship, prove themselves to be so. They should live simply, sell what they don't need, and not lay up earthly treasures, realizing how foolish that would be in light of eternity. They should give all they can to support the gospel intelligently and assist fellow believers who are suffering pressing needs. They should be content if they have no more than what they legitimately need. If they have more or gain more, they should keep only what they need, giving as God directs. This is the essence of what Christ and His apostles taught about money, possessions and stewardship.

I rest my case. All that remains now is this question: Are you through the needle's eye yet? In the next chapter, I want to tell you about my own journey.

TEN

My Journey

One of the people who read the manuscript of this book encouraged me to write a chapter about my personal journey through the needle's eye. It also occurred to me that other readers might be wondering if I actually practice what I preach. Thus the reason for this chapter.

As I confessed in the introduction, my journey through the needle's eye has not been an easy one, and I'm sure I'm still on the journey. For the progress I've made, however, I must give praise to God. Only with Him is such a passage possible. It is a miracle indeed when a camel makes it through the needle's eye. But "all things are possible with God." And may I interject that it is a terrible crime that Jesus' words, "All things are possible with God," are so often used by prosperity preachers to encourage wealthy people to have faith in God to receive more wealth. Jesus was actually talking about how God is able to motivate wealthy people to give all their money away, what would be impossible apart from Him (see Matt. 19:26; Mark 10:27; Luke 18:27).

Let me tell you my story.

I was raised in a middle-class American family of six. We lived, however, in an upper-class suburb, although our particular neighborhood put us in a lower segment of that upper class community. Growing up, I often wore hand-me-down clothes from family friends. We only owned one car (at a time) and it was always purchased used. We had one bathroom in our house. Consequently, I grew up often thinking we were somewhat poor because many of my school friends had so much more. I was completely ignorant of how the rest of the world lived.

In my junior year of high school, I was born again, and I felt called to vocational ministry while attending my first year of college. That led me to a popular Midwestern Bible School that is known the world over for its emphasis on faith and prosperity. During my two years there, it was continually emphasized that God would prosper us financially as long as we would apply the biblical principles for wealth. We could be rich, even by American standards. Setting the example of what we could expect if we too had faith, both the school's founder and his son (the executive president) enjoyed expensive wardrobes, lived in very upscale homes and drove brand new Jaguars.

I'll never forget when the school's founder once justified his luxury automobile by telling us, "Jesus drove the best during His earthly ministry." He went on to explain that the "best" in Jesus' day was a donkey, and the Bible talks about Jesus riding a donkey into Jerusalem. If Jesus were living in our day, we were told, surely He would have driven the best by our standards. It never occurred to me until years later that, as far as the Bible tells us, Jesus rode a donkey only one time, during His triumphal entry into Jerusalem. In so doing, He was fulfilling a messianic prophecy found in Zechariah 9:9 that specifically spoke of Him riding a colt. Additionally, Jesus didn't own the donkey upon which He sat. It was borrowed for the occasion. Thus, if you want to be "prosperous like Jesus," Scriptural precedent allows you to ride a borrowed donkey one time (and only if you are the Messiah).

Garbage In, Garbage Out

At Bible School we were told that if it was a sin to be rich, then God was the biggest sinner of all, because He owns everything. As King's kids, we had a right to material luxury.

As a young and impressionable Christian, I bought into it their doctrine hook, line and sinker. To me, prosperity became an indicator of spirituality and faith.

For the first decade of my ministry, I preached and practiced what I learned at Bible School. Although I never attained the level of wealth that some of my fellow graduates did (those who pastored larger churches), I probably exceeded the majority of them. I told the congregations which I pastored that it was God's will for them to prosper abundantly. Each time I received an offering, I never neglected to read a scripture that would build their faith to receive more financial blessings from God. I emphasized tithing as an investment plan that assured ever-increasing wealth. Higher-paying jobs, better cars, nicer homes and more "things" awaited those who "applied God's prosperity principles." Every promotion or acquisition was looked upon as an indication that our faith was working. It was occasionally mentioned that our prospering afforded us even more to give, but that was hardly our primary motive. Rather, our prospering afforded us more to spend on ourselves. We'd gladly part with ten percent of our increase if we could keep ninety percent of it. (What greedy person wouldn't?) Moreover, our giving was directed primarily toward our own church or ministries that, like ours, "preached the word" (that is, preached prosperity and everything else just as we did).

I could make scripture say just about anything that I wanted it to say. I had explanations for most of Scriptures' "hard sayings" regarding wealth. Some of my explanations were so absurd that it's a wonder no one challenged me on them. For example, I reconciled my theology with Scripture's commandment to be "content with what you have" (thus showing that your character is free from the love of money; see Heb. 13:5), with the profound statement: "I'm content, but just not satisfied." Other explanations were more sophisticated: It was OK to have things as long as things didn't have you. God is only opposed to greed, not to our ever-increasing personal wealth. Jesus only ever told one man to sell all he possessed. Many of the difficult scriptures I simply ignored. I kept building bigger barns.

A Dream House and a Prayer

My wife and I eventually bought ten acres of rural land on a hilltop and built our four-bedroom, three-bathroom dream house, assuming more debt than ever before. But we could afford the monthly payments, as I was making a good salary at my third pastorate. I often felt guilty in my heart as we built that house, inwardly questioning if it was God's will for us. Furthermore, as we endured significant difficulties as well as personal problems during its construction, I wondered if God was actually working against us. But we eventually moved in and began to enjoy our home in the country. We built a new church building around the same time, borrowing "only" $800,000 in the name of Jesus, requiring our congregation to make monthly payments of $7,000 for years while Jesus went hungry, thirsty and naked around the world.

But then something happened that set me on a different course. I sincerely prayed and asked God if there was anything I was doing that was displeasing to Him, and if there was, to please reveal it to me. (That is a prayer that God answers 100 out of 100 times when it is prayed.) The Lord soon began to open my eyes to the scriptures I had been ignoring or twisting, and I began to see my greed. My wife and I began to have serious discussions about our lifestyle. I felt convicted for the example I had set before my congregation and for much of what I had previously taught. I began preaching very serious sermons about stewardship. When I announced that my wife and I were going to sell our house because we felt it was a monument to our selfishness, I was surprised by many people's reactions. Rather than rejoicing that their pastor was actually beginning to obey Jesus, some were upset. I suppose our decisions were making them feel guilty.

We weren't able to sell our house immediately, as the entire interior needed to be painted for the first time. I also wrestled with my decision, and tried to find a way out of it. Perhaps, I thought, we could finish the basement and provide a place for some homeless people to stay temporarily. During that time we did take in a homeless Christian woman for six months until she was able to get back on her feet. In the end, however, we were convinced we should sell the house and scale down.

Scaling Down

During that same time, we began to take inventory of everything we owned, selling what we didn't need to give the money to poor believers in developing nations. The first thing to go was an antique 16-guage Winchester shotgun I had inherited from my father, who had inherited it from his father. I hadn't used it in two decades, so it seemed like it couldn't be anything but a "treasure" that I had laid up on earth.

I gave all but one suit and most of my ties to poor pastors in developing nations.

We got rid of our cats, feeling guilty that we were feeding animals while we were letting brothers and sisters starve in Sudan. My wife later became very involved with helping Sudanese refugees, five of the "Lost Boys," who had been relocated to our city. Another "Sudanese mother" like herself reported her experience with one of her thin, young Sudanese men the first time she took him to a grocery store. When he came to an aisle full of dog food, he stood in amazement and asked, "What kind of work do the dogs do here in America?"

We sold our antique dining room furniture that I had painstakingly refinished twenty years earlier. It was to us our most obvious "treasure" at the time, and we used the money for the Kingdom. It occurred to us that having a dining room that is used only once a month (we had a more-than-sufficient eat-in kitchen) is really an unnecessary luxury. But we were like so many Americans. We had good china that we used only when we had dinner guests, which was less than once a month. We needed a place to showcase that china, so we had a china closet. And of course we needed matching table, chairs, and buffet. All that furniture had to go somewhere, so we had to have a formal dining room included when we built our house. So the cost of owning that china amounted to about 10% of our monthly mortgage payment as well as what it cost to heat that dining room in the winter and cool it in the summer. Costly china indeed!

That pain of selling our treasured antique furniture was incomparable to the joy of using the proceeds to help an elderly woman in Romania, buy 25,000 gospel tracts for native Asian evangelists, ship Christian literature to pastors in Nigeria, and release seven young children from bonded labor in India.

Once our house was sold, we purchased the home my parents had bought when I was five years old. Since they also wanted to scale down, our arrangement was that they would move into the mother-in-law suite they had added for my grandmother when she was still alive. Currently, my wife and three children still live in that three-bedroom, one-bath home, and my parents still live with us in the mother-in-law suite. Our house is still very nice by the standards of much of the world. In fact, as I write these words, my wife and I are staying with a Christian Cuban couple in their Havana home which makes my house seem very luxurious. I take a little comfort knowing that my present home is worth about two-thirds the price of the median home in America and that it also houses our ministry office and book warehouse. But I would still be embarrassed to show my Cuban hosts a photo. Earlier this evening, we took another Cuban couple out for a pizza dinner and spent less than we would have spent at any fast food restaurant in the United States. Yet that total meal cost more than their monthly income. They live in an apartment with three tiny rooms, four children and no windows.

Convicted by a Book

It was during that period of my life when I began writing this book. When it was 90% complete, I gave up hope and stopped writing, believing that there were few people, if any, who would be interested in reading it. (I did eventually post the completed chapters on my website.) I resigned my pastorate then as well, and began doing full-time what I had been doing part-time for years, ministering to pastors in the developing world. We also began supporting orphans and meeting pressings needs of poor Christians (see www.HeavensFamily.org)

My dashed hopes of a readership were resurrected about five years later when I was invited to speak at a conference in Missouri at which the theme was repentance. The organizer specifically asked me to speak about stewardship, and to my surprise, my message was well received by several hundred people who had gathered from around the U.S. and Canada. Encouraged, I began writing once again, and as I reviewed what I had previously written, I fell under more conviction regarding my own stewardship. I had saved tens of thousands of dollars for retirement during the previous fifteen years. I was also spending money every month on life insurance and disability insurance. (Health insurance had been out of reach since I resigned my pastorate two years earlier.)

I was traveling around the world teaching pastors about making disciples, which included teaching them to obey what Jesus taught about stewardship. I was, of course, telling them not to lay up earthly treasures, but none of them had retirement savings, health, life, or disability insurance. I felt hypocritical. Are those things really necessary for those whose God is the Lord? Is the one who created us able to take care of us? Why should I, who never plan to retire, save money for retirement? Did Peter, James, John or Paul save money for retirement, have health, life and disability insurance? Do the billions of people who live on less than two dollars per day have them?

My wife and I wrestled with these things for several months. In the end, we decided to part with them all. It was a wonderful feeling, and every day we thank the Lord because He is trustworthy. Now we have more to give.

Are we foolish? If God can't be trusted, I suppose the answer might be *yes*. But it doesn't seem likely that God will soon renege on all of His promises to provide for, protect and preserve His children. Insurance companies make promises and people trust them. *Is God less trustworthy?* Moreover, He can provide what no insurance company would dare promise. People with health insurance are becoming ill as well as dying every year by the millions.

Had we been born in any one of thirty very poor nations of the world, we would probably have already lived out our life spans (currently I am age 47). So everything from here on is a bonus. On top of that, we're not afraid to die, because we believe in Jesus.

So we're going to try to give God every reason to keep us healthy and alive by trusting Him and bearing fruit for His kingdom, a very biblical idea. We are in His hands, and it feels wonderful to no longer be using God's money to bet against His promises. What we used to spend on insurance just in case God let us down, God can now use to keep His promises to widows and orphans. In eternity, it will be obvious if we were wise or foolish in the eyes of God.

It was during this same time when we also lost thousands of dollars that we had invested from the proceeds of the sale of our dream house. Our hope was to use those investments to help fund our ministry, but as the stock market further slumped and as a "too-good-to-be-true investment" turned out to be too good to be true, we watched much of it evaporate. It was a painful reminder of what the once-world's richest man said:

> Do not weary yourself to gain wealth, cease from your consideration of it. When you set your eyes on it, it is gone. For wealth certainly makes itself wings like an eagle that flies toward the heavens (Prov. 23:4-5)

We lost a wonderful opportunity to lay up treasure in heaven by taking a gamble. The only good result is that we will never make such a foolish mistake again, and we have asked for God's forgiveness. Thank God for His mercy.

Cars and Cubans

We decided long ago never to buy another new car, realizing that such a decision could enable us to give away tens of thousands of dollars during our remaining car-buying years. My wife and I need only one automobile,

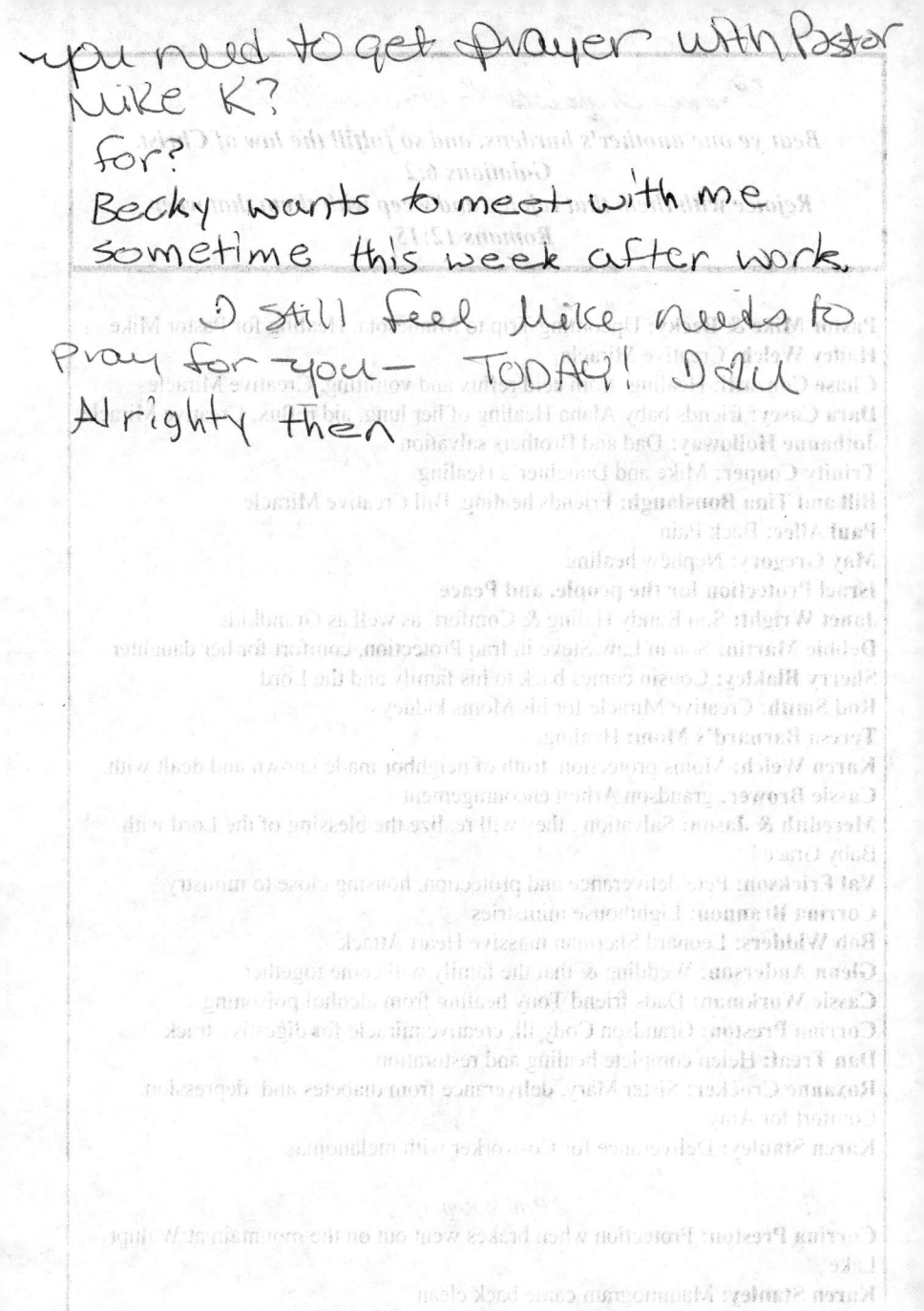

you need to get prayer with Pastor
Mike K?
for?
Becky wants to meet with me
sometime this week after work.
I still feel Mike needs to
pray for you— TODAY! I ♡ U
Alrighty then

Pastor Mike & Becky: Upcoming Trip to Minnesota, Healing for Pastor Mike
Hailey Welch: Creative Miracle
Chase Conzatti: Healing from acid reflux and vomiting, Creative Miracle
Dara Casey: friends baby Alana Healing of her lung, aid reflux, Creative Miracle
Johanne Holloway: Dad and Brothers salvation
Trinity Cooper: Mike and Daughter's Healing
Bill and Tina Bouslaugh: Friends healing, Bill Creative Miracle
Paul Allee: Back Pain
May Gregory: Nephew healing
Israel Protection for the people, and Peace
Janet Wright: Son Randy Haling & Comfort, as well as Grandkids
Debbie Martin: Son in Law Steve in Iraq Protection, comfort for her daughter
Sherry Blakley: Cousin comes back to his family and the Lord
Rod Smith: Creative Miracle for his Moms kidneys
Teresa Barnard's Mom: Healing
Karen Welch: Moms protection, truth of neighbor made known and dealt with.
Cassie Brower: grandson Arhon encouragement
Meredith & Jason: Salvation , they will realize the blessing of the Lord with Baby Grace
Val Erickson: Pete deliverance and protection, housing close to ministry
Corrina Brannon: Lighthouse ministries
Bob Widders: Leonard Sherman massive Heart Attack
Glenn Anderson: Wedding & that the family will come together
Cassie Workman: Dads friend Tony healing from alcohol poisoning
Corrina Preston: Grandson Cody ill, creative miracle for digestive track
Dan Treat: Helen complete healing and restoration
Roxanne Crocker: Sister Mary, deliverance from diabetes and depression.
Comfort for Amy.
Karen Stanley: Deliverance for Co-worker with melanoma

Praise Reports

Corrina Preston: Protection when brakes went out on the mountain at Walupt Lake
Karen Stanley: Mammogram came back clean
Hannah & John South: The Birth of Miss Ava Rose Thursday August 10th

as we both work from home for our ministry, *Heaven's Family*. Our current auto is six years old and has over 100,000 miles on it. But it looks good and is dependable.

My income is now about half of what it was a few years ago, at the peek of my pastoral ministry. The less I make, the more that our ministry has for good works around the world, so my goal is to reduce my income to the lowest level I can. We intend to continue on the path of scaling down. Laying up treasures in heaven is so much smarter. Living simpler is so much better. Adam and Eve had nothing and lived in a Paradise.

Living with less and giving more, we're happier than we've ever been in our lives. Today I sat holding back tears of joy for an hour and a half as I watched my wife give away reading glasses to Cuban pastors and their wives who could no longer read their Bibles. All it cost was one dollar per pair of glasses. An American friend who has joined us here just returned from filling up the trunk of our rented car with food for that Cuban couple who live in three windowless rooms with their four children. They were overjoyed in God's provision. He was overjoyed to be the vessel of God's love. It cost him thirty dollars. He can't wait to do it again tomorrow for another poor Cuban Christian family. He wouldn't have traded his experience today for two weeks on a Caribbean cruise ship.

Ministering to pastors all over the world has brought us face to face with very poor brothers and sisters in Christ, many of whom have pressing needs, and we cannot close our hearts. We have consequently launched a ministry called *Orphan's Tear*, through which we assist struggling Christian orphanages in numerous countries through the kindness of $20-per-month partners who sponsor one orphan. A second ministry, *I Was Hungry*, provides opportunities for Western Christians to supply food and meet other very pressing needs of fellow believers in developing countries, all administered through trusted pastors.[1]

Surely we will be even happier as God continues His miracle in us, purging us of our selfishness and making us more like Christ. May He complete the work that He has begun. We're going through the needle, glory be to God. If you're still reading, looks like you are too. *Glory be to God!*

[1] For more information, visit www.OrphansTear.org and www.IWasHungry.org.

Appendix: The Old Testament View

Although I rested my case at the close of the ninth chapter, it occurs to me that there are many professing Christians who resort to various Old Testament scriptures to justify their disobedience to Christ's commandments. I've already limitedly exposed the more common fallacies of those kinds of justifications, but I thought it might be helpful to examine a number of relevant Old Testament scriptures, anticipating that I might be accused of ignoring them. Thus the reason for this appendix. It can be used to better equip those who are defending the truth against those who are perverting it. The Old Testament, taken as a whole, absolutely annihilates the doctrines of modern prosperity preachers and condemns the self-indulgence of most Western evangelicals.

Allow me to begin by first asking a question. If we discover an Old Testament scripture that contradicts (either real or imagined) what Christ clearly taught, does our discovery give us the right to nullify Christ's and His apostles' teaching? Certainly not. If we can't find a way to reconcile what Jesus taught with what the Old Testament teaches, we would be foolish not to give prerogative to Christ. We are, of course, living under the new covenant and are supposed to be obeying Jesus' commandments.

We should also acknowledge that the New Testament upholds a somewhat higher standard of holiness than the Old, and from us to whom much has been given shall more be required (see Luke 12:48). For example, God obviously permitted the polygamy of some Old Testament leaders such as Jacob, David and Solomon, but New Testament overseers must be "the husband of one wife" (1 Tim. 3:2). We don't we justify having multiple wives and concubines based on Old Testament scriptures. Is it not because we have more divine light?

God permitted His old covenant people to acquire slaves from surrounding pagan nations (see Lev. 25:44). Shall we justify doing the same based on what God allowed them to do? Is God telling Christian believers to invade neighboring nations as a means of His judgment upon them as He did the people of Israel? Obviously not.

We who are indwelled by God's Spirit have a higher capacity to live godly lives. Jesus gave us a *new* commandment, which is to love each other even as He has loved us (see John 13:34), a very high standard indeed. Why would we ever imitate some patriarch, wealthy only by the standards of his own day, who did not have the spiritual revelation, spiritual help, or God-given responsibility that we possess, when we have Christ, our sinless Shepherd and Lord, to follow and imitate?

Moreover, by a very large majority, the people who lived before and during the Old Covenant were not wealthy. They generally lived by similar standards that many citizens of the developing world do today. What grounds do prosperity preachers have to single out a few Old Testament kings from among millions of other Old Testament people and use them as examples of God's will for all New Testament believers?

Throughout our Old Testament survey, we'll discover ancient endorsements of what Christ taught, but every person about whom we read will not necessarily attain to His new covenant standards. Some scriptures will answer a few nagging questions that remain or tweak our understanding more closely to a perfect biblical balance. This survey will also help us to identify the Old Testament scriptures that are so often misused to support modern prosperity teaching. A careful and honest examination of those passages will expose the many modern fallacies that are used to justify greed.

A surprising amount of information is found in the Old Testament that is relevant to our topic of money, possessions and stewardship. Hundreds of scriptures could be listed under the heading of "Personal Stewardship." I have thus avoided commenting on a number of those scriptures that added nothing to balance or enhance truths we've already learned. I've also avoided quite a few scriptures that are accountings of offerings to God, even though they certainly buttress Christ's teaching on stewardship. I have not, however, avoided scriptures that could be considered contradictory to what Christ taught. I think it will be well worth your time to read this entire appendix.

Genesis

2:4-3:24 From the first pages of the Old Testament, we note that when God created the first two humans, He gave them only what they needed—food, and human and divine companionship. Later, after their fall when they needed it, He provided clothing. The climate in the garden of Eden must have been perfect, the temperature fluctuating only slightly through the day and night (see Gen. 3:8), so Adam and Eve needed no clothing. Perhaps God gave them or they constructed some kind of a dwelling, but we have no record of this. Their water was pure[1] and all the food they needed was waiting to be picked nearby. Their time would have been occupied by enjoying God's creation, fellowshipping with Him and one another, cultivating the garden of Eden, perhaps some limited animal husbandry, and a few other necessities—eating, bathing and so on. In short, they would have been subsistence farmers living in a tropical paradise, having very few, if any, possessions.

Obviously, having just the essentials must not be so bad, because that is all God gave Adam and Eve. We have been duped by our materialistic culture into thinking that happiness is made possible by owning material things. Adam and Eve could have been perfectly happy with what God gave them. And what God gave them was essentially all that most people have had over the past 6,000 years, and all that most people in the world have today. Why do we believe we need so much to be happy? Why do we buy more of what we don't need when there are so many people who

[1] Note that their water would have been pure because it was unpolluted by industry that produces all the products we love. The cost of modern products is much more than the money we pay for them at the cash register. Much of the creation is being destroyed as we crave more stuff.

are lacking basic essentials whom we could help? Why are we discontent even with all we have?

Indeed, discontentment was Adam and Eve's undoing. The serpent seduced Eve into believing that there was something beyond what God had given her that could make her happy. So she ate what God forbade, expecting to find fulfillment, and her husband followed suit. Neither trusted that the Lord had told them the truth in His previous warning, and their unbelief and discontentment resulted in their expulsion from Paradise. How many of us have suffered because of our own discontentment? I suspect all of us.

4:2-5, 20-22 We read in verse 2 of the very first sectored economy. For some reason, perhaps natural inclination, survival, mutual benefit, or material gain, Abel and Cain are found in different vocations. By the time we come to 4:20-22, it seems that diversified economics had established a course of no return in early civilization. Technology also had its beginning, and here are the roots of capitalism. Enterprising individuals could benefit by providing some useful goods or service to others.

It has been suggested that the parents of Cain and Abel learned about bringing God offerings of animal sacrifices when He clothed them with the skins of slain animals after their fall. Perhaps He gave them a lesson on how their sin and shame could be covered and what they needed to do if they sinned again. Regardless, Cain and Abel obviously knew about bringing the Lord offerings, something stipulated later in the Law of Moses by God Himself. Offerings could be brought to God for various reasons—for thanksgiving, atonement and so on—but in every case there was an acknowledgment of the worshiper's stewardship and God's ownership. The worshipper relinquished something he possessed and would watch his offering go up in smoke "to God" as it were. Regular offerings were a regular safeguard against attachment to material things and a continual reminder of God's lordship over one's possessions. This practice is something that God established from the dawn of human history, and it was practiced prior to the Law by Noah, Abraham, Isaac and Jacob (see Gen. 8:20; 12:7-8; 13:4, 18; 22:9; 26:25; 33:20; 35:1, 3, 7), making it no insignificant concept.

13:1-12 Abram was an elderly chieftain who headed a nomadic community of perhaps more than one thousand souls (he was able to muster an army of 318 fighting men from among their number according to 14:14). He probably inherited his leadership position and much of his wealth at the death of his father, Terah.

Abram's community lived in tents because they would have needed to move periodically to find pasture for their livestock, the basis of their livelihood. They would have been sustained by eating their animals and consuming or utilizing the animal products, and by selling some of their animals or animal products, using the money they gained to purchase other necessities.

They apparently were able to graze their animals on land they didn't own or lease, and as their herds and flocks naturally multiplied, Abram and Lot found that they needed to separate out of necessity. The arid land simply could not sustain their combined livestock, which must have numbered in the thousands of animals.

Thus we read that "Abram was very rich in livestock, in silver and in gold" (13:2), but one could hardly call his lifestyle luxurious or self-indulgent. The entire community lived in tents pitched in remote areas, sleeping on some sort of mats or rugs on the ground. They had no running water, refrigeration, electricity, and so on. They ate, not at tables, but sitting on rugs or mats. Perhaps they had a few tents they used as toilet tents. I always have to chuckle when I hear some prosperity preacher talk about how we can be rich "like Abraham." Would you trade places with Abram to have his wealth?

Compared to others in his community, Abram was the richest, being the owner of the livestock. But to maintain and gain wealth, he needed his community, and the community needed his wealth to survive. It was a mutually beneficial relationship. Thus, Abram was comparable to an owner of a modern, mid-sized business. Using his God-given resources, he created jobs. He hired people to take care of necessary responsibilities, and they joined his community for their economic wellbeing and physical safety. Abram had great responsibility—hundreds of people depended on him for their lives, and he took care of them all. It was not as if Abram was living in a luxury palace along the Mediterranean Sea, collecting weekly profit checks that were mailed from his slaves who eked out a living in the wilderness. He was not like modern CEOs who make 400 times the salary of their average employee. He gained his wealth justly, and used it for the benefit of an entire community. In that respect, Abram was a wonderful example for modern Christian business owners to imitate.

Neither does it appear that money was Abram's God. He graciously offered Lot his choice of pasture when they needed to separate their flocks and herds (see 13:8-12). He paid tithes to Melchizedek the priest from the spoils of his just war with the four kings (see 14:20), and he wouldn't accept payment from the king of Sodom for his invaluable service to him (see 14:21-24). We really don't have any conclusive information from Scripture that this blessed man whom God commanded to "be a blessing" (12:2) was greedy.

But was not Abram's wealth "in silver and in gold" (13:2) the equivalent of earthly treasures? Even if it was, how much of the New Testament had Abram ever read? (In fact, how much of the Old Testament?) Are we to follow Abram's example or Christ's? We know that Abram twice lied about his relationship with his wife, saying she was his sister (see 12:10-20; 20:1-5). Moreover, Abram had a sexual relationship with his wife's Egyptian maid (see 16:1-4) and kept concubines (see 25:5-6). Shall we follow his example in those cases in disregard of Christ?

Finally, here are a few questions for which we don't have certain answers: How many (if any) of Lot's flocks and herds came as a gift from his uncle, Abram? Were there any impoverished people in Abram's day, and if so, did Abram know about them, and if so, did he ignore their plight?[2] How many of the hundreds who lived with him had perhaps been destitute before he offered them employment? In regard to his silver and gold, how much capital did he need to have in liquid assets in order to continue to operate his business, like any other modern business owner? Could his wealth in livestock, silver and gold have been the equivalent of a modern person's business capital, when perhaps millions of dollars are tied up in inventory, equipment or buildings, while the owner has little personal wealth by comparison? (Meanwhile, because of his initiative, hundreds of people are employed and providing for their families.) And why is Abram chosen by modern prosperity preachers as the norm when Abram clearly was not the norm even among his own people? Why don't they mention that he lived in a tent all his life?

14:17-20 Hundreds of years before the Law of Moses was given, we find Abram paying tithes to an authentic priest and king of Salem (the future city of Jerusalem). Tithing was originally either a human or divine idea. Since its practice was later stip-

---

[2]If there were no impoverished people, or if there were some that Abram wasn't aware of, he was under no

ulated in the Law of Moses, I would prefer to think that tithing was a divinely-given concept rather than a pagan one that God adopted for His worshipers. Archeological discoveries reveal to us that the Chaldeans of the city of Ur, the hometown of Abram and his father, Terah, actually tithed to their pagan priests. So perhaps tithing was something Abram learned in Ur. Abram's example of tithing was passed down to his posterity, at least, to his grandson, Jacob (see Gen. 28:22).

Tithing was always an acknowledgement of God's ownership and the worshipper's stewardship. Since God is the source of all provision and blessing, He deserves to be honored by the giving of tithes. Tithing isn't a new covenant practice, but certainly not because God expects less devotion from His new covenant children than from His old covenant servants. Tithing is a great starting place in stewardship, but the Christ who indwells Christians whom He abundantly blesses will not be satisfied only to tithe. He who indwells us is not any more greedy than He was when He walked the earth two-thousand years ago.

15:13-14 More than half a millennium before it occurred, God revealed to Abram that his descendants would become a race of slaves in a foreign nation (not exactly a promise of prosperity). But the God of justice would judge their oppressors, and His settlement with the oppressing nation would include their having to pay "back wages" to the slaves whom they exploited to enrich themselves. God kept His promise, and at the Exodus, the Israelites "plundered the Egyptians" (Ex. 12:36).

Certainly there are many parallels between the Exodus story and New Testament redemption. Like the Israelites, we have been released from slavery and an oppressing kingdom. Our slavery, however, was to sin; the kingdom from which we were set free was Satanic, not Egyptian. Prosperity preachers like to add, however, that we, like the Israelites, should expect to become rich once we're delivered from the kingdom of darkness.

The delivered Israelites, however, weren't exactly made wealthy to the point of being able to live in luxurious self-indulgence as they wandered in the wilderness, or even once they settled in Canaan. During and after the Exodus, God provided what the Israelites needed to live and what they needed to construct the Tabernacle for Him. But they ultimately complained about the food that He supplied in the wilderness, and in Canaan, they lived like people do today in the developing world.

We too should expect that our new Father will take care of our needs and equip us for every preordained good work, just as He did for the Israelites in the wilderness. But most likely, we've been wealthy all our lives, always having much more than we needed. We are much more like the Egyptians, who became rich at the expense of others, than we are like the impoverished Israelite slaves. Thus, we should not expect that God will make us richer. Rather, like repentant Egyptians, we should be using the wealth we already possess to help set oppressed people free from sin and supply their needs. If God entrusts us with even more money, then we have even more to use for His purposes.

18:1 Here is *wealthy* Abraham (formerly *Abram*), still living in a tent, twenty-four years after the Lord first spoke to him (see 12:4; 17:1). His nephew, Lot, has a house in the city (see 19:1-11) that will soon dramatically depreciate in value when God rains fire and brimstone upon Sodom, forcing him to retreat to the comfort of a cave (see 19:30).

20:14-16 With Abimelech's gift, Abraham now has even more sheep and oxen to look after, which is probably why Abimelech also gave him servants (employees), knowing he needed more help to take care of his new livestock. Abraham's community is growing, and he now has more people than ever who are dependent upon him for their livelihood. Perhaps Abimelech also gave Abraham those 1,000 pieces of silver knowing that he would need it to cover the new expenses associated with his growing community. Or perhaps God was blessing Abraham through Abimelech because Abraham was a blessing to so many people. God had previously said to Abraham, "I will bless you….so you shall be a blessing (Gen. 12:2), or literally, "so be a blessing." God blesses people to make them a blessing to others.

Incidentally, Abraham returned some of those sheep and oxen to Abimelech in 21:27.

23:3-20 If wealthy Abraham owned any other real estate from age 75 until his death at age 175, scripture is silent about it. His wealth consisted of livestock, silver, gold and servants (see 24:35).

24:22, 35, 53 See my comments on 13:1-12.

26:12-17 Isaac's God-granted wealth, like his father Abraham's, consisted of livestock and "a great household" (26:14), that is, a large community of people that he headed. Like his father, he also lived in tents as a nomadic chieftain. I doubt that any reader would want to trade places with him in order to have his wealth.

There is no indication that Isaac hoarded his growing wealth or used it to live in luxury. Like his father, he would have been somewhat comparable to a modern owner of a mid-sized business who continually reinvests his profits into his growing operation. Isaac provided a living for many people. There is no evidence that he misused his stewardship.

Even if Isaac wasn't a good steward of his wealth, that wouldn't change what Jesus commanded His followers to do with their wealth. Scripture never states that Isaac is a model that New Testament Christians should imitate. Why do prosperity preachers set Isaac up as a standard for Christians, yet ignore, for example, Isaac's many servants, who owned much less? And why have we never heard any prosperity preacher say, "Have faith in God so that you can be rich like Isaac, living in a tent in remote areas as you follow your herds and flocks from place to place!"?

28:20-22 Although one could easily critique the merits of Jacob's vow as well as his character, to his credit it can be said that he only hoped that God would supply his basic needs of food, covering and safety. Also to his credit, Jacob promised that if God did provide those things, he would tithe. Jacob apparently knew about tithing hundreds of years before its practice was stipulated in the Law of Moses.

30:43 Like his father and grandfather, Jacob's prosperity also consisted of an abundance of livestock and servants who worked for him. According to his testimony before his wives and father-in-law recorded in 31:4-13, 36-42, God justly transferred to him the wealth he produced for dishonest Laban (see 30:27-30).

Because Jacob owned many sheep, goats, camels, oxen and donkeys, does that prove it is God's will for every Christian to own many sheep, goats, camels, oxen and donkeys? If not, then what gives anyone the right to say it proves it is God's will for all of us to hold more modern forms of wealth purely for the sake of self-indulgence, especially in the light of all Christ and His apostles taught? Because Jacob had two wives, does that prove it is God's will for every Christian man to have two wives?

Similar to Abraham and Isaac, Jacob also was somewhat equivalent to a modern mid-sized business owner. His servants were his employees and his business was raising livestock. He could consume the products of his animals, sell their products or sell the animals themselves and thus make a living. He may have been wealthy by the standards of his day, but would you trade places with him? Note how he described his "luxurious life" of tending Laban's flocks and herds: "By day the heat consumed me, and the frost by night, and my sleep fled from my eyes" (31:40).

34:25-29 Who would maintain that Jacob's sons acquired this wealth legitimately? This was nothing less than cold-blooded murder and thievery, motivated by revenge. Even worse, it was an unjust revenge, as an entire city was punished for one man's misdeed. I wonder, why don't prosperity preachers use these rogues as examples for us to follow to attain divine prosperity?

39:2-6, 21-23 God prospered Joseph and made him successful in Potiphar's house and in prison, yet there is no indication that his success resulted in the increase of his personal wealth in either place. Rather, it was Potiphar's wealth that seemed to have increased because of God's blessing on Joseph (see 39:5). Even if Potiphar did reward Joseph financially, Joseph lost it all when he was thrown into prison, where he spent several years, at least (see 41:1).

Why do some prosperity preachers use thirty-year-old Joseph as a model of God's will for all Christians? What about the first twenty-nine years of his life? Was there some deficiency in his faith for his first twenty-nine years that stopped him from experiencing "God's best"?

Joseph was indeed successful in all that he did, always increasing in favor before his superiors as he faithfully fulfilled his responsibilities. He was obviously a man of high character who maintained a good conscience before God. In regard to any money that the Lord may have entrusted to him, I suspect that Joseph was just as faithful in his stewardship before God as he was before men.

41:42-49 Joseph was now a rich, powerful man with a pagan wife, the daughter of the priest of On. He also had the most important job on the face of the earth, administrating the greatest relief effort to that point of history and perhaps of all time. Joseph was responsible to store huge quantities of excess grain for seven years in order to provide food for the world during the seven years of famine that would follow. He knew that he had been given much, and from him much would be required, later declaring to his brothers, "God sent me...to preserve life" (45:5). He recognized, unlike so many of us, that God gave abundance, not for self-indulgence, but in order to meet the pressing needs of others.

How sad it is that some prosperity preachers focus on Joseph's wealth while ignoring his service to the hungry, his extraordinary generosity (see 42:25; 44:1; 45:21-23; 47:12), and his prophetic significance, as he stands out as preeminent type of Christ found in the Old Testament. Here was a man who was rejected by his own, sold for some pieces of silver, but who was received by and exalted among the Gentiles, becoming their "savior." Joseph's rule foreshadowed the time when Christ will rule over the entire earth from Jerusalem, when "all the nations will stream to it" (Is. 2:2), just as the nations streamed to Egypt to buy grain (see Gen. 41:56-57).

Joseph is indeed a model for any Christian who has been entrusted with much. His story, however, is certainly not recorded in the Bible to encourage rich North Americans to "believe God" for more wealth with which they can further indulge themselves, while millions starve and face eternity without Christ.

47:13-26 Did Joseph become greedy, shrewdly taking advantage of desperate people to gain immense wealth for himself? Why didn't he give away grain rather than sell it?

Perhaps because it wasn't his to give. It belonged to Pharaoh, considered a god by the Egyptians, and Joseph worked for him. The profits belonged to Pharaoh as well, not Joseph (see 47:14, 19-20, 23, 24). As the famine continued year after year, Pharaoh eventually owned all the money, all the livestock, the majority of the land, and practically all the people of Egypt. Amazingly, the Egyptian citizens did not hate Joseph, but appreciated him for saving their lives (see 47:25). They didn't consider what he did to be unfair.

Everyone agrees that Joseph's story is a marvelous foreshadowing of Christ's story, as the similarities are unmistakable. Is it not possible that this section of the story foreshadows the time when Christ will rule over the kingdom of His Father, when everyone will personally own nothing, true stewards of what rightfully belongs to Him, glad to be servants of the one who has saved them? The events of the historic story are so remarkable that one can't help but wonder if God orchestrated them precisely only to that end.

To use the story of Joseph to prove that God wills for all His children to be immensely wealthy is unwarranted. Why not also say that God wants all His children to be sold into slavery by their own families, or be falsely accused of attempted rape? Where does Scripture teach that we are to be imitators of Joseph? And even if any of Joseph's actions stand in contradiction to what Christ taught, does that relieve us of responsibility to obey our Lord?

One truth that surfaces in this story, a truth that is consistent with the rest of Scripture, is that God supplies the needs of His people. Long before the seven-year famine, God made plans to preserve the lives of Israel and his sons through an unselfish man named Joseph. God cares about us, and we don't need to worry about food, drink or covering, just as Jesus taught (see Matt. 6:25-34), even in the midst of famine.

Exodus

3:7-8, 16-17 God's goodness is revealed in His plan to deliver His people from their Egyptian taskmasters and to bring them into a land where they could be free to enjoy the fruit of their labors. The Lord would abundantly supply all their needs in the Promised Land. Although it "flowed with milk and honey," ultimately the Israelites would still have to run the risk of getting kicked by a hoof or stung by a bee to enjoy that milk and honey! God wasn't promising an idle life of ease, but one of productive opportunity. Then, however, they would face a new danger. Later on, He would sternly warn the former slaves not to forget Him once they prospered (see Deut. 8:7-20).

3:21-22; 11:2-3; 12:35-36 Here is an unmistakable example of God blessing His own materially. I like to think of the silver, gold and clothing that the Egyptians gave to the Israelites as being the payment of "back wages," since the Israelites had worked as slaves for so many years. The Egyptians had enriched themselves by the Israelites' hard work; now God acted in perfect justice. But their blessings were given to them for another reason as well: God would soon be commanding Moses to receive offerings from the people of Israel in order to construct the Tabernacle in the wilderness (see 25:1-9).

Should we expect, once we've become Christians, that God will make us wealthy like the Israelites, as some prosperity preachers claim?

First, I don't see that the Israelites became instantly wealthy when they plundered the Egyptians. They received clothing and articles of silver and gold. Yet at the Exodus, they left their homes and any large possessions behind. They would be living in tents in the desert as they journeyed to the Promised Land. Would you trade places with them so you could enjoy their wealth?

Second, as I've previously stated, the large majority of North Americans are much wealthier than any Israelite was even after the Egyptians had been plundered. We are much more like the Egyptians in the story, who profited from the labor of slaves. Thus, we ought to be sharing our abundance with the needy among God's people, not expecting that God will give us more so that we can indulge ourselves to an even greater degree.

Third, if the Israelites' plundering of the Egyptians at the Exodus is the pattern for New Testament Christians, why don't the prosperity preachers encourage their followers to request clothing, gold and silver from their neighbors, as God did the Israelites? Have you felt led to plunder your neighbors?

What we should expect, once we become Christians, is that God will take care of our true needs, because that is consistent with all of Scripture. And if God adds to that blessing, then we have the blessed opportunity to be a blessing to others.

15:22-25; 16:2-3, 12-35; 17:1-6 In the hot desert, God supplied Israel's need for water and food, yet He first allowed them to become thirsty and hungry, testing them (see 15:25; Deut. 8:3).

God's instructions regarding the gathering of manna reveal His desire that they trust Him for their "daily bread," as He provided only what they needed for one day. The exception was on Friday morning, when the Israelites would gather twice as much as they needed for their households, and the extra manna didn't become foul the next day, which was the Sabbath rest. The Friday gathering required trust as well.

The apostle Paul found new covenant application in this story, mentioning in his second letter to the Corinthians that when the Israelites gathered the manna for the first time, some gathered much and some gathered little (see 2 Cor. 8:13-15). Yet when each Israelite's gathered manna was measured, each had exactly one omerful. It was a miraculous redistribution, a clear reminder or God's love for every Israelite.

Likewise, the Corinthians, from whom Paul was requesting monetary gifts on behalf of poor saints in Jerusalem, should understand that God has the right of redistributing His provision through their generosity. God loves all His children, and thus it should be obvious that His children who have more than they need should share with His children who have less than they need. Paul reminded the Corinthians that the time might come when their roles would be reversed with the Jerusalem saints (see 2 Cor. 8:14), not exactly something any modern prosperity preacher would teach.

20:17 The tenth commandment, prohibiting covetousness, reveals that God is not only concerned about our outward actions, but also our inner attitudes and hidden thoughts. The sins of theft and adultery begin with the desire to possess what belongs to another. Resentment, jealousy and hatred may also have their roots in covetousness. Contentment is the cure.

The tenth commandment also indicates God's sanction of the private ownership of property. There is nothing wrong with having a house, livestock or even servants. (Note that there were many other commandments in the Law regarding how one treated his servant, revealing that servants were much closer to employees than slaves.)

Keep in mind, however, that when God spoke these words to Israel, there was no great disparity in wealth between individual families of Israelites. At the exodus, there is no indication that there were rich and poor Israelites. All of them had just come out of slavery and all of them had just plundered the Egyptians. In the wilderness, God gave each family equal portions of daily manna. In Canaan, God divided up the land equally among the tribes and families. And finally, knowing that there would inevitably be disparity of wealth among the Israelites, God made provision in the Law for a regular release of debts and the restoration of one's property previously sold out of economic necessity. God leveled the playing field, as it were. What else would we expect from our loving God?

All this is simply to say that the tenth commandment cannot legitimately be used to prove God's sanction of the selfish amassing of wealth. It is simply a prohibition of covetousness.

21:2-6 Certainly this ordinance concerning the release of Israelite slaves after six years of service indicates that God considered such slavery to be less desirable than freedom. Keep in mind that Israelites could only become slaves by choice, not by force. And the only reason one would become of slave of a fellow Hebrew was due to economic necessity. If one incurred debt that he could not repay, for example, he could always sell himself as a slave in order to pay his debt, and he would have a fresh start in six years. Thus this ordinance was given because of God's concern for those facing financial hardship.

It is also clear that such arrangements were nothing similar to the kind of slavery of which we are familiar from American history. At the six-year release date, a slave might love his master so much that he might decide to serve him permanently. He was more like an employee who loved his job rather than a slave.

Why would a Hebrew buy another Hebrew as a slave? Most likely because he needed another person to take care of his crops or livestock. He knew very well that the initial purchase and on-going expenses of keeping his slave would cost him money. Thus his decision to purchase a slave required the same kind of foresight needed by modern employers. Economic forces bearing on available slaves and prospective buyers would determine the price of a slave.

21:33-22:15 Like the tenth commandment, these ordinances regarding individual property rights also reveal God's sanction of privately-owned property. They do not, however, sanction selfishness. The early Christians held private property, but "not one of them claimed that anything belonging to him was his own; but all things were common property to them" (Acts 4:32). Note that individual Christians had things that belonged to them, indicating private ownership, but they shared to the degree that they considered their private belongings to be common property. This was not the forced collectivism of communism, but the free expression of Christ-like love, born from hearts that were released from selfishness.

22:21-27 God's special concern for strangers (foreigners, refugees and travelers), orphans, widows, and other poor people was (and is) so strong that the man who oppressed such people had committed a capital offence. Moreover, the Israelites were forbidden to charge interest on loans made to the poor, as that would be profiting by another's misfortune, a violation of the second greatest commandment.

One could, however, receive from a poor borrower a "pledge" of repayment, some token of good faith, held as collateral until the loan was repaid in full. But in the case when the borrower was so poor that he had nothing better than his own cloak to give as a pledge, the lender was required to return his cloak before the sun set, as the cloak was the poor borrower's only means of keeping warm as he slept. Clearly, such a borrower was one who was extremely poor. Money that he borrowed would be for absolute necessities to sustain him until his fortune changed, or for capital to be used to begin making a living.

22:29-30 We will eventually read the many laws regarding the offerings of the first-fruits, which belonged to God, just as did the first-born animals and sons (who weren't sacrificed, but redeemed).

Imagine making your living by raising sheep and one of your sheep giving birth to a first-born lamb. You are required by God to sacrifice it, offering it up to Him. You would be losing your lamb, and if you had much intelligence, you would probably realize that God wasn't gaining a lamb. What then was the reason for such a requirement? The offerings of the first of the harvest and flock served as a continual reminder that God was the source and rightful owner of every material thing, and that those entrusted with such blessings were His stewards. God wants our hearts in heaven with Him, not on earth with material possessions. One's relationship with God is not right if his attitude and actions regarding his possessions are not in line with these facts.

23:3-8 All injustice is a violation of the second greatest commandment. Although the poor are often robbed of justice by the rich, the rich can also be robbed of justice from those whose compassion for the poor influences them to be partial in a legal dispute. God declares that rich and poor are entitled to equal justice. Being poor does not give one the right to steal what belongs to another, for example. If a poor thief was caught, he could be sold as a slave, and his selling price used to make restitution if he had no other means (see 22:3).

Even one's enemies are entitled to fairness, and just because the livestock of my enemy wanders into my field, I have no right to keep them (see 22:4). I would be stealing, regardless of my justification. (This commandment certainly stands in contradiction to the playground ethic of "Finders: keepers, losers: weepers.")

Using money as a bribe also violates God's justice.

23:10-11 Here God states that the primary reason He required the people of Israel to allow their land to lie fallow every seventh year was so "the needy of your people may eat" (23:11). Certainly this reveals God's special concern for the very poor and His plan to provide for their needs through the sharing of those who had more. God still cares about the poor, and it is still His intention to supply their needs through those who have more than they need.

Note also that, in the wisdom of God the poor were required to gather food for themselves from the fallow fields. People who lacked food because of laziness received nothing. Neither were the industrious poor completely stripped of their dignity by receiving handouts. In most cases, providing opportunities for the poor to earn their living is better than simply giving them what they need.

23:23-33 God, the owner of all land, certainly has the right to take away anyone's land and give it to someone else. In this case, His reason for doing so was because of the sins of the inhabitants of Canaan. He used the Israelites as the means of His judgment upon them, not driving them from their land, but destroying them on their land. The Israelites would then receive the land as God's gift.

This passage, among many others, also illustrates God's desire that His people all have some capital by which they can make a living. In an agricultural economy, people need land. In an information/technological economy they need an education.

25:1-9 How is it that the Israelites, who had been slaves a few days earlier, now owned gold, silver, bronze, scarlet material, fine linen, and so on? Most of those things were likely gained when God granted them favor among the Egyptians, who freely gave them valuable items at the Exodus (see 12:35-36). God intended that at least some of that plunder would be used for the construction of the Tabernacle and its furnishings. He blessed His people so they could be a blessing (see also 35:20-36:7).

Note, however, that God only wanted those "whose heart moves him" (25:2) to give, that is, those who had a heart-felt desire to make a contribution because they loved God. God still wants His people to give as they "purpose in [their] heart[s], not grudgingly or under compulsion," because He "loves a cheerful giver" (2 Cor. 9:7). Those who give cheerfully are those who give because they love God and fellow man.

34:21 God's commandment to rest from labor each seventh day served to safeguard against becoming too focused on work and gaining wealth. Here we read that even during critical times of planting and harvest, when the temptation to work seven days was especially strong, the Sabbath rest should be observed.

Leviticus

1:1-7:38 The burnt, grain, peace, sin and guilt offerings all had at least one thing in common—they all cost the worshipper something. It was *his* sheep, goat, bull or agricultural produce that went up in smoke "to the Lord" (2:9). This practice continually helped the Israelites maintain the proper perspective of their possessions in relationship to God. Each time they brought an offering, they were saying to Him, "You are the source and rightful owner of my wealth and possessions. You have the right to direct the use of what you have entrusted to me. You are worthy to be honored by my relinquishing material things to give them to you."

19:9-10 As in Exodus 23:10-11, we again read of God's means of providing for the poor through His own people's obedience. Note that God expected the poor to work for their food. Although they didn't have to plant crops, they did have to harvest or gather them. God does not want to subsidize laziness. So much of modern charity encourages irresponsibility, thus sustaining what it should be eliminating. When the poor are able to work and work is available, they should be expected to work. Paul wrote, "If anyone will not work, neither let him eat" (2 Thes. 3:10).

19:18 This commandment that Jesus said is the second most important commandment (see Mark 12:31) is found in the Old Testament only once, whereas it is found in the New Testament eight times. Using ratios for comparison, it is found once every 23,145 verses in the Old Testament and once every 994 verses in the New Testament, or 23 times more frequently in the New than in the Old. Paul wrote that this one commandment summarizes the whole Law (see Rom. 13:9; Gal 5:14). James called it the "royal law" (Jas. 2:8).

As the commandment is found here in Leviticus 19, it seems to be a summary of verses 9-18. Loving my neighbor as myself includes doing none of the following: bearing a grudge, taking vengeance, hating my brother in my heart, slandering, showing partiality, disrespecting the handicapped, mistreating employees, stealing from, oppressing or lying to my neighbor, and neglecting the poor.

"Who is my neighbor?" (Luke 10:29) asked a Jewish lawyer of Jesus. Are neighbors only people who live in our neighborhood? Are they only "our kind of people"?[3]

Jesus responded by telling him the Parable of the Good Samaritan (see Luke 10:30-37), a man who loved his neighbor, and it cost him time and money. Jesus made it clear that neighbors may be members of groups of people that are hated by our closest neighbors. Moreover, neighbors may not live in our neighborhood. They may live many miles away from us. Today, in our global community, our neighbors are everywhere on the Earth. Would it not be foolish to think that in a world where our selfishness affects people on the other side of the globe that we have no responsibility to love the people on the other side of the globe? For this reason, those of us who claim to be lovers of God and neighbor must live as simply as possible, sharing our excess by feeding the hungry, clothing the naked, and so on, as well as supporting the spread of the gospel to those who have never heard it yet. If we don't, how can we claim to be obeying the commandment our God considers to be the second most important commandment that He ever gave?

25:10-17, 23-34 The year of Jubilee was instituted by God to safeguard every Israelite from temporary and life-long financial destitution. It also prevented economic domination by a few who might amass all the capital, which, in an agricultural economy, is the land. The Jubilee clearly expressed God's desire for economic justice. Every fifty years, the playing field was supposed to be leveled again.

When the Israelites conquered Canaan, each family was given a portion of land, the basic capital from which they could derive their living. If an Israelite met with financial hardship, he could sell part of his land, but God did not allow land to be transferred permanently. If the man had a relative who was able to purchase it back for him, that relative was expected to do so. In the event that there was no "kinsman redeemer," at the fiftieth year, the year of Jubilee, all land that had been sold over the past fifty years reverted back to its original owner or his heirs. Thus, land values were based on the years left before the Jubilee, and purchasers were more like renters than owners. Additionally, if a person who had been forced to sell his land out of necessity recovered the means to redeem it, he had that right at any time.

Let us imagine an Israelite who finds himself facing a financial crisis. He is unable to feed his family. His problem is solved by selling part of his land to a fellow Israelite for ten years, the number of years that remain until the Jubilee. Let's say he sells a portion of his land for $10,000, which would amount to $1,000 for each year left until the Jubilee. He can now feed his family with his cash. He then hires himself out or hopes that next year will bring a bumper crop on his remaining land. At the end of one year he has the right to repurchase his land for $9,000. If his expenses over the past year did not exceed his income plus $1,000, he can redeem his land.

Note that God declared that the land was His (see Lev. 25:23). He graciously lent it to His people, and from it they derived their food, fuel, animal feed, and building

[3] The Jewish lawyer could have found his answer by reading Lev. 19:34.

materials for homes and tools. God never wanted any of His people to lack what they needed. But they had to work.

Everyone needs some capital from which he can earn his livelihood. Capital can be land, a piece of machinery, or a marketable inventory of goods, a skill, or knowledge. Realizing this, we can help lift the poor if we provide them with some kind of capital. Many Christian organizations are doing this around the world by the means of micro-loans, money lent to impoverished yet industrious people at interest rates that match inflation. Micro-loans have proven to be a very successful way of helping the poor help themselves, preserving their dignity while improving their lives. All of us can help the poor by giving to the micro-loan funds of Christian ministries.

25:35-55 Here we read of further provisions God made to assist Israelites who faced financial difficulties. All Israelites were commanded to sustain fellow Israelites (as well as strangers and sojourners among them) who met with hard times. If they lent such a person money or food, they were not permitted to charge any interest (see 25:35-38).

A person meeting severe financial hardship (apparently having had to sell all his land out of necessity to pay debts) could, as a last resort, sell himself as a slave to either a fellow Israelite or to a stranger or sojourner among Israel. For a price, he would agree to serve as a slave for six years or until the year of Jubilee (see Ex 21:2-6; Deut. 15:12-18), when he could rightfully reclaim "the property of his forefathers" (25:41), getting a fresh start. In essence, he would be renting himself for a specified time and would receive a lump sum that was equivalent to an advance on his full wages. His Israelite purchaser was forbidden to sell him or treat him severely, and was required to treat him, not like a slave, but like a hired man. According to Deuteronomy 15:18, a slave did twice the work of a hired man.

Selling oneself as a slave to a stranger or sojourner among Israel would be done only as a very last resort, and God compassionately made additional provisions for such a desperate person. His relatives had the right to redeem him fairly at any time, freeing him from his obligation to his purchaser. Also, if the man's fortunes reversed, he had the right to redeem himself fairly at any time.

All of these regulations reveal God's special concern for the poor and His desire for economic justice.

We also note that the Israelites were permitted to acquire male and female slaves from surrounding "pagan nations" and from "the sojourners" living in their midst (see 25:44-46). Particularly in regard to the "sojourners," keep in mind that there were other laws that made provision for their compassionate treatment by the Israelites (see Ex. 22:21; Lev. 19:9-10, 33-34; Deut. 26:12). Thus we can safely assume that sojourners who became slaves of Israelites did so voluntarily and out of economic necessity, rather than by force.

26:3-5, 14-15, 20, 26 Here we see the obvious correlation between obedience and material provision. If the people of Israel obeyed God, He assured them that He would supply their material needs. They would have sufficient food from their harvests. If they did not obey Him, however, they would suffer scarcity of food as well as many other hardships. Likewise under the new covenant, God promises to supply our need for food and covering if we seek first His kingdom (see Matt. 6:32-33).

Numbers

7:1-88 I've passed over a few previous passages that mention the giving of offerings, but this one can't be overlooked. It, like those I've passed over, once more illustrates that devotion to the Lord under the old covenant involved the giving up of material things. In fact, such giving was central to old covenant worship. *It cost something to have a relationship with God.* Here we find an entire chapter devoted to enumerating the specific offerings that the tribal leaders brought at the dedication of the Tabernacle. That this was recorded in Scripture reveals that God must have taken notice and considered their sacrifices significant.

8:24-26 Here is the only passage concerning retirement in the Old Testament. We are told that individual Levites were only to serve in the Tabernacle until they reached the age of fifty. After that, they were permitted to assist the younger men who worked in the Tabernacle, but they were prohibited from performing the work itself, which is somewhat of a vague commandment.

We are not told the reason for this commandment. Perhaps it was because the work was too strenuous for the average person over fifty. Regardless, we should certainly not assume that retired Levites were unproductive and lived idle, self-indulgent and meaningless lives. They were still obligated to serve the Lord like any other Israelite.

How does the modern concept of retirement compare to this? When people lived simple lifestyles and were sustained by their own land, there was no great need to save money for retirement. One owned his house, field, and animals, and his capital sustained him until death. Even if one may have become gradually incapable of working in his field and taking care of his animals, he could likely hire someone to do it for him or could easily be sustained by his grown children who would have inherited his land.

Modern retirement differs in that we do not live modestly and thus need continued large incomes to sustain luxurious lifestyles during retirement. Moreover, we most often retire out of desire rather than necessity, and so we race to save huge amounts of money in order to retire as soon as possible. Beyond that, we rarely retire gradually due to old age, but fully retire on a given day. Finally, modern retirement is often considered to be a time for daily self-indulgence and personal entertainment and amusement. How tragic it is that those who should be wise with years, who know they are closer to eternity than most, should spend their final years in continual testimony to their atheism.

The follower of Christ should consider God's will in the matter of retirement.

If you are currently retired, you are highly privileged, more privileged than the majority of people who live in the world today, as well as the majority of people who have ever lived. To have been able to save enough money so that you don't have to work any longer in order to earn a living is a testimony to your wealth. In developing countries, most people work until they die, and their life spans are much shorter than ours. If they become unable to work, they rely on their families to support them.

A principle of stewardship that certainly applies to retirement is, "From everyone who has been given much shall much be required" (Luke 12:48). The retired person, if in good health in mind and body, has much more discretionary time than one who must earn his living. Therefore, he will have to give account for that time, and God will expect that he use it for His glory. He may even consider going back to work in order to have more to give and share. If he isn't using his time to earn money to share, he should use his time in other ways that serve God's kingdom.

But what about those who are not yet retired? Is there anything wrong with saving money for retirement? This is not the simplest question.

First, the non-retired person should consider his reasons for wanting to eventually retire. If it is so he can spend all his time in the pursuit of leisure and self-indulgence, then he needs to repent and be born again. He is no disciple of Jesus Christ.

If one hopes to retire in order to spend the majority of his time serving others and God, that is certainly more virtuous.

It would seem impossible, however, to save money for retirement without laying up earthly treasures. (Obviously, Social Security and many non-optional company retirement plans relieve one's individual responsibility in this matter.) Thus it would seem advisable that working persons plan to retire only out of necessity, remaining financially fruitful until death in order to always have something to share. This does not require that every believer remain in a job that he hates until his death.[4] Rather, if he is older, out of debt, and has no children to support, he can probably find a way to sustain himself working part time and thus have more time to devote to ministry and service. If he has had his own business in operation for many years, he may be able be to continue earning his living with much less effort than when he began it, or he may be able to scale down his business but still have sufficient income.

It could be argued that saving money for retirement is wise in our modern non-agrarian economy, because most of us do not own land that is our capital, nor do we own our own businesses, things that could support us when we are unable to work. Additionally, saving for a time when one is unable to earn a living so as not to be a burden on others is a way of loving one's neighbor as one's self (see 1 Thes. 4:11-12; 2 Thes. 3:12).

Both of these arguments, however, are based on the assumption that one will eventually experience a time when he will be unable to work. If you expect that will happen to you, then I suppose that you should make plans to be sustained by some means. Personally, I prefer to trust God's promises in this regard, not the least of which is Psalm 92:12-15:

The righteous man will flourish like the palm tree,
He will grow like a cedar in Lebanon.
Planted in the house of the Lord,
They will flourish in the courts of our God.
They will still yield fruit in old age;
They shall be full of sap and very green,
To declare that the Lord is upright;
He is my rock, and there is no unrighteousness in Him (emphasis added).

The key to enjoying the benefit of yielding fruit in old age is righteousness. To expect to become incapacitated and unable to earn a living is not exactly an evidence

---

[4] In my opinion, the person who hates his vocation should find one that he enjoys. Too many stay saddled to jobs they hate only because they love the money those jobs provide.

of one's faith in God! Many insurance salespeople make their living from people young and old who dwell upon fears of what the future holds. Do we ever consider how much money Christians spend on health insurance, for example, money that often ultimately does nothing more than keep us suffering in hospital beds when we could be in heaven? That same money could be used to spread the gospel and feed orphans, laying up treasure in heaven.

11:1-35 Here is a classic example of discontentment followed by greed. Forgetting God's goodness in their deliverance from slavery, the Israelites complained about manna and wished for meat. We don't have to wonder how God felt about their discontentment, as "the fire of the Lord burned among them and consumed some of the outskirts of the camp" (11:1).

Prosperity preachers sometimes like to point out the great abundance of quail that God provided, but they fail to see that the quail were more of a punishment than a blessing. God warned that He would give them meat "until it comes out of your nostrils and becomes loathsome to you" (11:20). And when they greedily gathered much more than they needed, "the anger of the Lord was kindled against the people, and the Lord struck the people with a very severe plague" (11:33) so they died. God considered people to be greedy if they gathered more food than what they reasonably needed, and He killed them for it. Why don't prosperity preachers mention that fact?

18:8-28 By receiving certain offerings as well as the tithes of all the people of Israel, the Levites were sustained and enabled to perform their ministry at the Tabernacle. Clearly, it was the duty of every Israelite to tithe and thus insure the continuation of God's intended ministry. Surveys show that the large majority of professing evangelical Christians in America do not come close to attaining even this old covenant standard of giving.

22:4-9 Here is yet another story that illustrates God's view of discontentment. Suffering His judgment, Israelites died because of their discontentment. How must God feel about prosperity preachers who fuel the discontentment of people who are already among the world's richest?

22:1-24:25 Balaam was obviously tempted to fulfill King Balak's request to curse Israel and thus gain riches and honor for himself (see 22:17), but throughout these chapters, he resisted. Scripture reveals, however, that he soon gained the riches he had forfeited by counseling Balak that the only sure way to cause Israel to fall was by getting the Israelites to sin and thus incur God's wrath (see Num. 31:16; Rev. 2:14). Balak followed Balaam's advice, and his plan worked to some degree—24,000 Israelites who yielded to the temptation of idolatry and immorality lost their lives (see 25:1-9). Shortly thereafter, Balaam was killed in battle, and he is remembered in Scripture as a fool who traded God's approval for earthly wealth (see 2 Pet. 2:15; Jude 11). Beware of the deceitfulness of riches!

33:54 True to His love and justice, God commanded that Canaan's land be divided fairly among the families of Israel. No one was favored. Then what must be God's view of the great disparity of wealth that exists today among those who profess to be His children, some of whom have much more than they need, and others of whom are lacking basic necessities?

Deuteronomy

6:10-15 Here is a promise of prosperity coupled with a warning. If the people obeyed God, they would inherit the homes, cisterns, vineyards and orchards of the evil Canaanites whom they would dispossess. They would then have more than they needed. But there was a real danger that their prosperity might distract them from their devotion to the Lord. We, too, need to guard against that same danger.

7:12-13 Just as Jesus promised to supply all the material needs of His followers if they would seek first for His kingdom, God promised Israel blessing on their agricultural pursuits if they would obey Him. But should we conclude that God would want Israelites who were blessed with superabundant harvests to tear down their barns and build bigger ones so they could retire early? (If you don't know the answer to that question, see Luke 12:16-21.)

8:1-20 Again we find a promise of prosperity joined with a warning. If there was danger of forgetting God due to prosperity during a time when prosperity could be defined as having food without scarcity, "good houses" (that had no running water, glass windows, air conditioning, electricity or appliances), multiplying herds and flocks and multiplying silver and gold, then how much more danger exists for people living in the kind of prosperity to which we are accustom? God wanted the Israelites never to forget where they had come from and who had brought them out of Egypt. It is sad that modern prosperity preachers often use God's words in 8:18, "You shall remember the Lord your God, for it is He who is giving you power to make wealth," as a means of proving that God wants to prosper us, but they ignore the context, neglecting to mention what God was warning of before and after that verse. So many of the modern followers of such preachers have forgotten God and His Son's commandments relative to stewardship as they pursue greater wealth in order to lay up more earthly treasures, proving their devotion to mammon. They consequently set themselves up, not for more prosperity, but to perish, as God promised in 8:19-20. We should understand, however, that if God is the one who gives us the power to make wealth, then God has the right to tell us what to do with the wealth He has empowered us to make.

11:13-17 This is more of a promise of provision rather than prosperity. As long as Israel obeyed God, they would have plenty to eat. Otherwise, they would face deprivation.

12:6 Again we see how stewardship under the old covenant included so many different kinds of giving by those who worshipped the Lord: burnt offerings, sacrifices, tithes of every agricultural product, heave offerings, votive offerings, freewill offerings, and the giving of the firstborn of every animal.

13:12-18 I can't help but wonder why prosperity preachers pick and chose what they want from the Old Testament to find application for their modern audiences. One could just as easily find application from verses like these to justify killing prosperity preachers who are trying to lead us astray to follow the god of mammon! And why do prosperity preachers not find some message for New Testament believers in the material goods that were "under the ban" and to be publicly burned in 13:16-17? Is there nothing "under the ban" for us?

14:22-29 These instructions regarding tithing seem contradictory to what we have previously read in Numbers 18:21-28, where God said that all the tithe of Israel belonged to the Levites. Here we read of tithes being used by tithers for a big feast, and of every third year the tithe being given not only to Levites, but also to aliens, orphans and widows. Commentators debate how to reconcile these apparent contradictions. I speculate that, because there was no way for a family to eat a tenth of all their annual increase in one feast, each family used a small portion of their tithe for a feast that included Levite guests, and then all of the remainder was given to the Levites. Then, as believed by some Jewish commentators, every third year a second tithe was received that was given to the Levites, aliens, orphans and widows in one's own town.

15:1-18 This passage gives us a balanced picture of God-pleasing prosperity and stewardship. First, note that every seven years, every indebted Israelite became debt free. God leveled the playing field, because He is a God of love and justice. He didn't want some to grow richer as others grew poorer. Keep in mind that Israelites only went into debt because of necessity, not because of purchasing luxuries.

Second, note that Israel's prosperity depended on their obedience (see 15:5), which would include their obedience to His laws in this very chapter that relate to remitting debts every seven years and taking care of the poor. *Prosperity was promised only to those who cared for the poor* (see 15:10).

Third, note that lending money to a poor person could easily become an act of giving if the year of remission was near. In such cases, God forbade prosperous Israelites from hardening their hearts against their poor brethren.

And fourth, any Israelite who became a slave (which would have been only because of economic necessity) was to be set free after six years of service, and at that time, his master was commanded to provide him liberally with food and animals to sustain him. This, again, reveals God's concern for the poor and for economic justice.

16:9-15 At the annual, one-week Feast of Weeks, we see that the Israelites, blessed with abundance, were to remember the less fortunate and include them in their celebration. When there are so many scriptures in the Old Testament that speak of God's concern for the poor, why do prosperity preachers focus on those that speak of God's promises of prosperity?

16:16-17 All Israelite males were required to appear before the Lord in Jerusalem three times a year, but never "empty-handed." God expected them to bring an offering according to His blessing upon them. This was giving beyond the tithe, and another reminder to the Israelites that they were only stewards of all God had entrusted to them.

17:14-17 All of these things which God forbade the future king of Israel to do, Solomon did. He multiplied horses, wives and silver and gold for himself. The world's wisest man became the world's most foolish man, laying up earthly treasures, and he ultimately became an idolater.

20:10-14 One means God used to prosper Egypt's former slaves was through the plunder they gained when besieging pagan cities. Since some prosperity preachers find all the support for their doctrine in the Old Testament, why don't they encourage their followers to attack their pagan neighbors, kill the men, and take their women, children and possessions for themselves, so that they might prosper according to

God's will? If you asked them, they would reply that such a practice is unscriptural under the new covenant, and they are correct. They rightly negate an Old Testament practice by considering New Testament truth. My question then is this: Is it safe to assume that the means have been negated but not the ends? Didn't Jesus forbid new covenant followers to lay up earthly treasures, telling them to sell what they have in order to give to charity? Did God ever say such a thing to the people of Israel?

24:10-13 The "pledge" mentioned here is what we would call collateral to secure a loan. God's special concern for the very poor is revealed by His prohibition against keeping a poor man's cloak, given as a pledge, overnight. For what purpose would such a poor man be borrowing money? Probably for the most basic essentials.

24:14-15 God's special concern for the poor is again revealed by His commandment to pay a poor worker before the sun sets.

24:19-22 We are certainly finding more scriptures in the Old Testament that speak of God's concern for the poor and His expectations for generous giving and lending than we are scriptures that promise prosperity. If prosperity preachers would simply read all that the Old Testament has to say on the subject of stewardship, they would have to make major adjustments to their theology.

Notice again the wisdom of God. The poor should be given an opportunity to work, and they must work if they are going to eat.

26:1-15 This is another beautiful passage regarding stewardship. In recognition that every material blessing came from God, Israelites were instructed to bring an offering of their first fruits to the Lord. When they did, they were to make a declaration that contrasted their former lot in life as slaves with their present blessed position, and then share the first fruits with Levites and strangers. Similarly, when the second tithe was given every third year, a declaration was to be made after that tenth had been given to Levites, strangers, orphans and widows. This was followed by a prayer for God's blessing—blessing that was obviously contingent upon obedient stewardship and a genuine concern for the poor.

28:1-14 Here we find God's promises of national blessing to the people of Israel, contingent upon their corporate obedience. As the entire nation obeyed God's commandments, they would, as a nation, be "set...high above all the nations of the earth" (v. 1), defeat national enemy armies (v. 7), and "lend to many nations" (v. 12). Obviously, God was not promising individual Israelites that they, as individuals, would lend to many nations (see 28:13). However, as the nation was materially blessed, obviously all individual Israelites would be blessed. Take note that these blessings were contingent upon Israel obeying all of God's laws, not excluding His numerous laws of stewardship that we have already read.

Christians, unlike old covenant Jews, live in many nations of the world, and so it is impossible to find any direct application from this old covenant promise. And when we find so many scriptures in the New Testament that clearly show that very obedient people sometimes become or remain very poor, we know we would be abusing Scripture to use this passage to prove that God will give big houses and new cars to every Christian who has faith for prosperity.

28:15-68 In contrast to the national blessings in the first part of this chapter, we now read the national curses that are promised to Israel upon their disobedience. A popular modern doctrine promoted primarily by prosperity preachers couples this passage with Paul's words in Galatians 3:13, where it is said, "Christ redeemed us from the curse of the Law." Because the curse of disobeying the Law included poverty (see vv. 31, 38-44, 68), we are redeemed from poverty, they say. We should thus expect more abundant material things.

Even if this particular interpretation is true, I must wonder how many Western Christians are suffering the kind of poverty described in these verses. I would venture to guess that none of them are, and that most are probably much, much closer to (if not far exceeding) the level of material blessing described in the first part of chapter 28. In fact, we've likely never found ourselves needing to be redeemed from the poverty described in chapter 28, and most of us have enjoyed a level of prosperity that exceeds what is described in the first part of chapter 28 even prior to salvation.

31:20 Note that God knew that when Israel became prosperous, they would then reject Him.

32:13-15 Here again, in the Song Of Moses, it is clear that God knew Israel's downfall would occur when they grew prosperous. Could the same thing have happened to the Western church?

Joshua

6:15-19, 24, 7:1-26 Here is a sobering Old Testament lesson in stewardship! What was Achan's sin? He kept some silver and gold, which was supposed to go into the treasury of the Lord, for himself. We should not assume that just because we are given an opportunity to enrich ourselves, God wants us to use that opportunity to do so. Nor should we assume that our only obligation is to tithe such material windfalls. God may bring such opportunities solely to enrich His kingdom. (Incidentally, at the conquest of the next city, Ai, the people of Israel were permitted to keep the spoil for themselves [see 8:2] as well as from subsequent cities [see 11:14].)

Ruth

2:2-17 Ruth's opportunity to glean was made possible, not only because of Boaz's kindness, but because God commanded Israel to care for the poor in that way (see Lev. 19:9-10, 23:22). In this case, the gleanings of a poor woman not only provided her and her mother-in-law's needs, but set the stage for a love story that would culminate in the birth of Christ, a descendant of Ruth the Moabitess.

1 Kings

3:5-14 Note that God promised to grant Solomon riches and honor because Solomon didn't request either, preferring wisdom to serve God's people. The Lord also granted him the wisdom he desired, but unfortunately Solomon didn't always walk in his divinely-given wisdom. Had he done so, he would have obeyed God's commandments concerning his wealth. In the Law of Moses, the Lord specifically said of Israel's future king, "He shall not multiply horses for himself....He shall not multiply wives for himself, or else his heart will turn away; nor shall he greatly increase silver and gold for himself" (Deut. 17:16-17). Solomon eventually did all these things, and his 700 wives and 300 concubines ultimately turned his heart from God and he became an idolater (see 1 Kings 4:26; 11:1-10). Thus it could be said that the wisest man who ever lived became the greatest fool who ever lived. Solomon's misuse of wealth was his downfall. He should have used his money to love his neighbor as himself. Instead, he made life easy for himself and hard for millions of others who at his death, were happy that he was gone (see 1 Kings 12:1-16). He loved himself and effectively robbed 999 other men of wives.

9:15-22 As I pointed out in the fifth chapter of this book, the only way for a person to become extremely wealthy is to profit, directly or indirectly, from the labor of others. Here we see a prime example of that very phenomenon, Solomon's "forced laborers" from among the Amorites, Hittites, Perizzites and so on. I am not going to assume that just because God *promised* Solomon wealth that Solomon *gained* all his wealth according to God's will anymore that I'm going to assume that Abraham, although promised a son by God, became the father of Ishmael according to God's will. Solomon may well have abused his power to gain wealth just as he abused his power to gain hundreds of pagan wives in opposition to God's will (see 1 Kings 11:1-10). I think it is quite likely that a person who would be so selfish as to effectively rob 999 other men of their potential wives is also quite likely to have been equally selfish in how he gained and used his wealth.

10:21, 27 Like silver in Solomon's day, when something that was once scarce becomes abundant, its value decreases. The amount of silver that people previously would have given weeks of their labor to obtain, they would now give only hours for, simply because there was more of it on the market. Those who bought silver before the market was saturated watched their investment erode in value right before their eyes. This is a small picture of what will happen to everyone's wealth when they die. What they gave their entire lives to own will become utterly worthless to them in a moment.

We see that earthly value is determined by supply and demand. This is precisely why, for example, the flow of diamonds to the world market is carefully controlled, otherwise the greater supply would drive down the price of diamonds and the profits of those who control the supply. The actual value of diamonds is far below their current price. How foolish it is to give weeks or months of one's labor for what would be worth a fraction of its current price if the diamond supply were not controlled, and for what will ultimately be completely worthless when one dies, especially when one could have given the same labor in laying up eternal treasure in heaven.

17:1-16 Here are two inspiring examples of the Lord supplying the needs of Elijah in two supernatural ways while all of Israel languished in drought. Note that in both cases, Elijah had to obey the Lord's instructions in order for his needs to be met. Likewise, the widow whom God used to supply Elijah's needs had to obey Elijah's instructions and have faith, and she and her son consequently also benefited. Perhaps this is what Jesus had in mind when He said, "He who receives a prophet in the name of a prophet shall receive a prophet's reward" (Matt. 10:41). If so, in this case the reward was food.

21:1-24 Before Ahab broke the sixth and eighth commandments, he broke the tenth, which prohibits coveting (see Ex. 20:17). Evil deeds are born from evil desires, and so the way to avoid evil deeds is to extinguish evil desires. Greed always begins in the heart and then manifests itself in evil deeds. Thus Scripture warns against the *desire* to be rich and teaches contentment (see 1 Tim. 6:8-9). If we are content, greed has no garden in which to grow.

2 Kings

4:1-7 Here is another marvelous example of God's compassion on the poor and His miraculous provision. Prosperity preachers often encourage their followers to imitate the widow's faith as a means to greater prosperity, but they fail to point out the fact that she was not trusting God for more luxuries. Rather, her situation was tragic and desperate, and the Lord delivered her from the impending crises of her deep poverty, providing what she needed as she followed Elisha's instructions.

5:1-27 What was wrong with Elisha or Gehazi taking a gift from Naaman after he was healed? Naaman's owning the silver and clothing didn't prevent him from *being healed* of leprosy, so why would Gahazi's owning just a portion of it result in his *being stricken* with leprosy?

The answer is found in verse 26: it was the wrong time to receive such gifts. God didn't want Naaman or anyone who heard of his healing to think that such divine blessings could be purchased for a large sum. That would send the wrong message to everyone, and especially to the poor. God wants to be known as a God of grace, not as a God whose benefits can be bought with silver. The severity of Gehazi's punishment sheds light on how grievous this was to God. How must He feel about TV evangelists and prosperity preachers who continually sell God's blessings?

6:20-23 Here is an Old Testament example of loving one's enemies by means of feeding them. Apparently, the love that was shown had the desired effect, just as is promised in Proverbs 25:21-22: "If your enemy is hungry, give him food to eat; and if he is thirsty, give him water to drink; for you will heap burning coals on his head, and the LORD will reward you." One can't help but wonder what would happen if the money nations spend on war would be spent on providing the needs of their enemies.

6:24-7:16 The four lepers mentioned in this story felt guilty for hoarding their abundance with the full knowledge that other citizens were starving. The difference between them and so many of us is that they repented after a few hours, while year after year we keep on hoarding our prosperity, knowing full well the plight of our spiritual family in developing nations.

8:1-6 Here is another inspiring story of God's provision. Take note that the Shunammite woman had to obey God's instructions through Elisha in order for her needs to be supplied during the seven-year famine. Also note that it was obviously God's will for her to have some capital, in this case land to grow crops, as indicated by the providential way her land was restored to her. The very best way to help the poor is not to give them money, but to give them a means to earn a living.

20:12-19 Because this description of Hezekiah's personal wealth contains no moral commentary, should we assume that God preferred that Hezekiah hoard it rather than use it to love his neighbor as himself? That is doubtful, and this passage certainly does not give us who are under the law of Christ the right to follow Hezekiah's example. Clearly, Hezekiah "laid up" (see 20:17) "treasure" (see 20:13, 15) on the earth, something Christ forbade His followers to do. 2 Chronicles adds an interesting commentary about this incident:

> Even in the matter of the envoys of the rulers of Babylon, who sent
> to him to inquire of the wonder that had happened in the land,
> God left him alone only to test him, that He might know all that
> was in his heart (2 Chron. 32:31).

God left Hezekiah alone, that is, He didn't interfere or intervene. Rather, He simply observed Hezekiah's actions to learn what was in his heart. What do you suppose was revealed to God about Hezekiah's heart? What could have motivated Hezekiah to show his treasures to the envoys from Babylon? Do you suppose that God was pleased with what He observed?

Interestingly, God told Hezekiah through Isaiah that all his treasures would eventually be carried away to Babylon, an event that would occur because of God's judgment. Is it possible that this revelation was part of God's test of Hezekiah? Is it not possible that God was trying to help him understand that of all his treasures were temporal? Would it not have been wise if Hezekiah had thus concluded, "All of this will one day be carried away to Babylon and neither I nor my heirs will own it, so why should I cling to it any longer?" But Hezekiah had no such reaction to the divine revelation. Rather, his perspective remained selfish, as he thought to himself that the foretold loss would not occur within his remaining years. Do you suppose that Hezekiah passed God's test?

24:14 I can't resist pointing out that it was only the poor who were not deported by Nebuchadnezzar during God's judgment upon Judah. They were apparently considered invaluable and of no threat to Babylon. As the rich and middle classes were marched away in chains, I wonder if for the first time in their lives they envied the poor?

1 Chronicles

22:14 Obviously, no expense was too great for the temple that David wanted built for the Lord. I think it is safe to say that David could have kept all this wealth for himself, but he didn't because of his love for God.

29:1-17 Here we read of a high point of Old Testament generosity as David and other wealthy Israelites willingly gave for the embellishment of the temple. It appears that David gave all of his remaining personal silver and gold (v. 3), and his sacrifice inspired others to follow his example. He knew that his wealth and the wealth of his fellow Israelites had come from God (vv. 12, 14, 16), thus their wealth was actually belonged to God (v. 16) and should be used to glorify Him. David also knew that God was looking at his heart (v. 17), and he acknowledged the transience of life in his prayer (v. 15), both of which no doubt motivated him to give so generously. Wealthy professing Christians who continue to lay up earthly treasures will find no solace from reading passages like this! Prosperity preachers who hold David up as their model of wealth should read this!

2 Chronicles

1:15 During Israel's "golden era" under Solomon's early reign, all of Israel prospered. When we read that silver and gold in Jerusalem became as plentiful as stones, that did not mean that everyone was fabulously wealthy, because we read earlier that the abundance of silver significantly lowered its value (see 1 Kings 10:21, 27).

More likely it meant that everyone had plenty, and their needs were well provided. Consequently, there would have been less need to share. If no one is suffering poverty because everyone possesses all he needs, then the ideal has been attained. But that is just not the case in our day. Thus, when prosperity preachers cite this verse to prove that God wants their audiences to become rich while they make no mention of the needs of the poor among their own family, they do injustice to the truth. They should rather use this scripture to prove that God wants *all* His children to have their needs supplied, and so those who have more than they need should help those who have less than they need.

14:13-15 There isn't any doubt that after the invasion of Ethiopia that Judah prospered with plunder. But did this windfall give them the right to use that windfall selfishly and disobey the second greatest commandment? God's blessing carries with it responsibility.

17:5, 11, 18:1 All of these verses that speak of Jehoshaphat's increasing wealth are mentioned nowhere in the New Testament as being the exemplary standard for believers. Why then do prosperity preachers point to such verses to prove that there must be nothing wrong with believers growing wealthy and keeping the majority of their wealth for themselves? And why do they assume that is what Jehosphaphat did? If Jehoshaphat, who spread the Law's teaching (see 17:7-9), kept the Law himself, there is no doubt that he shared a significant portion of his wealth, as that is what the Law prescribed.

31:4-10 All times of true revival (see 29:1-31:21) are accompanied by revived giving because a true relationship with God demands it.

32:27-31 God did indeed make Hezekiah wealthy, but we read here that God tested him to know what was in his heart when he showed his wealth to the envoys of Babylon. If God increases your wealth, it is also a test of your heart. Do you love God or mammon? As I commented when we read the parallel passage in 2 Kings 20:12-19:

> Interestingly, God told Hezekiah through Isaiah that all his treasures would eventually be carried away to Babylon, an event that would occur because of God's judgment. Is it possible that this revelation was part of God's test of Hezekiah? Is it not possible that God was trying to help him understand that of all his treasures were temporal? Would it not have been wise if Hezekiah had thus concluded, "All of this will one day be carried away to Babylon and neither I nor my heirs will own it, so why should I cling to it any longer?" But Hezekiah had no such reaction to the divine revelation. Rather, his perspective remained selfish, as he thought to himself that the foretold loss would not occur within his remaining years. Do you suppose that Hezekiah passed God's test?

Nehemiah

5:1-13 *Usury*, as the word is used here (see vv. 7, 10), was not the practice of charging exorbitant interest as it is often defined today, but was the practice of charging *any* interest on a personal loan, something that was forbidden by the Law of Moses for Israelites to do in regard to fellow Israelites (see Ex 25:25, Lev. 25:35-37, Deut. 23:19-20). Keep in mind that only those facing desperate personal misfortune and who lacked necessities borrowed money in that day, as exemplified in this story. Lending a fellow Israelite money at interest would be taking advantage of him and not loving one's neighbor as himself. Proverbs 28:8 warns, "He who increases his wealth by interest and usury gathers it for him who is gracious to the poor."

Because only those facing desperate personal misfortune borrowed money in that day, the ethics of the Mosaic Law regarding lending at interest should not be applied today to anything but loans made to fellow believers who are forced to borrow because of personal misfortune and who are lacking basic necessities. Additionally, the modern manipulation of currencies by governments and their subsequent inflation, not a factor in ancient times, should also be considered by modern Christians who are trying to follow the ethics of the Mosaic Law in this matter. If a borrower repays a lender in currency that has lost some of its value, he should repay the equivalent *value* of the original loan, otherwise he is taking advantage of the lender.

5:14-19 Nehemiah turned down money that could have been his out of love for his fellow Israelites, not wanting to burden them as did former governors. Every opportunity to prosper is not necessarily from the Lord, but may well be a test from the Lord. Will you refuse to enrich yourself at the expense of others even when doing so is perfectly legal?

13:10-13 How quickly and predictably Israel backslid in Nehemiah's day. One of the first indications of their relapse was their neglect of tithing.

Esther

9:22 Although God's name is never mentioned once in this biblical book, we do find a reference to His concern for the poor, as sending gifts to them became part of the tradition of the Feast of Purim, established to commemorate the Jews' victory over their enemies during Esther's time.

Job

1:1-3 No one can debate that Job was a very wealthy man in his day, and yet God considered him to be the most righteous man on the earth. How was that possible?

First, Job gained his wealth righteously. Like some other patriarchs, Job's business was animal husbandry, and his wealth consisted mostly of his inventory, his livestock (see Job 1:3). His enterprise provided numerous jobs, and he and his servant-employees had a mutually dependent relationship. There is no evidence that Job exploited his employees (see Job 31:13-15, 31) or that he lived at a significantly higher level of comfort than they did.

Second, Job used his wealth righteously. There isn't any question that Job possessed a sincere concern for the poor. He said,

> Some remove the landmarks;
> They seize and devour flocks.
> They drive away the donkeys of the orphans;
> They take the widow's ox for a pledge.
> They push the needy aside from the road;

The poor of the land are made to hide themselves altogether.
Behold, as wild donkeys in the wilderness
They go forth seeking food in their activity,
As bread for their children in the desert.
They harvest their fodder in the field
And glean the vineyard of the wicked.
They spend the night naked, without clothing,
And have no covering against the cold.
They are wet with the mountain rains
And hug the rock for want of a shelter.
Others snatch the orphan from the breast,
And against the poor they take a pledge.
They cause the poor to go about naked without clothing,
And they take away the sheaves from the hungry.
Within the walls they produce oil;
They tread wine presses but thirst.
From the city men groan,
And the souls of the wounded cry out....
Have I not wept for the one whose life is hard?
Was not my soul grieved for the needy? (Job 24:2-12, 30:25).

But Job did more than lament the plight of the poor. He served them with his wealth. He had no need, like the rich young ruler, to repent and liquidate those possessions that testified of his selfishness and lack of love for his neighbor. Job had continually liquidated his personal wealth to meet pressing needs, doing everything within his power to serve orphans, widows, the handicapped and strangers. In his final defense before his accusers, he testified of himself:

When I went out to the gate of the city,
When I took my seat in the square,
The young men saw me and hid themselves,
And the old men arose and stood.
The princes stopped talking
And put their hands on their mouths;
The voice of the nobles was hushed,
And their tongue stuck to their palate.
For when the ear heard, it called me blessed,
And when the eye saw, it gave witness of me,
Because I delivered the poor who cried for help,
And the orphan who had no helper.
The blessing of the one ready to perish came upon me,
And I made the widow's heart sing for joy.
I put on righteousness, and it clothed me;
My justice was like a robe and a turban.
I was eyes to the blind
And feet to the lame.
I was a father to the needy,
And I investigated the case which I did not know.
I broke the jaws of the wicked
And snatched the prey from his teeth (Job 29:7-17).

If I have kept the poor from their desire,
Or have caused the eyes of the widow to fail,
Or have eaten my morsel alone,
And the orphan has not shared it
(But from my youth he grew up with me as with a father,
And from infancy I guided her),
If I have seen anyone perish for lack of clothing,
Or that the needy had no covering,
If his loins have not thanked me,
And if he has not been warmed with the fleece of my sheep,
If I have lifted up my hand against the orphan,
Because I saw I had support in the gate,
Let my shoulder fall from the socket,
And my arm be broken off at the elbow.
For calamity from God is a terror to me,
And because of His majesty I can do nothing.... (Job 31:16-23).

Have the men of my tent not said,
"Who can find one who has not been satisfied with his meat"?
The alien has not lodged outside,
For I have opened my doors to the traveler (Job 31:31-32)

There is little doubt that Job, like other patriarchs, was wealthy because of God's blessing him as a reward for his righteousness. Yet everyone who has read the book of Job knows that God did not want Job to serve Him only because of the material benefits, and thus Job was tested by means of losing almost everything he had. Those whom God has so blessed would do well to check their own motives for serving God, and they should be prepared for the possibility of being similarly tested by Him.

22:5-10 Here Job's friend Eliphaz enumerated some characteristics of a wicked person, although wrongly assuming they belonged to Job. They included withholding clothes from the naked, bread from the hungry and water from the thirsty as well as neglecting widows and orphans.

31:24-25 Job recognized that trusting in his wealth for his security would be a sin, as it would result in his not trusting in God. He also realized the danger of becoming proud because of his wealth. These twin temptations are also mentioned by the apostle Paul, who recommends overcoming them by the only means possible—through generous giving. He wrote, "Instruct those who are rich in this present world not to be conceited or to fix their hope on the uncertainty of riches [there are the twin temptations], but on God, who richly supplies us with all things to enjoy. Instruct them to do good, to be rich in good works, to be generous and ready to share, storing up for themselves the treasure of a good foundation for the future, so that they may take hold of that which is life indeed" (1 Tim. 6:17-19). Anyone who hoards wealth trusts in it and thus does not trust in God. Like greed, trusting in wealth is more than just an attitude. It is a condition of the heart that manifests itself by actions. Our father who feeds the birds and clothes the lilies will take care of us, so we have no need to place our trust in anything else.

Psalms

1:1-3 In order to experience the prosperity promised in verse 3, one must keep the conditions of verses 1-2, which would include keeping God's commandments regarding stewardship. And as he prospers, he will continue to use his prosperity for God's purposes, being "rich toward God" (see Luke 12:21), true prosperity.

15:5 See my comments on Nehemiah 5:1-13 regarding loans at interest.

17:13-15 Here David contrasted the purpose of his life with the purpose of those who don't know God. Their portion "is in this life," and they are satisfied with nothing higher than having children to whom they can pass on their accumulated material acquisitions. David, however, lived to see at the end of his life God's "face in righteousness," a goal worthy of imitation. Those who possess such a goal will of course lay up their treasure in heaven, not on earth.

34:9-10 Again note that the promise here is conditional. Those who seek the Lord and fear Him shall not be in want of any good thing. Of course, those who seek and fear Him will obey His commandments, including those that regulate their financial affairs. They alone are assured of not being in want. This then is not a promise of divine help to lay up earthly treasures.

35:27 This verse does not say, "The Lord delights in the prosperity of His disobedient and phony children." God delights in the prosperity of His *servants* because He knows their prosperity will be used for His glory.

37:11, 16 Jesus was perhaps quoting 37:11 when He said, "Blessed are the meek: for they shall inherit the earth" (Matt. 5:5). Obviously 37:11 is not a promise that has come to pass for every humble follower of God during his lifetime, but God will keep His promise when Jesus rules the earth. Then "the righteous will inherit the land, and dwell in it forever" (v. 29). In the meantime 37:16 certainly applies, because the righteous, who in this life have little, can look forward to abundant prosperity, while any abundance that the wicked might have is only temporary.

37:21, 25-26 There is a definite difference in the financial affairs of the righteous and the wicked. God provides for the righteous so they have no need to beg. And He provides them with more than they need, enabling them to give and lend to others. If one is not graciously giving, he does not fit the description of the righteous here.

39:4-6 Note the connection David made in these verses between the transience of life and the foolishness of amassing riches.

41:1-3 An alternate translation of verse 1 is, "How blessed is he who considers the poor." Those who do can expect to be rewarded with protection and healing from God. Who would have ever thought that health could be a benefit of helping the poor? That means that sickness could be a result of not helping the poor.

49:5-6 "Trusting in wealth" and "boasting in the abundance of riches" are again both spoken of as negative characteristics. The sure way to avoid both is to give one's wealth away.

49:16-20 In the light of scriptures like this, why has the theme of "success in life" (a euphemism for "getting rich") become so dominant in so many so-called Christian circles? Every person who dies successful in the eyes of man (v. 18) dies a failure and a fool in the eyes of God.

52:5-7 The person condemned in verse 7 "would not make God his refuge, but trusted in the abundance of his riches." Note the contrast. One cannot trust in the abundance of his riches while at the same time make God his refuge, that is, trust God. One who trusts in his abundant riches is one who believes that his future is secure because of his wealth. He has, he thinks, no need to trust God. Yet, as the psalmist makes so clear, his error is grave. It would have been better to trust God. Had he made God his refuge instead of wealth, he would not have hoarded his riches, as there would have been no need to hoard under God's care. Instead of hoarding, he could have shared his wealth and laid up heavenly treasure.

62:10 What does it mean to set your heart upon riches when they increase? Jesus gave us the answer. He said that where our treasure is, there will our heart be also (see Matt. 6:21). If we are laying up treasure on earth, it proves that our hearts are on the earth. If we are laying up treasure in heaven, it proves that our treasure is in heaven. So anyone who hoards his increasing riches has set his heart upon them in disobedience to the admonition here. Do not fool yourself, as so many have, into thinking that they have not set their hearts upon their increasing wealth as they cling to it.

73:3, 12 Prosperity is not always an indication of righteousness or of God's blessing.

112:1-9 Wealth and riches are in the house of the man who fears the Lord and who greatly delights in His commandments (vv.1-3), but for what reason? Note that as the psalmist mentions the specific godly characteristics of such a person, he focuses on his generosity and care for the poor, an indication of his greatly delighting in the second greatest commandment. He is "gracious" and "compassionate" (v. 4). He "lends" and gives "freely to the poor" (vv. 5, 9). As we have consistently witnessed throughout Scripture, those who give to the poor are blessed in return, and thus enabled to continue giving. The wealth and riches that God gives them are not for piling up in their houses, but for distributing to those in need. Prosperity preachers twist this biblical truth of sowing and reaping to make themselves and their ministries the object of giving rather than the poor. I can assure you, however, that God is not blessing people in order to repay them for enriching the self-indulgent lifestyles of prosperity preachers or for helping them spread their heresies.

119:72 How many Christians could honestly make this testimony?

Proverbs

The book of Proverbs contains hundreds of inspired axioms, none of which by itself is the sum of all truth. *Each contains one small aspect of truth.* That being so, it is quite easy to over-inflate a truth found in one proverb while ignoring the balancing truths found in others. Proverbs has thus become the preferred book of the Bible by prosperity preachers and Christian mutual fund salesman alike. It contains a gold mine of individual verses just waiting to be extracted, separated from their context, and selfishly exploited. You are much more likely, for example, to hear a prosperity preacher quote Proverbs 15:6, "Great wealth is in the house of the righteous," than hear him quote Proverbs 16:8, "Better is a little with righteousness than great income with injustice" or Proverbs 21:13, "He who shuts his ear to the cry of the poor will also cry himself and not be answered." When the book of Proverbs is considered as whole, it harmonizes quite well with the rest of Scripture. For the sake of our study,

I've divided just about everything that can be found regarding stewardship in the book of Proverbs into seven categories:

1.) Material blessing promised as an incentive for generosity and righteousness; material lack promised as in incentive against stinginess and unrighteousness.

2.) The believer's responsibility toward the poor and warnings against neglecting that responsibility.

3.) Observations regarding greedy behavior.

4.) Warnings against the desire to be rich and unethical means of gaining wealth.

5.) The superiority of wisdom, righteousness and contentment over riches.

6.) Admonitions to sluggards, slackers, the self-indulgent and stupid.

7.) Prudent business and financial practices.

Because these themes are found in so many of the Proverbs, I will not use space to discuss them all individually. Rather, I will consider some examples of proverbs that fall under each theme and then simply list the remainder of those that are similar. In that way we will cover every relevant scripture in Proverbs.

Stewardship Theme #1: Material blessing promised as an incentive for generosity and righteousness; material lack promised as an incentive against stinginess and unrighteousness.

Perhaps the most well-known and most abused scripture under this theme is Proverbs 3:9-10:

> Honor the Lord from your wealth, and from the first of all your produce; so your barns will be filled with plenty, and your vats will overflow with new wine.

First, to "honor the Lord from your wealth and from the first of all your produce" can only mean to make stewardship your highest priority, using your wealth in such a way that it honors God. This theme, as you know, resonates throughout the Bible. God blesses the obedient, and His blessing is what enables the obedient to continue to be a blessing. When your "vats overflow" as is promised in Proverbs 3:10, that means you have more than you need, and you have some to share.

Prosperity preachers always use this scripture to influence people to give to their "ministries," which are not really ministries at all since they promote what God hates—the love of money and the worship of the false god Mammon. We are not "honoring the Lord from our wealth" when we enrich greedy prosperity teachers. Rather, according to the book of Proverbs, one way that we honor the Lord is when we are gracious to the poor: "He who oppresses the poor taunts his Maker, but *he who is gracious to the needy honors Him*" (14:31, emphasis added).

Another proverb that falls under this same theme is the already-mentioned Proverb 15:6:

> Great wealth is in the house of the righteous, but trouble is in the income of the wicked.

This is clearly written as an incentive to be righteous and not to be wicked. However, if one does not obey God's commandments regarding stewardship, he is *not* righteous. This fact is endorsed in the book of Proverbs itself, as it tells us that one characteristic of a righteous person is that he is concerned for the poor, a characteristic not shared by the wicked (see Prov. 29:7, see also Ps. 112:1-9).

Thus only those who obey God as good stewards can expect to be rewarded materially. The wicked, and those who do not obey God's commandments regarding stewardship, have no such hope. God is more likely to make them like the poor whom they ignore, that they might be encouraged to repent of their selfishness.

We can clearly see how prosperity preachers abuse such verses. Twisting the Scripture, exploiting people's gullibility, piling up earthly treasures for themselves and not caring for the poor, they are not in the category of the righteous, but in the category of the wicked and greedy. Their wealth is not a blessing from God, but a consequence of their deception and greed, which leads me to another important point. This proverb was not given to us as a way to test who is righteous and who is wicked by means of measuring their net material worth. If that were the case, the Bible would be endorsing the delusion that drug lords, mafia kings, and prosperity preachers are examples of righteousness!

No, other scriptures found in the book of Proverbs and the rest of the Bible lead us to believe that it is not universally and always true that the righteous prosper while the wicked suffer lack. If such were the case, we would never find axioms in the book of Proverbs that say, for example, "Better is the poor who walks in his integrity, than he who is crooked though he be rich" (Prov. 28:6) or, "Better is a little with the fear of the Lord, than great treasure and turmoil with it" (Prov. 15:16).

We should also consider the fact that wealth, according to the Bible, is not always measured in material things. For example, we also read in the book of Proverbs, "Better is a dish of vegetables where love is, than a fattened ox and hatred with it" (Prov. 15:17). So according to the book of Proverbs, the true wealth of one's household consists of the love enjoyed there.

Thus we should not always assume that when the book of Proverbs speaks of the "wealth" or "riches" of the righteous that it is speaking of their material prosperity. Jesus Himself once told some very poor believers that they were actually quite rich, and He could only have been speaking of their spiritual wealth (see Rev. 2:9).

Finally, and along these same lines, although it is true that not all believers always enjoy abundant material prosperity, they can rest assured that one day they will inherit the earth (Matt. 5:5). Then will Proverbs 13:22 be fully realized, "The wealth of the sinner is stored up for the righteous."

The two primary proverbs we've considered under this theme (and others like them) were written to encourage readers to be generous and righteous so that they could experience the continued blessing of God's provision, as well as the blessing of giving and being re-supplied by God to give again. They are the equivalent of Jesus' words in the New Testament, "Seek first His kingdom and His righteousness; and all these things shall be added to you" (Matt. 6:33) and, "Give, and it will be given to you; good measure, pressed down, shaken together, running over, they will pour into your lap." (Luke 6:38). So we've really learned nothing new. Perhaps the proverb that best sums up this biblical theme is 11:24-25:

> There is one who scatters, yet increases all the more, and there is
> one who withholds what is justly due, but it results only in want.
> The generous man will be prosperous, and he who waters will
> himself be watered.

Other proverbs that fall under this same theme (at least to some degree) are 2:21-

22; 3:13-16, 33; 5:8-10; 8:12-21; 10:3, 22; 11:6, 26, 28; 13:21, 22, 25; 14:11, 24; 15:25; 17:2; 19:17; 21:20: 22:4, 9, 16, 22-23; 24:3-4; 25:21-22; 28:20.

Stewardship Theme #2: The believer's responsibility toward the poor and warnings against neglecting that responsibility.

As I stated when we considered the first stewardship theme of Proverbs, it is only the righteous who can expect God's material blessing. Since God has commanded that we share with the poor, however, only those who do so are in the category of the righteous. Those who do not are in the category of the wicked. They are actually promised punishment for their lack of compassion.

This theme is repeatedly emphasized in the book of Proverbs:

> He who is gracious to a poor man lends to the Lord, and He will repay him for his good deed (Prov. 19:17).

> He who shuts his ear to the cry of the poor will also cry himself and not be answered (Prov. 21:13).

> He who is generous will be blessed, for he gives some of his food to the poor (Prov. 22:9).

> He who gives to the poor will never want, but he who shuts his eyes will have many curses (Prov. 28:27).

> The righteous is concerned for the rights of the poor, the wicked does not understand such concern (Prov. 29:7).

We are instructed in Proverbs to give to the needy whenever we have opportunity and ability:

> Do not withhold good from those to whom it is due, when it is in your power to do it. Do not say to your neighbor, "Go, and come back, and tomorrow I will give it," when you have it with you (Prov. 3:27-28).

Proverbs tells us to be gracious to the poor even if they are our enemies:

> If your enemy is hungry, give him food to eat; and if he is thirsty, give him water to drink; for you will heap burning coals on his head, and the Lord will reward you (Prov. 25:21-22).

This just-quoted verse and second stewardship theme of Proverbs reminds us of Jesus' well-known words:

> But I say to you who hear, love your enemies, *do good to those who hate you*, bless those who curse you, pray for those who mistreat you....*Give to everyone who asks of you,* and whoever takes away what is yours, do not demand it back (Luke 6:27-28, 30, emphasis added).

Other scriptures in the book of Proverbs that fall under this same stewardship theme are 14:21, 31; 17:5; 19:17; 22:2, 22-23; 29:14 and 31:20.

Stewardship Theme #3: Observations regarding greedy behavior.

As we've learned in earlier chapters, greed is not just an attitude of the heart, but is always manifested by outward actions. The book of Proverbs includes some observations regarding the manifestation of greedy behavior, but they are observations that, in light of the rest of Scripture, can only be considered critical. For example, we read in Proverbs 10:15 the observation, "The rich man's wealth is his fortress, the ruin of the poor is their poverty."

Although this observation includes no moral commentary, it hardly seems right to think that it has no moral objective. It seems to say to us, "This may be how it is, but this is not how it ought to be, because this is not fair. The rich man, who clings to his wealth as a means of security, would be better to trust the Lord for his security and share his abundance with the poor who are being ruined due to their lack."

A later proverb uses a very similar expression as this one, but it includes some additional words that can only be considered to be a negative moral commentary regarding the rich man and his fortress: "A rich man's wealth is his strong city, and *like a high wall in his own imagination*" (Prov. 18:11, emphasis added).

The reason the rich man's wealth is like a high wall *in his own imagination* is because his wall doesn't exist anywhere in reality. His imaginary wall can't protect him from God's wrath, as other proverbs warn, "Riches do not profit in the day of wrath, but righteousness delivers from death" (Prov. 11:4) and, "He who trusts in his riches will fall" (Prov. 11:28).

Other examples of "observational" proverbs that surely contain some negative moral implications regarding the love of money are,

> Abundant food is in the fallow ground of the poor, but it is swept away by injustice (Prov. 13:23)

> The poor man utters supplications, but the rich man answers roughly (Prov. 18:23).

> The rich rules over the poor, and the borrower becomes the lender's slave (Prov. 22:7).

All of these "observations" beg to have the words added, "And this is terrible and ought not to be, because the source of these sorrows is greed."

Under this stewardship theme we also find observations that, when read for their subtleties, reveal how the love of money motivates rich and poor alike to be deceptive. For example:

> "Bad, bad," says the buyer; but when he goes his way, then he boasts (Prov. 20:14).

> There is one who pretends to be rich, but has nothing; another pretends to be poor, but has great wealth (Prov. 13:7).

In order to drive the price down, the buyer pretends to believe that he thinks the item for sale is of poor quality. After the sale, however, he boasts to others of his bargain. The love of money motivates him to be deceptive to the seller.

And the reason some poor people pretend to be rich is because they hope to impress others whose wealth is real, win their favor and friendship, and perhaps profit. (Perhaps this is why certain proverbs warn about giving to or flattering the rich; see Prov. 22:16; 23:6-8). And the reason some *rich* people pretend to be *poor* is because they want to keep all their wealth, and they don't want anyone expecting anything from them, nor do they want the kind of phony friends that rich people are plagued with. These phenomena are illustrated in other proverbs:

> The poor is hated even by his neighbor, but those who love the rich are many (Prov. 14:20).

> Wealth adds many friends, but a poor man is separated from his friend....Many will entreat the favor of a generous man, and every man is a friend to him who gives gifts. All the brothers of a poor man hate him; how much more do his friends go far from him! He pursues them with words, but they are gone (Prov. 19:4, 6-7).

The love of money makes people not want to associate with the poor, even if they are relatives, neighbors, or (former) friends, lest they feel an obligation to help them. All of these observations are obviously moral commentaries about the love of money.

Stewardship Theme #4: Warnings against the desire to be rich and unethical means of gaining wealth.

In the New Testament we read,

> If we have food and covering, with these we shall be content. But those who *want to get rich* fall into temptation and a snare and many foolish and harmful desires which plunge men into ruin and destruction. For *the love of money* is a root of all sorts of evil (1 Tim. 6:8-10).

> Let your character be free from *the love of money, being content with what you have*; for He Himself has said, "I will never desert you, nor will I ever forsake you" (Heb. 13:5).

Thus we should not be surprised to read these same themes in the book of Proverbs. They can indeed be found there:

> Do not weary yourself to gain wealth, cease from your consideration of it. When you set your eyes on it, it is gone. For wealth certainly makes itself wings, like an eagle that flies toward the heavens (Prov. 23:4-5).

> Two things I asked of Thee, Do not refuse me before I die: Keep deception and lies far from me, give me neither poverty nor riches; feed me with the food that is my portion, lest I be full and deny Thee and say, "Who is the Lord?" Or lest I be in want and steal, and profane the name of my God (Prov. 30:7-9).

One wonders how prosperity preachers can even dare to turn to the book of Proverbs and publicly read an out-of-context verse there when the danger exists that someone in their audience might accidentally read one of these two verses!

The way to avoid all the dangers that are attached with wealth is not to desire wealth in the first place. The many other sins mentioned in the book of Proverbs that fall under this fourth stewardship theme are only committed by those who have allowed a place in their heart for the love of money. Proverbs mentions many unethical means of gaining wealth, such as violence and murder (see 1:10-19), deception (see 11:18; 21:6), kidnapping (see 13:8), fraud (see 11:1; 13:11; 16:11), oppressing the poor (see 14:31; 22:16, 22-23), bribery (see 15:27; 17:8, 23; 29:4) and thievery (see 29:24). Only God knows how much of the wealth in the world has been gained, directly or indirectly, by these means. God promises that those who gain by these means will ultimately be the losers.

According to Proverbs, attempting to gain wealth hastily is also a manifestation of the love of money:

> An inheritance gained hurriedly at the beginning, will not be blessed in the end (Prov. 20:21).

> A faithful man will abound with blessings, but he who makes haste to be rich will not go unpunished (Prov. 28:20).

> A man with an evil eye hastens after wealth, and does not know that want will come upon him (Prov. 28:22). (The "evil-eye" or "bad eye" expression is found in other places in Scripture, and it is clearly an idiom for a greedy heart; see Matt. 6:23 and NASB marginal notes for Prov. 23:6 and Matt. 20:15.)

Those who attempt to prosper by "get-rich-quick-schemes" will suffer for it. God wants us to be faithful and work in order to prosper. This will become even more obvious to us when we consider Stewardship Theme #6, *Admonitions to sluggards, slackers, the self-indulgent and stupid.*

Stewardship Theme #5: The superiority of wisdom, righteousness and contentment over riches.

Pursuing wealth above virtue is another manifestation of the love of money. It is a million times more important that we be righteous than rich, because "Riches do not profit in the day of wrath, but righteousness delivers from death" (Prov. 11:4). You can go to heaven without riches, but you can't without righteousness. Thus,

> Better is a little with the fear of the Lord, than great treasure and turmoil with it. Better is a dish of vegetables where love is, than a fattened ox and hatred with it (Prov. 15:16-17).

> Better is a little with righteousness than great income with injustice....It is better to be of a humble spirit with the lowly, than to divide the spoil with the proud (Prov. 16:8, 19).

> Better is a dry morsel and quietness with it than a house full of feasting with strife (Prov. 17:1).

> Better is a poor man who walks in his integrity than he who is perverse in speech and is a fool....What is desirable in a man is his kindness, and it is better to be a poor man than a liar (Prov. 19:1, 22).

> A good name is to be more desired than great riches, favor is better than silver and gold (Prov. 22:1).

> Better is the poor who walks in his integrity, than he who is crooked though he be rich (Prov. 28:6).

The message is redundant and clear: Don't puruse wealth; pursue holiness. This is not a new theme to readers of Scripture. Paul, writing about the love of money, admonished Timothy, "Flee from these things, you man of God; and pursue righteousness, godliness, faith, love, perseverance and gentleness" (1 Tim. 6:11).

These verses in Proverbs obviously also dispel the idea that every believer should expect to become rich. Rather, each of them teaches that every believer should be content even with little. Again, I can't help but wonder how prosperity preachers dare open the book of Proverbs to read one of their out-of-context proof texts in light of such scriptures.

Other verses in Proverbs speak of the superiority of wisdom over silver, gold and jewels, because wisdom leads to righteousness, which is the most important thing (see Prov. 3:13-14; 8:10-11, 19; 16:16; 20:15). "All things desirable cannot compare with her [wisdom]" (Prov. 8:11).

Stewardship Theme #6: Admonitions to sluggards, slackers, the self-indulgent and stupid.

The New Testament teaches, "If anyone will not work, neither let him eat" (2 Thes. 3:10). The book of Proverbs repeatedly emphasizes that same principle, sometimes with sayings that seem intentionally humorous, what are sometimes referred to as the "sluggard scriptures." Here is a sample, serious and comical:

> Go to the ant, O sluggard, observe her ways and be wise, which, having no chief, officer or ruler, prepares her food in the summer, and gathers her provision in the harvest. How long will you lie down, O sluggard? When will you arise from your sleep? "A little sleep, a little slumber, a little folding of the hands to rest"—and your poverty will come in like a vagabond, and your need like an armed man (Prov. 6:6-11).

> The sluggard says, "There is a lion in the road! A lion is in the open square!" (Prov. 26:13).

> As the door turns on its hinges, so does the sluggard on his bed (Prov. 26:14).

> The sluggard buries his hand in the dish; he is weary of bringing it to his mouth again (Prov. 26:15).

Other "sluggard scriptures" are Prov. 10:4-5; 13:4; 19:24; 20:4, 13; 21:25-26; 22:13 and 24:30-34.

Closely related to the sluggard, who does nothing, is the slacker, who does something, but very little: "He also who is slack in his work is brother to him who destroys" (Prov. 18:9).

After the sluggard and the slacker is the self-indulgent. He loves pleasure too much. (Now we are getting into American territory.) Proverbs says of him:

> He who loves pleasure will become a poor man; he who loves wine and oil will not become rich (Prov. 21:17).

> Do not be with heavy drinkers of wine, or with gluttonous eaters of meat; for the heavy drinker and the glutton will come to poverty, and drowsiness will clothe a man with rags (Prov. 23:20-21).

> Have you found honey? Eat only what you need, lest you have it in excess and vomit it (Prov. 25:16).

Lastly under this theme, Proverbs addresses the "stupid," those who follow foolish plans in hopes of profiting when they should simply labor:

> In all labor there is profit, but mere talk leads only to poverty (Prov. 14:23).

> He who tills his land will have plenty of food, but he who follows empty pursuits will have poverty in plenty (Prov. 28:19; see also 12:11).

Stewardship Theme # 7: Prudent business and financial practices.

Most of the scriptures that fall under this heading speak of the folly of "becoming surety for a stranger," which is the equivalent of co-signing a loan (see 6:1-5; 11:15; 17:18; 20:16; 22:26-27; 27:13).

Beyond that, reasonable expectations, thoughtful planning, and acquiring of skill are also presented as desirable in business and financial affairs:

> Where no oxen are, the manger is clean, but much increase comes by the strength of the ox (Prov. 14:4).

> The plans of the diligent lead surely to advantage, but everyone who is hasty comes surely to poverty (Prov. 21:5).

> Prepare your work outside, and make it ready for yourself in the field; afterwards, then, build your house (Prov. 24:27; see also Prov. 27:23-27; 31:13-27).

Ecclesiastes

2:4-11 If there were ever an assertion of the emptiness of wealth by an authority on the subject, Solomon's words here would take the prize. Late in his life, after years of backsliding, idolatry, and accumulating more material things, Solomon realized it had all been "vanity and striving after wind." Yet prosperity preachers so often point to Solomon, during his vain years, as a model for New Testament Christians!

4:8 Here we find Solomon's observation of the folly of the workaholic.

5:10-20 Paul likely had verses 15-16 of this passage in mind when he wrote Timothy saying,

> For we have brought nothing into the world, so we cannot take anything out of it either. If we have food and covering, with these we shall be content. But those who want to get rich fall into temptation and a snare and many foolish and harmful desires which plunge men into ruin and destruction (1 Tim. 6:7-9).

Can you imagine a prosperity preacher quoting either of these passages? In regard to their doctrine and practice, they would be wise to heed Solomon's overriding conclusion:

> The conclusion, when all has been heard, is: fear God and keep His commandments, because this applies to every person. Because God will bring every act to judgment, everything which is hidden, whether it is good or evil (Ecc. 12:13-14).

Isaiah

Throughout the books of the major and minor prophets we find the recurring theme that disobedience results in material deprivation—primarily as a consequence of foreign invasion, destruction, and deportation. Similarly, we find God's promises of better things, such as peace and bountiful harvests, for those who will repent and serve Him. This is nothing new for those who have read other portions of Scripture. I will therefore not comment on the many passages within the prophets that reiterate these familiar themes, leaving them for the prosperity preachers to exploit. Rather, I will focus on those specific scriptures that speak of individual aspects of godly stewardship, about which prosperity preachers are strangely silent. Part of the reason God's judgment fell upon the nations of Israel and Judah (as well as other nations to whom the prophets addressed their words) was because of their poor stewardship. And God only blesses people who practice good stewardship and who continue the practice it as He continues to bless them.

1:16-17, 23 Defending widows and orphans is frequently listed in the prophets as a foundational aspect of righteousness. Older widows and younger orphans are especially vulnerable, having no means of self-support. Along with bribery, ignoring the needs of widows and orphans is an indication of the love of money, and this also attracts God's judgment.

2:6-8 Verse 7 can hardly be considered to be a positive statement in light of its context between verses 6 and 8. As they sought to enrich themselves materially, the Israelites had been influenced by the idolatry of neighboring nations. They ultimately used their gain to fashion idols.

3:15-23 I can't help but wonder if there is some continuity from verse 15 through verse 23. This passage, taken as a whole, may indicate that the excessive adornment of wealthy, proud and seductive Israelite women was made possible by means of "grinding the face of the poor." I happen to be in Pakistan as I write these words, a county where much of North America's clothing is manufactured. Garments workers here often work twelve-hour days, seven days a week, for as little as sixty cents per hour. Should we feel good about providing them with jobs (that is, until more desperate people can be found who will work for less)?

5:8-9 Although not as clear as we would prefer, these verses certainly condemn amassing wealth, in this case real estate, so that it results in hardship for others. When a few own a large percentage of the available land, others inevitably suffer. That is why God made provision in the Law of Moses for everyone's land to be returned to the original owner every fifty years.

5:16-17 Like the previous passage we considered, this one is also a condemnation of the rich amassing land. God promises to right this wrong in favor of the poor.

5:22-23 Bribery, here condemned in its more blatant form, is in its more subtle form characterized by any decision to compromise loving one's neighbor as oneself for the sake of material gain. Satan is continually offering bribes, isn't he?

10:1-3 Here is yet another condemnation of those who gain by means of oppressing the poor, particularly widows and orphans.

32:5-7 Neglecting to care for the hungry and thirsty are again listed as fundamental characteristics of the unrighteous. Where does this leave many professing Christians?

33:14-16 Those who excuse their unjust gain by claiming it is necessary for their survival have no legitimate excuse. Their unjust gain is only necessary to satisfy their *greed*. God promises here to supply the bread and water of those who resist this temptation, but only those who can be content with bread and water will resist.

39:1-8 See my comments on 2 Kings 20:12-19.

58:6-11 Here God attempts to help Israel, apparently overly-focused on fasting, to understand what He considers to be of greater importance. Not surprisingly, He mentions sharing food with the hungry, clothing the naked, and providing shelter for the homeless. God prefers that we fast from selfishness much more than that we fast from food. The Israelites were ignoring the former while practicing the latter and wondering why God was not responding.

Jeremiah

5:27-29 Here God credited the people of Jerusalem's deceitfulness, rather than their faith or righteousness, as being the reason they were rich and fat. Neither did the city's inhabitants care for orphans or the poor.

6:12-13; 8:10 Lacking contentment, the people of Judah were "greedy for gain," and practiced deceitfulness to acquire more. God promised to judge them by taking away what they possessed. Why don't prosperity preachers ever mention verses such as these?

17:11 The one who makes a fortune unjustly (by taking advantage of others), God promises to judge by means of taking away his fortune, making a fool out of one who was worldly wise.

22:13-17 Those who know the Lord do not take advantage of others and are not focused on bigger and better homes, what amounts to the laying up of earthly treasures. Rather, they are helping the less fortunate and laying up heavenly treasures. Have we heard this message before?

32:1-40 The purchase of his uncle's field was surely a bargain for Jeremiah, as property values would have significantly dropped due to the siege of Jerusalem by Babylonian armies. But more than that, Jeremiah's purchase served as a prophetic sign to the nation of Judah that God would eventually restore them to their land.

Ezekiel

7:19-21 When people are starving and no food is available for purchase, they gain a different perspective regarding the gold and silver that they had once so highly valued.

16:15-19 Here is a study in poor stewardship. The people of Judah took God's material blessing and used it for what He hated.

16:49 Until this point in the Bible, we would have thought that Sodom's only sin was sexual perversion. Single sins, however, are rarely found. Here we learn that Sodom's perverts had no concern for the poor and needy, and this also attracted God's wrath.

18:7-17 Once again we see that a sure characteristic of the righteous is their care for the poor, while a sure characteristic of the unrighteous is their lack of care for the poor.

22:12-13, 25, 27, 29 Another list of economic sins that all stem from greed. The love of money is indeed the root of all sorts of evil (see 1 Tim. 6:10).

34:17-22 Here we find a descriptive analogy of selfishness. There are likewise in the church today fat and lean sheep, and God will judge between them.

Daniel

4:27 It is illuminating that when Daniel told great King Nebuchadnezzar to break away from his sins in order to avoid inevitable judgment, the only specific action he mentioned to the king was that he show "mercy to the poor."

Hosea

2:8; 8:4 Another study in poor stewardship. The Israelites took the prosperity with which God had blessed them and used at least a portion of it to make idols. Professing Christians are no different when they use what God has given them for what pulls their hearts away from heaven.

Amos

2:6 It seems unlikely that any Israelites literally sold a needy person for a pair of sandals. This expression, however, certainly reveals God's perspective of the lack of concern the Israelites had for the poor and of their love of money.

4:1 Here God refers to the oppressive Israelite wives as "cows of Bashan," a picture of obesity and laziness. It is a rare person indeed in North America who views obesity as a sign of self-indulgence.

5:11-12 Here Amos contrasts the lifestyles of the poor with the rich who are wealthy at the expense of the poor. The rich can afford nice homes because of the high rent and taxes that they exact from their poor tenants.

6:4-7 These can hardly be considered words that are complimentary to the rich. Although Amos does not condemn here the means by which the rich gained their wealth, he does condemn them for the luxuries.

8:4-6 The love of money once more described.

Micah

3:11-12 When money becomes the driving motivation of spiritual leaders, the end is near.

Zephaniah

1:18 Although people who have hoarded their wealth feel secure, nothing could be further from the truth. They couldn't be more insecure, as they have been storing up wrath for themselves at the same time (see Jas. 5:3).

Haggai

1:2-11 The people of Judah were not "seeking first God's kingdom" as revealed by their priorities, spending their resources on their own paneled homes while the temple of God lay desolate. Because of their poor stewardship, God gave them lack, hoping to motivate them to repent.

2:7-9 Indeed, the silver and the gold, as well as the entire earth, is the Lord's (see Ps. 24:1), and thus He has the right to direct its use. In this passage, God reveals that He will one day direct it from the nations to Jerusalem to glorify the place of His temple and habitation. Prosperity preachers only quote verse 8, taking it from its context, and using it only to further their own greedy agendas.

Zechariah

7:8-10 Even as we come to the close of the Old Testament, God is still reminding us about the poor, the widows, and orphans.

Malachi

3:5-12 This classic and well-known text has often been rightly used to motivate Christians to give. It promises cursing for those who don't and blessing for those who do, certainly a recurring theme in Scripture.

What is often not said, however, particularly by pastors who are raising money for new buildings and various church programs, is that the tithes and offerings that were to be faithfully paid by the people of Israel, were not only to be given to the Levites in their service to the Lord, but also, at least in part, to aliens/strangers, widows and orphans (see Deut. 26:12-13). Notice that in this very passage that we are considering, the first verse (3:5) speaks of widows and orphans. (Verse 5 is rarely read publicly, and most pastors begin with verse 7.)

Pastors who teach that pastors are the modern equivalent of the levitical priests, and who thus monopolize the available funds for all ministry, should not forget that there are other ministries to which God calls vocational ministers, such as apostles, prophets, evangelists and teachers. If God-called ministers under the new covenant are the equivalent of old covenant priests, then apostles, prophets, evangelists and teachers have just as much right to people's tithes as do pastors, as they are just as much called to equip the saints for the work of service as are pastors (see Eph. 4:11-12). It is this monopoly by pastors of the finances of the body of Christ that keeps so many God-called apostles, prophets, evangelists and teachers *out* of God's will and serving as pastors, the only ministry for which they can be paid.

Is tithing required under the new covenant as it was under the old? See my comments on Hebrews 7:4-10 in chapter nine.

To learn more about the ministry of Heaven's Family,
please visit HeavensFamily.org